CW01481466

The Racialized Brain

For those whose bodies are read before their words are heard.

The Racialized Brain

The Neurosociology of Race and Racism

Rengin Firat

polity

Copyright © Rengin Firat 2026

The right of Rengin Firat to be identified as Author of this Work has been asserted in accordance with the UK Copyright, Designs and Patents Act 1988.

First published in 2026 by Polity Press Ltd.

Polity Press Ltd.
65 Bridge Street
Cambridge CB2 1UR, UK

Polity Press Ltd.
111 River Street
Hoboken, NJ 07030, USA

All rights reserved. Except for the quotation of short passages for the purpose of criticism and review, no part of this publication may be reproduced, stored in a retrieval system or transmitted, in any form or by any means, electronic, mechanical, photocopying, recording or otherwise, without the prior permission of the publisher.

ISBN-13: 978-1-5095-5794-3
ISBN-13: 978-1-5095-5795-0(pb)

A catalogue record for this book is available from the British Library.

Library of Congress Control Number: 2025936662

Typeset in 10.5 on 12pt Sabon LT Pro
by Cheshire Typesetting Ltd, Cuddington, Cheshire
Printed and bound in Great Britain by CPI Group (UK) Ltd, Croydon

The publisher has used its best endeavours to ensure that the URLs for external websites referred to in this book are correct and active at the time of going to press. However, the publisher has no responsibility for the websites and can make no guarantee that a site will remain live or that the content is or will remain appropriate.

Every effort has been made to trace all copyright holders, but if any have been overlooked the publisher will be pleased to include any necessary credits in any subsequent reprint or edition.

For further information on Polity, visit our website:
politybooks.com

Contents

Acknowledgments

About ten years ago, at a local arts festival in Atlanta, I met an author promoting a blackout poetry book. Blackout poetry involves taking a page of text and blacking out most of the words to reveal a new poem. As I bought his book, he took an old novel – its title now forgotten – and created a quick poem that read: "Fear is our curse." At the time, I admired the ease with which he found meaning, though I didn't think much more of it, perhaps because I was younger, and more naive. As the years went by, that one-sentence poem took on a deeper meaning in my life and now hangs on my bedroom wall. As life threw its usual challenges my way (or maybe I just started noticing them more), I started to understand that fear isn't just personal; it's something we inherit from the systems and structures around us. But just as we inherit fear, we also inherit resistance. Our resistance is also collective, communal, and intergenerational. People who stand beside you and behind you – sometimes with words, sometimes simply with their presence – remind you that fear does not have to define you. Even when the world tells you to shrink, to stay small, to doubt your worth, your community – whether chosen or by kin – certain people will remind you that you are still allowed to take up space, to dream, to speak, to be.

That is why, in this book, I want to acknowledge and thank all the people who stood by me and behind me, who pushed me and lifted me at times, and grounded me at others. Especially to my parents, Selahattin and Melahat, whose love was quiet but steady, and who taught me – without naming it – how to be resilient in the face of fear. They made hard choices so I could have the space to imagine new ones. And to my brother, Cafer, who grounded me, in presence and in shared memories, with a gentle kind of courage that spoke without words: *I've got you.*

To my mentors, colleagues, and collaborators – most notably Steven Hitlin, Bruce Link, Jennie Burnet, Victoria Reyes, Hye Won Kwon, and Kalina Michalska, among others – who challenged me, guided me, and made room for my voice. And to my students, who continually reminded me of the true value and reward in what I do. They gave me the kind of brightness I needed to pave a path forward in times of fear and uncertainty.

To the institutional funding support that I received along the way, including the grants I received from the Center for Health Disparities Research at the University of California, Riverside, through the National Institutes of Health, National Institute on Minority Health and Health Disparities grant # U54 MD013368. And, particularly to Dr. David D. Lo, who was the director of this Center, whose leadership and encouragement were instrumental throughout this journey.

To my friends – the chosen family who held space for every version of me. Especially, to my dearest friend Jazz, who taught me that healing is not linear and that being held is not a weakness but a strength. And to Yu-Chan, who kept showing up with steady love, care, and patience.

To the best boy, Vila the dog, who crossed oceans and state lines with me and made my heart full. And to my new companions, Shishi and Momo, whose playful chaos and soft purrs brought light and laughter to long writing days.

And finally, to all the authors whose words have left a lasting mark on my heart and mind, and the editors and copy-editors who work behind the scenes to bring those words to life. The published and unpublished work of so many others has inspired this book. This book would not exist without all of you.

Yes, fear may be a curse. But life is not about never fearing. It is about learning to move forward in spite of that fear. It is about facing fear and choosing courage anyway. Fear can be challenged. And with community, it can be transformed.

Thank you.

Introduction

I did not know I had a race until I moved to the United States. This realization was not just personal but deeply intellectual, shaping the very questions I would come to ask in my academic work. As a scholar, I recognize that my lived experiences shape the questions I ask, the theories I engage with, and the ways I interpret data.[1] My own journey – from experiencing racialization for the first time to navigating predominantly white institutions as a Brown, Middle Eastern, immigrant woman – has fueled my intellectual curiosity about race as a lived experience, a structural force, and a neural process. My experiences with migration, my academic training in both sociology and neuroscience, and my advocacy for incorporating positionality and reflexivity into the neurosciences[2] are not separate from my research; they inform it. This is why I begin this book with my personal journey.

At twenty-four, I left Istanbul – the largest city in Türkiye and home to over 15 million people – with nothing but two suitcases. It was my first time leaving my home country, my first time crossing an ocean, and one of only a handful of times I had even been on a plane. My father, a now-retired general surgeon, and my mother, a retired biology teacher, worked in Türkiye's public sector, where salaries were relatively modest. Though we were middle class, I did not grow up in affluence. My family, like many others in Türkiye, experienced structural constraints that shaped where we lived and worked. Public sector jobs in Türkiye, particularly in medicine and education, operate on a lottery system – a mechanism designed to ensure that doctors and teachers are available in underserved, rural areas. As a result, I was born in a small town in the Black Sea region and moved frequently throughout my childhood, living in seven different cities across the country. Some were large and liberal, others small and deeply conservative. These experiences, while at times unsettling, gave me a comparative lens through which to view inequality – not just as an abstract concept but as something deeply embedded in daily life, shaped by structural and cultural forces.

Despite growing up in such a diverse environment, race was never a salient category in my life – until I moved to the United States. In Türkiye, identity was primarily framed through ethnicity, religion, and class rather than race. Though ethnic tensions between Turks, Kurds, Armenians, and Arabs were prominent, racial discourse was largely absent. People in Türkiye, especially those who are educated, often resist identifying as Middle Eastern or as people of color. Yet the "phenomenology of whiteness," as described by feminist scholar Sara Ahmed,[3] operates in ways that transcend national borders. It is an invisible structure that positions whiteness as the default and desirable standard, shaping who belongs and who does not. This desire for whiteness has long influenced Türkiye's geopolitical positioning, particularly in its struggle for European Union membership. While official rejections of Türkiye from the European Union have been framed as political, cultural, or economic, they are also rooted in racialized exclusion – a refusal to accept Türkiye as part of a white European identity.[4] This phenomenology of whiteness leads to shifting and unattainable standards imposed on non-western states and peoples, perpetuating their exclusion from full participation in international systems. This forms a paradoxical situation[5] for non-western states and peoples, which are expected to align with whiteness while continuously being excluded from it. As Ahmed argues, whiteness is not just a racial identity but a system of power that determines global mobility, access, and legitimacy.[6]

This same paradox of whiteness was deeply embedded in my own experiences of racialization, even before I had the language to articulate it. I have a relatively dark skin tone by Turkish standards, even among my family and peers. While in Türkiye this difference was framed through color terminology rather than racial identity, it was still a constant marker of distinction. People with darker skin tones are often called *esmer* (meaning "dark") or *buğday tenli* ("wheat-colored," the Turkish equivalent of olive skin). However, my skin was considered darker than wheat, and, throughout my life, I was frequently referred to as "black girl" – not in reference to African heritage but as a literal descriptor of skin tone. Though often used descriptively, or even as a term of endearment, it was still a reminder of difference.

This became even more pronounced when I moved to the United States, where racial categorization is explicit, institutionalized, and unavoidable. While in Türkiye my skin tone was simply a variation within an ethnic group, in the United States it became a racialized marker that positioned me in relation to whiteness. The contrast became strikingly clear when a Transportation Security Administration (TSA) agent bluntly asked why I was "so dark" if I was from Türkiye – a question that revealed the US racial framework at play, where Middle Eastern and Turkish identities do not easily fit into the rigid Black/white binary.

This shift in perception – from being color-marked but not racialized in Türkiye to being racialized but not officially recognized in the United States – exemplifies how race operates differently across social contexts. In the United States, I was legally classified as white but socially perceived as non-white, while in Türkiye, whiteness was not a formal category but was still an unspoken hierarchical standard shaping social distinctions. This paradox highlights the global yet context-dependent nature of racial categorization, demonstrating that race is not simply about skin color but about the systems of meaning and power attached to it in different societies.

It was only when I arrived in the United States that I fully felt the weight of race as a lived experience rather than an abstract concept. It was not just a label – it shaped my interactions, opportunities, and even my physical movement through public space. The first time I entered the United States was through Chicago O'Hare International Airport. I stood in the long immigration line, my visa documents in hand, ready to begin my PhD program in sociology at the University of Iowa. When it was my turn, the officer took my passport, scanned my fingerprints, and asked why I was entering the country. After I answered, he called another agent, who took my documents and led me down a hallway to a secondary screening room.

For three hours, I sat on a bench with others, not knowing why I was there, not knowing if I had done something wrong. No one explained anything. When my name was finally called, the officer simply handed back my passport and told me I could go. This secondary screening experience repeated itself on multiple trips. The first time, I was confused. The second time, I was nervous but expected it. By the third, I understood that my racialized identity – my brown skin, Turkish passport, and Middle Eastern-sounding name – had placed me under suspicion. It was not until a Black TSA agent at O'Hare finally looked me in the eye and said, "I don't know why they keep pulling you in for secondary screening, but I'm going to fix that," that my experience changed. After that moment, I was no longer taken to the room. I remain grateful to that agent, but I also know that my experience speaks to a broader reality: Bodies that do not fit into the mold of whiteness are scrutinized, policed, and surveilled. These experiences at the border are not just random security measures; they are part of a global racial order that dictates whose bodies are free to move and whose are stopped, searched, and questioned. As Ahmed notes, "bodies 'move up' when their whiteness is not in dispute" (2007: 160). Mine was in dispute.

Within two years of moving to the United States – from the mega-city of Istanbul to predominantly white Iowa City – I developed a racial consciousness and realized, for the first time, that I had a race. This may seem obvious to many Americans, raised in a deeply racialized society, but, for many Middle Eastern immigrants, race is often dismissed in favor of explanations centered on ethnicity, religion, or immigration status. Sociologist Neda Maghbouleh describes this as "anything but race" discourse,[7] where systemic racialization is overlooked. However, focusing solely on anti-immigration sentiment or religious intolerance risks ignoring the broader structures of whiteness that continue to dictate who belongs and who is excluded – what Eduardo Bonilla-Silva calls colorblind racism.[8] This ideology, which suggests that race no longer matters, masks whiteness as an invisible norm while reinforcing its power – both in the United States and globally. During my PhD in Iowa City, I encountered many racializing experiences – constant questions about my accent, appearance, or origins, all of which reinforced my position outside the boundaries of whiteness. Though I often found these inquiries amusing or well intentioned, one moment cut deeper than the rest. I was visiting another Midwestern town with my then-partner, a white American man, to celebrate New Year's Eve. While we were dancing in a bar, a middle-aged white woman approached us. First, she asked if we were a couple. I said yes. Then she asked where I was from. Before I could process the shift in tone, she bluntly continued: "Are you Muslim?" Without waiting for my response, she added, "I don't care what your religion is as long as you don't go around bombing people." I was speechless. I simply looked at my partner and walked out of the bar.

The weight of this encounter hit me all at once. This woman, who had never met me before, felt entitled to interrogate, stereotype, and diminish me – not because of my faith, as she did not wait for my answer, nor my nationality, as she had no idea where I was from before approaching me, but purely because of what I looked like: a Brown, Middle Eastern woman. That night, I cried in anger and anguish, but I also had a realization – I was not white, and I was not welcome in white spaces. This realization was particularly jarring because, according to US government classifications, I was white. At the time – and still today – Middle Eastern and North African (MENA) individuals are categorized as white on official forms, erasing their lived experiences of racialization. Even in academia, my racial classification remained ambiguous. One of my former department chairs, recognizing this contradiction, told me she had to list me as "multi-racial" on paperwork because there was no other option. Despite the legal and institutional whitewashing of Middle Eastern identity, my lived experience told a different story – I was not white.

The promise of neurosociology

By introducing a neurosociological approach to race and racism – the interdisciplinary study of how social structures shape neural processes and vice versa – this book aims to bridge the gap between individual experiences of race and the larger structural systems that produce and maintain racial hierarchies. Traditional approaches to studying race often focus on either macro-level social structures (e.g., institutions, policies, and historical inequalities) or micro-level psychological processes (e.g., implicit bias, perception, and identity formation). Neurosociology offers a framework that integrates these levels, demonstrating how social environments and historical legacies become ingrained in the brain, shaping how race is perceived, internalized, and reproduced in everyday interactions.

Neurosociology is an interdisciplinary sub-field of sociology that examines the interplay between neural processes and social interactions. The term "neurosociology" was first coined by the American Sociologist Warrent TenHouten[9] in 1972 and later popularized by David D. Franks.[10] Much of earlier work on neurosociology was primarily theoretical, mostly bridging sociological theory with neuroscience methods, an approach extensively outlined in the first edition of the *Handbook of Neurosociology*, published in 2013.[11] However, despite its interdisciplinary promise, neurosociology initially struggled to gain traction within mainstream sociology. This lack of initial acceptance could be attributed to a variety of factors, including methodological challenges such as accessing and obtaining specialized training in neuroscience methodologies and insufficient empirical validation due to limited early experimental research.

However, another big reason for this reluctance is the historical misuse of biological and neuroscientific research to justify racial hierarchies. From the eugenics movement to phrenology, scientific racism attempted to rationalize white superiority through pseudoscientific claims about skull sizes, cognitive ability, and racial "fitness" – leading to devastating policies such as forced sterilizations and racial exclusion laws. Given this legacy of scientific racism, it is understandable why many sociologists, social scientists, and humanities scholars have remained skeptical of biological approaches to studying race. However, rather than abandoning the study of race and the brain altogether, this book argues for a critical, community-empowering, and anti-racist neurosociology – one that acknowledges historical injustices while using interdisciplinary tools to better understand and dismantle racial inequality.

Neurosociology allows us to see race not only as a category of classification but as a groupness of deeply embodied and affective experience.[12] This duality – the simultaneous invisibility and hypervisibility of race – highlights a core theme of this book: race as both a category and a group. As a category, race functions as a system of classification – a cognitive shortcut our brains use to organize the world. Neuroscience research shows that our brains categorize people automatically, but these categories are not biologically fixed; they are shaped by social structures, history, and lived experience.[13] The fact that race is not a biologically determined reality but a socially constructed one does not diminish its power. Instead, it underscores how race operates through learned associations that become deeply ingrained in neural pathways through repeated social exposure. As a group, race is an identity marker that shapes social belonging and exclusion. Racial identity is not simply an individual perception – it is a social reality enforced by institutions, reinforced by cultural narratives, and experienced in embodied ways. This explains why race can be both invisible (when it aligns with privilege) and hypervisible (when it marks individuals as "other" or a "problem group"). Neurosociology helps explain how these dynamics of group membership, exclusion, and racialization become encoded in the brain through emotion, perception, and social interaction.

The concept of "White Turks" versus "Black Turks" in Türkiye illustrates this well. The now well-known metaphor of "White Turks" and "Black Turks" emerged in the 1990s, originally rooted in social class distinctions rather than racial ones.[14] However, despite its economic and cultural origins, the metaphor carries clear racialized connotations, reflecting how race operates both as a category and as a group in social hierarchies. As a category, "White Turk" and "Black Turk" serve as classification markers that delineate social status, modernity, and political affiliation. As a group, these labels reinforce a sense of collective identity and exclusion, shaping how individuals perceive themselves and others in Turkish society. White Turks are associated with the elite, educated, urban, secular, and westernized social class, often positioned as the cultural and economic hegemons of Türkiye. They represent a racialized category of privilege – one that aligns itself with European identity and distances itself from the non-western and Islamic influences of the East. Black Turks, in contrast, represent the historically marginalized and rural populations, who are perceived as more religious, provincial, and economically disadvantaged. Although these terms do not map onto race in the same way as in the United States or Europe, their usage reflects the ways racial hierarchies and group boundaries are constructed through social, political, and geographical divisions. This categorization has been weaponized in Turkish political discourse. President Recep Tayyip Erdoğan, in a 2015 speech,[15] declared that he was "proud to be a Black Turk," reinforcing his populist appeal to the working-class and conservative segments of society. His statement highlights how racialized group identities are not just imposed from above but also embraced strategically to challenge elite status and power. In this sense, race as a group functions not only as an imposed identity but as a mobilized one, shaping political alliances and public discourse.

Moreover, while White versus Black Turk distinctions are often framed in terms of class, they also correlate with color and geographical lines in Türkiye. White Turks are more often associated with European heritage, lighter skin tones, and urban centers like Istanbul, Ankara, and Izmir, whereas Black Turks are often linked to darker skin tones, eastern and southeastern Türkiye, and ancestry tied to regions bordering Syria, Iraq, and Iran. This intersection of racialized geography and social stratification mirrors broader global patterns where whiteness is associated with modernity, privilege, and progress, while darker-skinned and non-western populations are often marginalized as backward or inferior.

Similarly, in the United States, racial categories also intersect deeply with geography, class, and social hierarchies. Historically marginalized groups, particularly Black and

Indigenous populations, have faced systemic exclusion, economic disparity, and geographic segregation – reinforcing racialized notions of who is deemed modern, privileged, or deserving of progress. The White Turk versus Black Turk metaphor thus exemplifies how race, even when not formally recognized in a society, still structures social, political, and economic inequalities. It also demonstrates how racialized categories are fluid and can be redefined based on shifting political and cultural landscapes. In Türkiye, as in many other nations including the United States, race is not solely a biological or phenotypical distinction but a historically and socially constructed system of power – one that both organizes and reinforces group-based hierarchies. The racial hierarchies that shape contemporary societies are not merely localized or national phenomena but are deeply embedded in the history of European colonial expansion and global power structures.

This complex nature of race – both as a fundamental reality and as a malleable categorical system – also underscores the symbolic nature of our brains. This ontology of "symbolic materialism" – that our material worlds, actions, feelings, and thoughts are shaped by the symbolic – is the embedded background theoretical position that underpins this book. Humans act toward things on the basis of the meanings they assign to them, or in other words symbols, and construct as well as modify and reconstruct these meanings through social interaction.[16] Inherent in these symbols are power hierarchies that people use to communicate status differences and reproduce inequalities[17] or, in other words, draw symbolic boundaries.[18] All objects (or subjects) that humans interact with within the external as well as the internal world (i.e., individual's thoughts), including race, are products of continuous social interaction processes that are symbolic in their nature.[19] It is our internal thinking system that simultaneously represents both the internalization of external social structures and our infinite capacity to create actions, thoughts, and feelings.[20] Race becomes a part of our second nature[21] that our bodies and brains produce and reproduce unintentionally or unconsciously. Our feelings, perceptions, experiences, and interactions are intrinsically racialized, whether we admit it or not, or if they are visible or not. Our brains are *racialized*, so to speak.

About *The Racialized Brain*

The integration of sociology and neuroscience, along with my lived experiences of marginalization, ultimately shaped my intellectual trajectory and the development of this book on the neurosociology of race and racism. The very point of this book is to make a case for a sociological or a neurosociological framework through which the brain is not only "racialized" but also itself a "racializing agent," patterning and structuring the feelings and impulses as well as attitudes and behaviors of the individual within the hierarchical order of modern, racialized society.

Through a unique lens that merges sociological and neuroscientific research and theories on race and racial inequalities, this book offers an "inside out" account of the racialized life of the human brain. Neuroscience research shows that people are not born with an automatic racial preference for their in-groups, neither do we have a "race center" in our brains. Racial categorization is a learned capacity. The circuitry of race in our brains is malleable because race is a social but not a biological or genetic reality. This book provides a road map to understanding how our brains came to be racialized and whether or not we can unlearn race, with an interdisciplinary framework that focuses on the two-way process between society and the brain. To be able to demonstrate that our brains can change and unlearn racism, we need to integrate our understandings of how the racialized brain operates (how the "inside" gets outside) and how society shapes a racialized life (how the "outside" gets "inside").

Accordingly, this book walks the reader through a step-by-step progression of the racialized lives of our brains and the ways to reduce racial biases via neuroplasticity. In chapter 1 ("Is the Brain Colorblind?"), the book begins by exploring how the human brain categorizes race as a cognitive shortcut, shaping social interactions and reinforcing biases. It introduces the concept of race as both a social category and a form of group belonging, explaining how racial perception is not just an individual process but is embedded in historical, structural, and institutional contexts. This sets the foundation for understanding racial cognition and its broader societal implications.

Building on this, chapter 2 ("The Moral Life of Our Brains") examines how racial categorization extends beyond simple classification to moral appraisals of group superiority and inferiority. It delves into the role of emotions in shaping racial group identity and bias, emphasizing how moral reasoning evolved to sustain coalitional dynamics. This chapter also explores how children develop racial group awareness and how socialization influences moral and racial perceptions from an early age.

Chapter 3 ("Race in the Making") expands on these ideas by arguing that race is not a biologically fixed reality but a dynamic social construct formed at the intersection of cognition, emotion, and structural forces. It explains how racial hierarchies are maintained through historical processes and psychological mechanisms like schemas and emotion-driven biases. Using real-world examples, this chapter illustrates how media and social narratives shape racial perception, reinforcing stereotypes and structural inequality.

Chapter 4 ("The Aftermath of Race") brings our attention to the aftermath of racialized cognition and emotion. It discusses how racialized group membership influences access to healthcare, exposure to stress, and biological responses to discrimination. Drawing from public health research and neuroscience, the chapter highlights how racism impacts both physical and mental well-being, reinforcing intergenerational health inequities.

The book continues in chapter 5 ("Rewiring Our Brains") by exploring the potential of neuroplasticity to combat racial bias and systemic discrimination. It introduces the 3E framework – empathy, empowerment, and equality – as a scientifically grounded approach to reducing bias and fostering long-term change. This chapter critiques traditional bias reduction strategies and emphasizes the need for interventions that target both individual cognition and structural inequalities.

In the concluding chapter, I offer a critique of systemic biases in neuroscience methodologies and three strategies to promote equity in neuroscience research, namely, community-empowering research, color-conscious leadership, and intersectional solidarity. I conclude the book by reflecting on this emergent dynamic and contribution from integrating sociological and neuroscientific literature on race. Focusing on this two-way process offers a complete story of the racial life of our brains all the way from the patterned ways the institutions operate to create inequalities to interpersonal and intrapsychic forms of racial bias that reinforce these structural inequalities and some research-driven ways to combat them.

By integrating sociology and neuroscience, we can move beyond simplistic debates about nature versus nurture and recognize that race is learned, reinforced, and – most importantly – changeable. Through the lens of neurosociology, we can begin to dismantle the racial structures embedded in both our institutions and our neural circuits, rewiring our brains – and our societies – for a more just future.

1

Is the Brain Colorblind?

On March 29, 2024, Beyoncé released her new album *Cowboy Carter*, sparking significant controversy. The critiques questioned not only the musical characteristics of the album, that is, if it fell within the genre of country music or not, but also its message around racial identity and the authenticity of this message. The album cover features a silver-white-haired Beyoncé in a white cowboy outfit adorned with the colors of the American flag, as she rides a white horse while carrying the flag. Given the strong association of country music with whiteness and the historical perception of cowboys as white, straight men, this album received backlash from both some die-hard country fans and from Black rappers like Azealia Banks, accusing Beyoncé of "white woman cosplay."[1]

Music genres are not colorblind. There are in fact many studies that reveal the associations between racial identities and taste in music. These studies confirm the common intuitions that genres like country, rock, or classical music are more popular among white people, while rap, soul, and R&B are often identified with people of color.[2] The billboard charts of different music genres are in fact pretty good indicators of this racial music divide. Knowing this well, Beyoncé announced in an Instagram post in March of 2024 that she feels "honored to be the first Black woman with the number one single on the Hot Country Songs chart,"[3] and that her hope is "that years from now, the mention of an artist's race, as it relates to releasing genres of music, will be irrelevant." Much of the debate about *Cowboy Carter* and Beyoncé's public reaction underscores the central question this book seeks to answer: Is race a natural and unavoidable way of sorting people – in other words, hardwired in our brains – or does it function as a malleable group position shaped by historical and social forces? The answer, as this chapter explores, lies in understanding how race is processed in the brain and shaped by society.

The dual nature of race

The key argument that this book will make is that race operates in the brain through a dual mechanism: it functions on the one hand as an automatically processed category and, on the other, as a form of "groupness" tied to identity (in terms of both a person's sense of self and a person's identity in relation to other people). In other words, race is both a cognitive category and a social position, shaping how our brains interpret and experience it. Race as a category influences how people perceive one another and engage in social interactions, as the brain responds to race-related cues in social situations. Much of the psychological and social psychological research discussed here treats race primarily as a category, examining how it shapes biases, behaviors, and emotions. However, this does not mean that racial categories are static or unchangeable. Rather, as will be explored in the following sections, race functions as a heuristic cue – often in the form of stereotypes – that influences in-the-moment interactions.

What makes race a particularly powerful analytical tool is that categorical perception extends into group perception. Physical differences that are outwardly visible or audible, such as skin tone, hair, facial features, or accents, become markers of group identity. These markers are then embedded within social hierarchies that distinguish moral superiority from inferiority, not only shaping but also legitimizing the unequal distribution of resources. In this way, race is not just a perceptual category but a socially constructed system that reinforces power structures and social inequalities.

Race as a category refers to the way race is perceived and used as a classification system based on physical traits (e.g., skin color, facial features) or ancestry. This concept has been extensively studied in psychology and later in neuropsychology, particularly in the study of stereotypes. Stereotyping is primarily a cognitive process and, as I will explain in this chapter, relies predominantly – though not exclusively – on cognitive-processing regions of the brain. Research in psychology and neuroscience has explored both automatic (fast) and controlled (slow) mechanisms of stereotyping and bias. Many studies have examined how individuals unconsciously associate racial categories with stereotypes, leading to biases that shape interpersonal behavior. This chapter outlines such studies and explores the neural correlates underlying how our brains process race categorically. However, it is important to remember that racial categorization and the associated stereotypes are neither fixed nor static; they are socially constructed labels that evolve over time while continuing to function as cognitive and social heuristics. Understanding race as both a cognitive category and a social construct highlights the possibility of change. Shifts in racial hierarchies can also challenge cultural representations – such as the long-standing association between whiteness and country music. Increasing visibility of Black artists in country music – as exemplified in Beyoncé's *Cowboy Carter* – can push against rigid racial boundaries. If Beyoncé's vision holds, future generations may no longer see Black women in country music as an anomaly but rather as part of a broader and more inclusive tradition.

Race as groupness, on the other hand, refers to the collective identity and consciousness that emerge among individuals who share similar racialized experiences. This concept is studied more extensively in the social sciences, including sociology and political science. One key argument in this body of literature is that racial judgments are inherently moral in nature and reinforced by societal norms, such as meritocratic ideals. These norms contribute to biases that seek to justify social inequalities under the guise of moral superiority, such as blaming marginalized groups for their disadvantages. The brain's moral-emotional infrastructure, particularly the ventromedial prefrontal cortex (vmPFC), plays a crucial role in these processes, making them subconscious yet deeply influential – a topic that will be explored in detail in the following chapter.

While these two processes are interconnected, they develop at different stages in human life – categorization emerging first – and are supported by two distinct yet related neural pathways. This developmental sequence raises a fundamental question: are humans biologically hardwired to categorize by race? While racial categorization appears earlier in infant brain development than racial group processing, as I will explain in the next section, human babies are not born with an inherent racial bias. Just as we live in a social world, so do our brains – shaped, influenced, and developed within social environments. Racialized group relationships form within existing social systems that are shaped by historical hierarchies and systems of oppression. These social structures divide the world into moral hierarchies, assigning labels that define certain groups, appearances, and behaviors as "normal," "right," and "good." These divisions – what I will refer to in the next chapter as moral boundaries – create the content and the labels for racial categorization. Rather than racial categories being biologically predetermined, they emerge from broader social and historical contexts, building on the brain's existing infrastructure for general social categorization.

The development of race as a category in our brains

From billboard charts to interactions with the police to many other daily aspects of our lives, race is ubiquitous in our lives. Race is one of the first things most people notice when they meet a new person. In fact, even children often show racial preference early on in their lives. The doll test conducted by psychologists Kenneth and Mamie Clark in the 1940s is one famous example of how children not only recognize but also prefer one racial group over another. Drs. Kenneth and Mamie Clark conducted a series of experiments with Black children aged three to seven by showing them dolls that were identical except in skin color and asking which doll they preferred. The majority of the children in these experiments preferred the white doll over the Black doll.[4] Does this evidence of racial categorization early on in childhood mean that racial preference is innate? Are humans born with an ability to racially categorize?

Despite the pervasiveness of racially biased perceptions and behaviors, research shows that humans are not born with a racial preference. Many studies have examined racial categorization in infants. Research shows that while newborns are capable of recognizing faces (from non-faces) and show a preference for their mothers' faces, they do not exhibit a racial preference for faces.[5] Within the first three months of their lives, babies "learn" to distinguish in-group from out-group racial faces, primarily through exposure to their own race.[6] This is the process called racial categorization introduced above – perceiving race as a category. These findings are most evident in racially homogenous societies (where there is a majority racial group) and have been replicated across different cultural contexts, including the United Kingdom, Ethiopia, and China.[7] An interesting discovery from studies with infants is that, starting at three months old, babies can not only distinguish between different racial groups but also perceive differences between faces *within* racial groups – a skill known as individuation. However, this ability to individuate, or recognize distinctions within racial groups, tends to decline at about eight to nine months of age if babies are not regularly exposed to faces from other racial groups.[8] This phenomenon – where individuals recognize faces of their own race more easily than those of other races – is called the "other-race effect." It is also well documented in adults.

Humans are born with a sensitivity to facial features. This is why we are all familiar with the tendency to see faces in everyday objects – whether it's an electrical outlet, the folding clip of a Tupperware box, or the famous "man in the moon." However, we are not born with a specialized center for processing race in our brains. Racial categorization (and processing race as a social group, as will be explained in the next chapter) develops over time through exposure to (or lack of exposure to) in-group and out-group races. This means the brain can "think" race as a category (and as a group position) without a hardwired system for race. Or, in other words, the brain becomes racialized over time. More importantly, however, infants can also learn to individuate – that is, to differentiate between members of out-group – if given sufficient exposure. For example, after just three weeks of brief exposure to unfamiliar Asian female faces (through video presentations), white infants aged eight to ten months showed improved recognition of the Asian faces they were shown.[9] Human brains did not evolve to categorize race specifically. The phenotypic (physical) diversity seen in human racial features – presumed to have resulted from the geographic dispersion of people from Africa to other continents – simply did not exist long enough in evolutionary history to drive such selection.[10] However, over the course of their lives, humans quickly learn to categorize race automatically and develop racialized perceptions, thoughts, feelings, and behaviors, either voluntarily or involuntarily. Categorization is a natural and automatic cognitive process that helps humans make sense of the world, including the people around them. Although newborns are capable of recognizing facial features, this attention to faces does not translate into social – and thus racial – categorization until around six months of age.[11] This is because, while babies are born fully equipped with the cortical brain regions responsible for visual face processing (such as those in the occipital lobe),[12] the brain regions responsible for social categorization (e.g., the frontal parts of the brain) take longer to develop. Research shows that myelination – the formation of a fatty sheath around nerve fibers (axons) that facilitates faster signal transmission – occurs in a back-to-front progression in the brain: it begins in the cerebellum at the back of our brains, then extends to the occipital areas responsible for visual processing (about three to six months of age), and later reaches the temporal and frontal lobes responsible for social categorization (about six to eight months of age).[13] Thus, while babies are not born with an innate capacity for racial categorization, their ability to identify faces – and so to, eventually, engage in social categorization – emerges within the first few months of life.

The automatic categorization of objects, events, places, animals, people, and other elements provides a significant advantage to the human brain when making inductive inferences about novel experiences.[14] This process allows our brains to efficiently and quickly process new information, functioning almost like a cognitive shortcut for navigating the complex world around us. For example, the ability to instantly recognize the shape of a predator lurking in the bushes or to distinguish a poisonous plant from an edible one could mean the difference between survival and danger. Social categorization is a further elaboration of this, when we classify people into groups based on facial features or other physical characteristics. We sort people into not only racial groups but also various other social categories like gender, age, social class, and so on. Unfortunately, social, and particularly racial, categorization can have unintended consequences, such as racial bias and discrimination.

However, while racial categorization-based preferences are observed in children as early as three years old, group-based identification and bias emerges later in life (as will be explained in more detail in the next chapter). Research shows that preschoolers, around the age of three, can demonstrate awareness of social hierarchies and higher social status (i.e., which groups have higher rewards) and thus can make categorical inferences about which racial groups are more desirable (i.e., the doll experiments by Kenneth and Mamie Clark).[15] This is evident not only in white children but also in children of other racial backgrounds.[16] Somewhere between the ages of three and five, children begin to develop more robust racial preferences. For example, a research study found that while three-year-old children showed a preference for same-gender (but not race) children for friendship and social activities, those who were four years old demonstrated both gender and racial preferences.[17] By the time they are five years old, children show explicit preferences for in-group race members.[18] Generally, children begin to develop more complex racial attitudes from the ages of five to seven[19] and show a preference for in-group races,[20] which coincides with the time they enter first grade and begin internalizing the racial biases that exist in their environment.

Race as a category: stereotypes

Stereotypes are overgeneralized and oversimplified (essentialist) beliefs about categories of people that include assumptions about how individuals can, do, or should behave in certain situations. They function as the cognitive components of racialized thinking, akin to bits of information stored in our brains. For example, stereotypes such as "women cannot drive," "older people are not tech-savvy," or "Asian people are good at math" are common in western cultures. Stereotypes are activated automatically within a split second. When we see a person, we form an immediate impression based on our preconceived notions about their categorical group membership (e.g., race, age, gender). Psychologists call this automaticity, and in stereotyping it speeds up cognitive processing, making information handling more efficient. However, even seemingly positive stereotypes can have harmful effects.[21]

People begin forming stereotypes about members of other groups early in life, often during childhood, and continue acquiring new ones throughout their lives.[22] These stereotypes are learned through families, peers and friends, schools, and the media – broadly speaking their social environment. For example, children may learn gender stereotypes from toys and cartoons that depict boys as adventurous and girls as nurturing. They might adopt racial or ethnic stereotypes from media portrayals that associate certain groups with specific behaviors or occupations. Additionally, schools and textbooks can reinforce stereotypes by underrepresenting women and minorities in historical narratives, while family interactions may further shape children's perceptions of different social groups.

The perpetuation of stereotypes through social interaction and exposure to stereotyped beliefs is not random. While our brains process stereotypes as heuristic shortcuts that enhance information efficiency, stereotypes themselves are not created in a vacuum based on objective observations or facts. Instead, they are shaped and circulated within an ideological system of power and domination, reinforcing hierarchies that favor some groups over others.[23] For example, during the 1930s and 1940s, Nazi propaganda used toys, games, and caricatures to depict Jewish people in dehumanizing ways, reinforcing the stereotype of "the Jew" as evil and money hungry. In visual imagery, Jewish individuals were often portrayed with exaggerated facial features, such as a large, hooked nose and dark curly hair or beards. Additionally, many caricatures depicted Jewish people as animals, frequently as pigs – an animal considered unclean and unholy in Judaism – deliberately stripping them of their humanity.

Many of these propaganda materials, including objects, paintings, and newspaper cartoons, can be found in the United States Holocaust Memorial Museum.[24] Similarly, during the trans-Atlantic slave trade and the Jim Crow era, a variety of stereotypes about Black people were created and circulated to justify slavery and systemic oppression. These included depictions of Black individuals as lazy, ignorant, violent, or criminal – characterizations designed to uphold their subjugation.[25] However, seemingly positive stereotypes also played a role in oppression. One of the most insidious examples is the Mammy stereotype – a fictionalized image of a Black woman, usually middle-aged or older, with a relatively large body and dark skin (see Figure 1.1). She was often depicted as warm, nurturing, and deeply devoted to caring for white children, prioritizing the white family's needs over her own, even at the expense of her own Black children.[26] The Mammy figure was deliberately portrayed as desexualized, despite often being shown as a mother herself. The image was a dominant stereotype used throughout slavery and the Jim Crow era, appearing in caricatures, postcards, toys, and household items. The Jim Crow Museum at Ferris State University houses over a hundred such objects, including ashtrays and dolls, featuring the Mammy image.

Perhaps the most famous Mammy portrayal was by actress Hattie McDaniel, who played the role in the 1939 film *Gone with the Wind*. Another widely recognized example is the Aunt Jemima brand, an American pancake mix and syrup product first introduced in 1888 by Pearl Milling Company and later acquired by Quaker Oats in 1925. Based on the Mammy stereotype, the Aunt Jemima character appeared on the product's packaging and advertisements for over 130 years. On February 9, 2021, PepsiCo (Quaker Oats' parent company) announced it would retire both the Aunt Jemima name and imagery, acknowledging its roots in racial stereotyping.[27]

Many stereotypes change over time. Race and racial stereotypes are historically constructed, embedded in social

MAMMY JANE

Figure 1.1 The Mammy stereotype in historical images

Sources: Cover illustration of a sheet music book from 1918, Gaylord Music Library; 1910 photograph from the Schomburg Center for Research in Black Culture in Harlem, New York Public Library Digital Collections; 1938 Aunt Jemima Pancakes advertisement in *Life* magazine. Daniel D. Teoli Jr. Archival Collection.

institutions such as slavery. Since these institutions evolve over time, stereotypes – like race itself – are fluid and subject to change. The study of stereotypes has a long history in psychology. American psychologists, particularly in the post-slavery era, focused on the stereotypes white Americans held about Black Americans. Much of this research in the United States comes from studies conducted with college student populations, primarily because researchers – often university professors – had easy access to these participants. However, relying solely on college students to study psychological concepts has significant limitations. For example, psychologists Joseph Henrich, Steven J. Heine, and Ara Norenzayan have argued that such samples are W.E.I.R.D. (Western, Educated, Industrialized, Rich, and Democratic) and therefore not representative of wider society or the rest of the world.[28] However, in the case of racial stereotypes, studying local college populations does offer some advantages – particularly in revealing how racial categories and stereotypes operate in homogenous, educated groups. Research suggests that higher education levels are associated with a decreased likelihood of explicitly endorsing stereotypes.[29] However, this does not necessarily translate to support for racially egalitarian policies such as affirmative action, implying that highly educated individuals might have more sophisticated strategies for defending the status quo.[30] Therefore, when even highly educated college students report blatant racial stereotypes, it suggests these biases are deeply embedded in broader society.

To illustrate how stereotypes have changed over time, Table 1.1 summarizes findings from six studies on US college students spanning approximately seven decades (from the 1930s to the early 2000s). The table highlights the most frequently reported stereotypes about Black and white (or "American") groups, as perceived by white college students across these studies. Although these findings do not represent the entire US population, they provide valuable insight into how racial stereotypes have persisted and evolved over time. The first two columns in this table come from one of the earliest and most influential studies on racial stereotypes conducted by Daniel Katz and Kenneth Braly at Princeton University in the 1930s.[31] Their findings showed a stark contrast between

Table 1.1 US college students' stereotypes over time

Katz and Braly (1933)*		Gilbert (1951)*		Maykovich (1972)		Clark & Pearson (1982)		Devine & Elliot (1995)		Madon et al. (2001)	
B	A	B	A	B	W	B	W	B	W	B	A
Superstitious (84%)	Industrious (48%)	Superstitious (41%)	Materialistic (37%)	Musical (38%)	Materialistic (67%)	Aggressive (27%)	Materialistic (68%)	Athletic (74%)	Not measured.	Musical (28%)	Materialistic (54%)
Lazy (75%)	Intelligent (47%)	Musical (33%)	Intelligent (32%)	Aggressive (32%)	Aggressive (46%)	Loyal to family ties (26%)	Ambitious (30%)	Rhythmic (57%)		Loyal to family ties (22%)	Lazy (30%)
Happy-go-lucky (38%)	Materialistic (33%)	Lazy (31%)	Industrious (30%)	Impulsive (32%)	Pleasure loving (32%)	Very religious (26%)	Aggressive (30%)	Low in intelligence (46%)		Loud (21%)	Individualistic (29%)
Ignorant (38%)	Ambitious (33%)	Ignorant (24%)	Pleasure loving (27%)	Persistent (24%)	Ambitious (30%)	Progressive (18%)	Industrious (26%)	Lazy (45%)		Tradition loving (21%)	Pleasure loving (28%)
Musical (26%)	Progressive (27%)	Pleasure-loving (19%)	Individualistic (26%)	Pleasure loving (22%)	Industrious (30%)	Ambitious (18%)	Conventional (24%)	Poor (40%)		Very religious (19%)	Industrious (23%)
Princeton University		Princeton University		Sacramento State College		Wake Forest University		University of Wisconsin-Madison		Rutgers University	

B = Black; A = American; W = white.

* Katz and Braly (1933), Gilbert (1951) and Madon et al. (2001) papers used the term "Americans" instead of "white."

In cases where the universities from which these samples were drawn were not explicitly reported, institutions were inferred where possible based on the author's affiliations and descriptions of sampling procedures, using careful judgment.

stereotypes about Black people and those about Americans in general. The three most commonly reported stereotypes about Black people were *superstitious*, *lazy*, and *happy-go-lucky*, whereas the top three stereotypes about Americans were *industrious*, *intelligent*, and *materialistic*.

By the 1990s, some negative stereotypes persisted; for example, in 1995,[32] Black people were still perceived as *lazy* and *less intelligent*. However, over time, there seems to be less consensus over attributing these stereotypes to Black people. In 1933, 75% of participants in the Katz and Braly study attributed *laziness* to Black people while, in 1995, only 45% of participants in the Devine and Elliott study did so. Moreover, seemingly positive stereotypes like *musical* (or *rhythmic*) remained persistent, or new positive ones like *athletic* seemed to appear for Black people. Stereotypes about white or "American" identity, on the other hand, consistently emphasized traits such as *materialism* and *industriousness* – two attributes that appeared across all studies spanning seven decades.

The hidden harm of positive stereotypes

While some stereotypes are positive, this does not mean they are harmless. A series of experiments with North American (United States and Canadian) participants demonstrated how positive stereotypes reinforce essentialist beliefs about racial differences.[33] In this study, participants were presented with fake news articles about a fictional scientific study that confirmed either: (1) a positive stereotype (e.g., *Black people are superior athletes*); or (2) a negative stereotype (e.g., *Black people have lower intelligence and academic ability*).[34] Findings showed that people were more likely to accept the positive stereotype as true while questioning the negative stereotype. So, they were less skeptical of positive stereotypes. However, those exposed to the positive stereotype (i.e., athletic ability) were also more likely to attribute racial differences to biological (natural) causes than those who read the negative stereotype. Positive stereotypes led to more essentializing beliefs about the biological differences between racial groups, which have historically served as a foundation for racism and harmful racial prejudice, reinforcing notions of inherent superiority and inferiority.

A follow-up experiment within the same study tested what influence these positive stereotypes might have on broader racial judgments. Participants were asked to read two news articles, one containing positive news about athletic performance and a second negative one about higher violent tendencies among Black people. After reading these articles, they were asked to rate fictitious profiles of Black men on kindness, cheating, criminality, or volunteering at a charity. Surprisingly, those exposed to the positive stereotype (athletic ability) were more likely than those exposed to the negative stereotype to rate the Black profiles higher in cheating and criminality.[35] This suggests that even seemingly harmless stereotypes can reinforce negative biases and shape perceptions in damaging ways.

Stereotype knowledge versus endorsement

It is important to note that knowing a stereotype exists is different from endorsing it. Psychologists distinguish between stereotype knowledge (awareness of cultural stereotypes) and endorsement (personal belief in those stereotypes). Simply being aware of a stereotype does not mean an individual endorses it or acts on it.[36] For example, as seen in the chapter's opening discussion of *Cowboy Carter*, Beyoncé's foray into country music was widely recognized as unusual or unexpected within mainstream cultural narratives, but that awareness did not necessarily mean that everyone viewed it negatively or opposed her presence in the genre. However, even when people do not personally endorse stereotypes, they can still have detrimental consequences. Even after winning the 2025 Grammy Award for Album of the Year, Beyoncé faced widespread questioning, with some critiques saying the album "is just a gimmick"[37] and does not feel like authentic country music.[38] Even if these reactions were not always driven by overt malice – for example, some critiques praised Beyoncé's excellence in the R&B genre and suggested she should stick with it[39] – they contributed to a broader pattern of skepticism and lack of recognition. This illustrates how deeply ingrained stereotypes can shape perceptions and responses, often in ways that reinforce exclusionary norms.

One well-documented example of the harmful effects of stereotypes – even in the absence of personal endorsement – is stereotype threat. First identified by psychologists Claude Steele and Joshua Aronson in 1995,[40] stereotype threat occurs when individuals underperform due to fear of confirming a negative stereotype about their group. It operates much like a self-fulfilling prophecy. This effect is particularly well documented in academic performance. When the categorical membership of a student (e.g., gender or race) is brought to their attention during an assessment, they perform worse. In their iconic study, Steele and Aronson found that Black participants performed significantly worse than white participants on a difficult verbal test when it was described as an "intelligence test." However, when the same test was not framed as a measure of intelligence, the racial performance gap disappeared. In other words, when participants were reminded of the stereotype about Black people being less intelligent, they performed worse – even though they did not personally believe in the stereotype. Since Steele and Aronson's original study, hundreds of studies have replicated stereotype threat across various performance domains, including math tests among women and cognitive tasks among older adults.[41] These findings offer critical insight into why racial and gender achievement gaps persist in education and professional settings.[42]

A personal example from my own life strongly resonates for me with these studies. When I was in elementary school in Türkiye, I remember my teacher punishing me for struggling with math. Her being mad at me over a geometry assignment that I got wrong is still a vivid memory in my mind. Of course, at the time I didn't explicitly think, "I am bad at math because I'm a girl," but over the years, as this pattern continued, I began to internalize the idea that math just wasn't for me. Looking back, I can see how the stress and lack of confidence I experienced were intertwined with the pervasive stereotype that girls aren't naturally good at math, even if no one ever said it outright. Despite this, my math skills improved in high school, and I even began scoring highly on standardized tests, which ultimately earned me scholarships to college. However, even then, I always saw myself as a qualitative critical scholar, believing that I would have little to do with numbers. It wasn't until I started my PhD program at Iowa, taking statistics courses from women professors and seeing other female graduate students excelling in math and statistics, that I began to think, "Oh, I actually really enjoy numbers." Despite all my preconceived notions – both personal and societal – about women not being good at math, I realized that I was actually a quantitative thinker. I also learned that one can apply quantitative methods while still being a critical scholar.

These "aha" moments ultimately shaped my research agenda, which applies a critical, quantitative methodology to studying race relations. Unfortunately, I still see many undergraduate and graduate students – particularly women and those from underrepresented racial or socioeconomic backgrounds – who falsely believe they are not good at math. Ironically, I have also observed some white male students displaying false confidence in their math abilities, even when they are not particularly strong in the subject. In fact, I have seen this overconfidence negatively impact some male graduate students' academic success. Often, their belief in their superior math skills prevents them from seeking help or utilizing resources such as professors or university support services for assignments and research papers.

Thus, my personal experiences align with existing research on the harmful effects of stereotypes even in the absence of explicit endorsement. Stereotypes – whether negative or positive – not only shape individual perceptions but can also impact academic achievement, confidence, and opportunities for growth in unexpected ways. Even when people do not believe in stereotypes, their mere existence in society can negatively impact performance, self-perception, and opportunities for success. Understanding how stereotypes evolve, persist, and influence behavior is crucial for addressing racial and gender disparities in education, employment, and broader social structures.

Implicit bias

While traditional studies of stereotypes have primarily relied on explicit measures, such as checklist reports (offering a list of stereotypes that participants can pick from) or survey questions, a new research paradigm focusing on implicit or automatic stereotypes (or bias more generally) emerged in the 1990s.[43] The idea behind these newer measurements and implicit bias theories is that contemporary racism is often more subtle, sometimes even occurring outside people's conscious awareness. In fact, even individuals who explicitly endorse racial equality may still exhibit implicit biases in their behavior. For example, a job interviewer may strongly value racial equality and consciously reject racial discrimination. However, during an interview, they might still exhibit non-conscious bias through their facial expressions (e.g., how much they smile) or body language (e.g., more open and engaged versus closed and guarded posture). According to the implicit bias framework, these subtle behaviors – even in the absence of explicit biases – may indicate an unconscious bias at play.

Implicit bias is most commonly measured using the implicit association test (IAT), developed in the late 1990s by American psychologists Anthony Greenwald and Mahzarin Banaji.[44] The IAT is a computer-based test designed to measure automatic, subconscious reactions to different social groups using a priming technique. Participants are asked to quickly match social categories (e.g., *Black vs. white people, men vs. women, young vs. old*) with different attributes (e.g., *positive vs. negative, strong vs. weak, good vs. bad*). The key idea is that the test does not assess explicit prejudice but rather the speed and ease with which participants associate different groups with positive or negative attributes. The speed at which individuals make these associations – referred to as reaction time – is used as an indicator of implicit bias. Since people are generally expected to link all groups to positive attributes, any differences in reaction time reveal implicit biases rather than intentional discriminatory beliefs. For example, if a person has an implicit bias against a racial minority, they may take longer to associate that group with positive attributes compared to negative ones. The IAT technique has been widely used to demonstrate implicit bias against Black people in the United States.[45]

An even more striking line of research builds upon implicit priming techniques to measure a phenomenon known as "weapon bias." In one set of studies, participants were shown images of Black and white men holding either a weapon or a non-threatening object (e.g., a cell phone). They were then asked to "shoot" if the individual was carrying a weapon and "not shoot" if they were not.[46] Findings revealed that participants were more likely to mistakenly shoot an unarmed Black person than an unarmed white person and were slower to withhold fire when the unarmed person was Black, compared to when the unarmed person was white. In a follow-up study, researchers extended this experiment to actual police officers in the Denver area.[47] The results showed that while police officers were less likely than civilians to make erroneous shots at unarmed Black individuals, their response times still showed bias – they were slower to decide not to shoot an unarmed Black person compared to an unarmed white person. These studies highlight the real-life implications of implicit bias, especially in high-stakes situations such as policing and criminal justice.

Despite its widespread use, the IAT has also faced criticism. Some researchers argue that the test may not measure personal bias as accurately as it claims. Instead, they suggest it might reflect familiarity with stereotypes rather than personal belief in them (stereotype knowledge rather than stereotype endorsement) or cultural knowledge of how certain groups are perceived in society.[48] However, even if the IAT primarily captures cultural knowledge rather than personal endorsement of stereotypes, this is still highly relevant. Stereotype knowledge plays a crucial role in shaping societal norms, institutions, and behaviors, making it an important factor in understanding racial dynamics. It is just another example of how the brain and its processes are entangled in the social worlds we live in, demonstrating the complex interplay between cognition and culture.

How our brains "see" race as a category

Brain imaging

There is no specific "race center" in the human brain. As explained at the beginning of this chapter, babies are not born with racial bias and are unable to code race. However, we are still able to process race as a category using facial categorization, memory, threat/salience detection, and cognitive perspective-taking regions of our brains. Our understanding of the brain regions involved in racial processing and social behavior has advanced significantly thanks to brain-imaging technology developed toward the turn of the twenty-first century. In 1991, functional magnetic resonance imaging (fMRI) was developed using the magnetic resonance imaging (MRI) scanner, a technology originally invented in 1984 to produce detailed images of the body. fMRI is a specialized type of MRI that detects the blood flow changes in the brain.[49]

One of the groundbreaking discoveries of the early 1990s was that oxygenated and deoxygenated hemoglobin (red blood cells) exhibit different magnetic properties. When a certain brain region becomes more active, such as while processing visual stimuli, it requires more oxygen, which is delivered through increased blood flow (oxygenated hemoglobin). The fMRI scanner is a giant, powerful magnet (see Figure 1.2) that can detect these changes in the blood flow, called the blood oxygenation level-dependent (BOLD) signal, and thus make inference about neural activity. Researchers analyze these data statistically to create high-resolution functional activity maps of the brain. Unlike other imaging methods, fMRI scanning measures both brain function and anatomy, making it particularly valuable for studying racial bias and social cognition in psychology.

Despite its revolutionary contributions, fMRI has several limitations. It is a correlational and indirect method because it measures changes in blood flow and oxygenation rather than direct neuronal activity. While fMRI is excellent for identifying where brain activity occurs (spatial resolution), it is less effective at capturing when activity happens (temporal resolution). The technique is also highly sensitive to motion artifacts, requiring participants to remain completely still inside

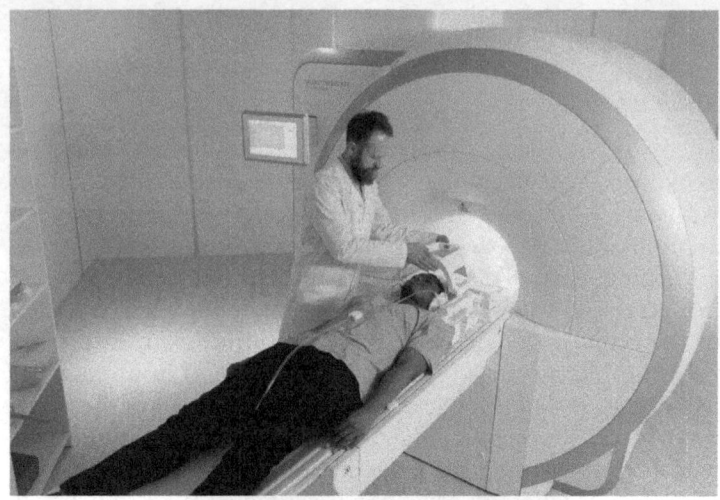

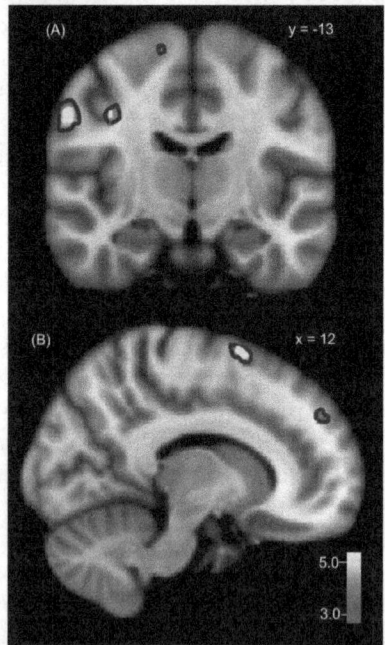

Figure 1.2 Functional magnetic resonance imaging scanner, and an example of functional activity maps obtained through fMRI scanning

Source: Mart Production, Pexels; PLOS, Wikimedia Commons (Ellert Nijenhuis)

the scanner, which can be difficult during long experimental sessions. And, more controversially, the fMRI analyses can be susceptible to erroneous results and misinterpretations due to the very large volume of the data. Because the fMRI takes snapshots of the brain every few seconds from three different angles, it produces three-dimensional voxel data (volumetric pixel), which can range from a few hundred thousand to millions of data points in a single experiment. Without proper statistical corrections, false positives might emerge from the data, showing activation when there is none.

One of the infamous examples of statistical errors in fMRI research is the "dead salmon" controversy. In this experiment, researchers scanned a dead Atlantic salmon while it was "shown" photos of individuals in various social situations and was "asked" to identify the emotions they were experiencing – a social perspective-taking task – inside an fMRI scanner.[50] When statistical thresholds were not properly applied, the analysis falsely indicated brain activity in the dead fish. Researchers referred to these misleading results as "voodoo correlations." Publication of this paper led to many rebuttals of the fMRI technique and its accuracy.[51] However, the real implication of this study is that it is extremely important to apply appropriate analytical strategies and cross-validating findings from one study with other imaging studies or other neuroscientific evidence, such as that coming from non-fMRI studies, for example, lesion studies, which behaviorally observe patients with brain damage, or the electroencephalogram (EEG), which measures electrical activity in the brain.

Despite these limitations, fMRI has revolutionized neuroscience by allowing researchers to explore brain connectivity, activation patterns, and cognitive functions without requiring invasive procedures. Compared to older imaging techniques like computed tomography (CT) or positron emission tomography (PET), which expose the body to radiation, fMRI is considered much safer and non-invasive. It provides whole-brain imaging, allows researchers to focus on specific regions of interest, and can map connectivity between brain regions, making it an essential tool for studying human cognition.

However, fMRI research faces challenges related to cost and accessibility. fMRI machines are extremely expensive to purchase, maintain, and operate, limiting access, especially for researchers in underfunded disciplines such as sociology. As a result, most fMRI studies on race and bias come from psychology and neuroscience, fields that focus on how the brain categorizes race rather than the broader societal, structural, and historical factors shaping racial cognition. While fMRI research has greatly contributed to understanding how the brain processes race categorically, it has been less concerned with societal context and historical institutions that shape racial perception (something addressed in the next chapter).

Processing racial categories in our brains

Many neuroimaging studies since the early 2000s have focused on the perception of race as a category. Researchers began shifting their attention to the brain to understand racial categorization and bias, partly due to the increasing influence of implicit bias research, which gained both scientific and popular traction. Experiments such as the IAT provided strong evidence that implicit biases are widespread and require attention, demonstrating that measuring racial bias through explicit questionnaires was often ineffective, as most people would not openly admit to racial bias. As a result, neuroscientists began exploring brain activity during racial bias tasks. Many of these studies used IAT-style experiments in which participants viewed Black and white faces and were asked to associate them with positive or negative adjectives, revealing a distributed neural network that processes race as a category. This network includes the fusiform gyrus, temporal lobes, temporal pole, amygdala, and dorsomedial prefrontal cortex (dmPFC) (see Figure 1.3). These regions are not an exhaustive list of all brain areas involved in stereotyping, nor do they include the brain regions involved in processing race as a group, which will be discussed in the next chapter, or the regulation and inhibition of bias, which will be covered in chapter 5. Identifying the regions more frequently involved in one type of racial processing over another helps us understand how the brain enables two different constructs of race (i.e., as category and as groupness).

Sensory cortices, such as the visual cortex, and the fusiform gyrus are critical for social categorization, particularly in processing facial features. The fusiform gyrus[52] helps to

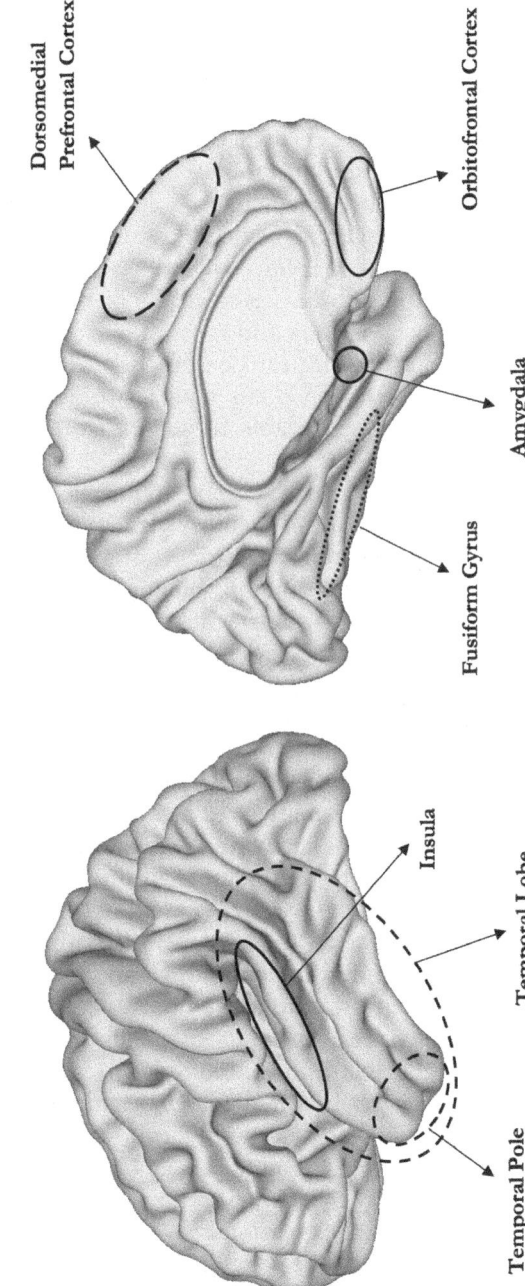

Figure 1.3 Neuroanatomy of the racial category processing regions of the brain

Source: Adapted from the Harvard-Oxford atlas developed at the Center for Morphometric Analysis (CMA) and distributed with the FMRIB Software Library (FSL) (Bakker, Tiesinga, and Kötter 2015); 3D Surface View (Majka et al. 2012)

assign individuals to different social groups, including racial groups.[53] It is located basally on the surface of temporal and occipital lobes and is connected to the anterior temporal lobes[54] as well as to the amygdala.[55] Within this region, the fusiform face area (FFA) is specialized for face recognition. Remarkably, this region responds to faces even in people who are blind from birth when they touch a three-dimensional sculpture of a face.[56] Electrically stimulating the FFA of the brain leads to distortions of facial perception, giving them a "metamorphosed" appearance.[57] Research suggests that the FFA is especially crucial for sex and race categorization, and its function in racial categorization corresponds with implicit racial bias: more biased individuals tend to show stronger FFA activation and are better able to categorize faces into racial groups.[58]

Stereotyping processes also rely on semantic memory processes – a type of long-term memory that stores general information about concepts or categories that are not tied to personal experiences. After sorting people into racial groups, semantic processing occurs by retrieving general knowledge about these groups from memory. Semantic processing occurs largely in the temporal lobes and the temporal pole of our brains. The temporal lobe, located on the sides of the brain near the temples, is responsible for auditory processing, language, memory, and emotions. The lateral temporal lobes and the temporal pole are also involved in automatic processing of social information.[59] The anterior part of our temporal lobes plays a crucial role in representing information about a person,[60] and maintaining stereotype knowledge about groups, which is then relayed to higher-level cognitive areas such as the medial prefrontal cortex (mPFC) and the dmPFC. Studies have shown that the anterior temporal lobe and temporal pole exhibit increased activation during race-related IAT experiments.[61] Furthermore, inhibiting anterior temporal lobe activity using transcranial magnetic stimulation, a non-invasive technique that disrupts neural activity in specific brain regions, has been found to reduce biased responses on gender-based IAT tasks.[62] These findings underscore the importance of temporal lobes, particularly anterior temporal lobes, for semantic categorization and conceptualization of social knowledge.

The amygdala is one of the most widely studied brain structures in racial bias research and plays a central role in processing race as both a category and a group. This almond-shaped structure, located deep within the medial temporal lobes, has strong connections with the prefrontal cortex and several subcortical structures, including the hippocampus.[63] The amygdala is primarily associated with processing emotions, especially fear, and emotional memory,[64] and plays a crucial role in evaluating social trustworthiness and approachability based on facial cues. People with bilateral amygdala damage struggle to assess trustworthiness[65] and fail to recognize fearful facial expressions,[66] highlighting its role in social evaluation. Many neuroimaging studies on racial bias have shown that the amygdala exhibits heightened activation in response to out-group faces, particularly Black faces in the United States.[67] Moreover, amygdala activation is more strongly linked to implicit racial evaluations, such as those measured by IAT scores, rather than explicit racial attitudes.[68] However, some studies have also found increased amygdala activation in response to in-group faces, particularly in comparisons between white and Asian individuals.[69] This means that both white and Asian participants showed greater amygdala activation when viewing faces of their own racial group compared to out-group faces. These findings suggest that the amygdala has a broader function in detecting and evaluating emotionally salient information and is involved in retrieving emotional memories, including implicit or non-conscious associations with racial categories.

The dmPFC, a region in the prefrontal cortex situated in the top and medial section of the frontal lobes, plays a significant role in processing race as a category. This region is involved in understanding personality traits and mental states – a function of what psychologists call theory of mind, or the ability to infer what others might be thinking or feeling.[70] The dmPFC is also associated with categorizing objects, events, or behaviors into broader and more abstract groups[71] (e.g., while an individual act of violence is a specific instance, the concept of violence as a trait represents a higher-level abstraction)[72] and forming social impressions about people.[73] Research suggests this process of abstraction extends beyond social groups; the dmPFC is also involved in constructing abstract categories not only for people but also for objects and animals.[74] This supports the idea that social categorization and stereotyping are not uniquely about race but rather are general cognitive mechanisms for organizing information efficiently.[75]

Interestingly, brain-imaging studies on racial stereotyping show that the dmPFC activation increases when people encounter information that does not match established stereotypes (e.g., associations of Black people with positive versus negative adjectives).[76] This effect is even more pronounced among individuals who have a strong tendency to apply biases.[77] These findings suggest that the dmPFC is crucial not only for creating abstract categories but also for integrating social knowledge with personal biases and motivations in shaping social behavior and interactions. However, while much of the research on social categorization and stereotyping has focused on singular social identities – such as race alone – real-world identities are rarely so simple. People do not just belong to one category; they hold multiple, intersecting social identities that shape their experiences in complex ways.

A note on intersectionality in the brain

As discussed earlier, the brain regions involved in how we "see" race are not specialized for race alone – they also process other social categories, such as gender. This underlines an important point: there is no specific "race center" in the human brain. Instead, our brains categorize people across multiple dimensions simultaneously, shaping how we perceive and interact with others. But it also means we should stop for a moment to think about what it means for the brain to be processing these multiple forms of social category.

Intersectionality, which is a concept coined by Kimberlé W. Crenshaw in 1989,[78] explains how multiple aspects of a person's social identity such as gender, social class, race, age, disability status, and so on interact to shape their experiences of privilege and oppression. We all hold multiple social identities at the same time. For example, I identify as an immigrant, a Brown woman, and a middle-class person, due to my higher education. The combination of these intersecting identities shapes my sense of self and my social experiences in a way that no single identity could fully capture on its own. Depending on the context, certain aspects of identity may become more prominent than others, creating a unique social position that influences how I navigate the world. Especially when multiple marginalized identities intersect, such as being both a woman and a racial minority, the unique intersectional experience extends beyond simply adding these identities together. The interactions between these identities create a distinct social position that shapes lived experiences in ways that cannot be reduced to the sum of their parts. Intersectional identities can be both sources of oppression and empowerment, depending on the social context and individual agency. For example, feminist scholar Patricia Hill Collins[79] argues that Black women, despite facing oppression from Eurocentric and masculinist perspectives, cultivate a form of collective empowerment through their everyday roles as mothers, educators, church leaders, and community organizers. Through these roles, they actively build and sustain communities that foster resilience and shared consciousness. This collective awareness not only enables them to navigate systemic oppression but also strengthens their capacity to challenge and redefine dominant narratives about race, gender, and power.

Intersectionality has been a central focus in sociology and feminist studies, yet it remains relatively underexplored in neuroscience, despite growing psychological evidence demonstrating its effects on cognitive processing. For example, in one foundational study, white participants associated the categories of "Blackness" and "maleness" more closely together, reinforcing the stereotype that Black individuals – regardless of gender – are perceived as more physically dominant or aggressive. They also perceived both Black men and women as more masculine than their white counterparts and rated Black women as less attractive than white women,[80] while Asian men in contrast, as shown by different research, are often perceived as more feminine compared to other racial groups. These findings suggest that race and gender are not processed as independently but interact in a complex matrix, where different racial and gender combinations elicit distinct, intersecting biases rather than fitting into a single linear comparison. However, neuroscience research has yet to fully integrate an intersectional framework into the study of how these identities shape perception, cognition, and bias.

Few neuroscience studies have explicitly applied an intersectional approach to understanding the brain. One such study examined how the brain processes overlapping social categories, such as race and gender, by examining neural responses associated with these categories.[81] Participants were shown faces varying in gender (female, male), race (Black, white, Asian), and emotions (angry, happy) with twelve category combinations (e.g., Asian woman with angry face) while inside an fMRI scanner. After scanning, the participants were asked to categorize all faces by gender, race, and emotion using a mouse click. Their hand movements were tracked to measure how much their response was influenced by the other unselected category before making a final choice (e.g., how much their mouse moved toward "male" before they made their final selection of "female"). Similar to previous research, participants showed more biased responses in rating male and Black faces as more angry, Asian faces as more female, and female faces as more happy categorizations. Moreover, multiple social categories were co-activated in the brain, even when only one is explicitly being selected. For example, the brain activity when seeing a Black face resembled the activity when seeing a male face, reinforcing how stereotypes shape perception at a neural level.

Despite the evidence on the intersectionality of social categorization processes in our brain, there is still very limited research that intentionally examines how multiple social identities interact to shape neural outcomes. Neurofeminisim, a critical neuroscience approach, calls for attention to intersectional research on the brain, emphasizing the need to move beyond single-category analyses.[82] Neurofeminists argue that traditional neuroscience has largely overlooked the ways in which multiple identities intersect, both in research design and analysis, leaving gaps in our understanding of social perception. Women, particularly women of color, are often underrepresented in neuroscience and psychology studies on race. Many of the images used in classical experiments, such as the IAT or facial recognition tasks, primarily feature male faces unless the study is explicitly about gender stereotypes or prejudice, in which case racial diversity is still often overlooked. Similarly, the intersectional identities of the researchers conducting these studies and the potential influence of their positionality on the study population are rarely acknowledged in mainstream neuroscience research. While there have been more recent efforts to recognize power dynamics in knowledge production,[83] the majority of studies do not include information on these dimensions, nor does the field widely consider how power influences the construction of scientific knowledge. These issues present important future directions for neuroscience, particularly in the study of race, gender, and social cognition.

Summary

This chapter has introduced the idea that race operates both as a cognitive sorting mechanism and a socially constructed group position without a hardwired center for race. Humans are not born with an innate sense of race, though categorization is a natural brain function. Studies on infants show that racial categorization emerges through exposure to specific social environments. For example, the "other-race effect," where individuals recognize faces of their own racial group more easily, develops through early exposure but can be mitigated with diverse interactions. Yet this cognitive sorting does not imply inherent bias. Research shows racial preferences in social interactions emerge only after two and a half years, pointing to social learning as a key factor. These findings emphasize that race is not biologically fixed but is learned through societal exposure and experiences.

This chapter distinguished between race as a social category – where stereotypes shape automatic racial perceptions – and as a social group, driven by historical power dynamics that foster in-group favoritism and prejudice. Stereotypes are cognitive shortcuts that allow the brain to process information quickly, but they are deeply shaped by societal contexts. For instance, the enduring stereotype of Black athleticism versus intelligence reveals how racial categories are reinforced by historical and cultural ideologies. Stereotypes, though seemingly efficient, often perpetuate harmful biases, such as stereotype threat, which impacts individual performance and self-concept.

Advancements in brain-imaging technologies have equipped researchers with amazing tools to understand contemporary racial bias, which is more subtle and implicit yet still pervasive. As I tried to convey in this chapter, our brains have not evolved a specific race cognition center that is responsible for racism. The natural processes for categorizing, face perceptions, memory, emotions, and social cognition have become the infrastructure for racial categorizing in the brain. Without neurosciences, we would be unable to understand how these mechanisms operate and would be making erroneous assumptions on the nature of bias and group identities. However, much of this neuroscience research also does not provide the full picture. Neuroscience studies are often individualistic, fail to include real-life contextual information or even multiple categories or identities (e.g., intersectionality), and mostly ignore the socially constructed nature of race. Most of this research focuses on race as a somewhat static category.

Beyond cognitive categories, however, race also functions as a group position. Rooted in historical struggles, collective consciousness, and institutionalized moral ideologies, racial groupness goes beyond individual categorization or simple sorting of individuals to a shared sense of belonging, solidarity, and position within a social hierarchy, which also leads to moral boundaries that divide racial groups. Pervasive moral ideologies of meritocracy influence our brains via shaping moral emotions, which serve, justify, and sustain racism. Modern racism disguises itself under socially acceptable moral codes and reasoning. While this chapter has shown how race operates as a cognitive sorting mechanism in the brain, the next chapter will focus on how moral boundaries and societal systems influence these brain-level mechanisms, shaping modern forms of subtle racism.

2

The Moral Life of Our Brains

The previous chapter introduced some of the ways we process race as a social category, a process enabled by our brains' readily available capacity for social categorization. This cognitive ability provides shortcuts that automatically divide the world into groups, which can reinforce and perpetuate racialized perceptions and biases. This chapter shifts our attention to how our brains can "think" race as a social group – an alternative yet interconnected aspect of racial processing. Thinking about race as a social group goes beyond mere categorization; it embeds race within a broader social, cultural, and historical framework of group relationships. When we process race in this way, we do not merely identify racial groups or feel a sense of belonging to them; we also attach moral appraisals of inferiority and superiority, shaped by the emotional significance of group membership. As discussed in chapter 1, racial categorization is primarily a cognitive process (though not exclusively so), whereas racial groupness is fundamentally a moral and emotional one.

Think of the most recent, 2024, US presidential elections. Group- and identity-based politics played a central role in presidential debates and public discourse. For example, one of the key narratives promoted by then-presidential candidate Donald Trump and the Republican Party was the suggestion that most immigrants are violent criminals. In a particularly controversial statement during the September 10, 2024 presidential debate, Trump alleged that Haitian immigrants in Ohio were stealing and eating pets. This assertion sparked significant public backlash, generating widespread debate across social media and news platforms. Such rhetoric illustrates how negative emotions and perceived moral superiority (e.g., a US-born American over an immigrant) are employed to racialize groups, inciting anger and avoidance toward members of racialized communities perceived as violating prized societal norms and values.

Distinguishing between processing race as a category versus as a group in real-life situations can be challenging since the two processes often influence each other. However, one of the key distinctions lies in their nature: racial categorization and the stereotypes associated with it do not necessarily have to be endorsed by individuals who are aware of them, meaning they are not inherently self-referential. In contrast, racial groupness is a self-referential process that involves social comparisons between the in-group and the out-group. Race as a social group is collectively constructed through historical processes in which the dominant racial group defines its position in opposition to subordinate racial groups. This historical process, shaped by key societal events, can foster in-group favoritism and prejudiced emotions.[1] American psychologist Gordon Allport[2] famously described prejudice as a "feeling, favorable or unfavorable, toward a person or thing, prior to, or not based on, actual experience."

Race, as a social position shared (to varying degrees) by members of a group, elicits similar positive feelings toward in-group members while generating antagonistic or aversive emotions – such as prejudice – toward out-group members. This chapter argues that racial groupness is processed and enacted in our brains – not because we possess a dedicated neurological structure for racial identity, but because our brains are biologically equipped to form and sustain coalitions and moral frameworks. Evolutionary psychologists suggest that various aspects of moral cognition – such as punishing free-riders, enforcing moral norms, and endorsing social conventions – evolved because they helped maintain group cohesion and cooperation.[3] In other words, morality serves group interests. As a result, moral judgments, emotions, and intuitions are deeply intertwined with our sense of group identity.

Humans are inherently social animals who evolved in small, isolated groups that were genetically and culturally (and, by extension, ethnically and racially) diverse.[4] To coordinate actions for mutual benefit – such as competing more effectively for resources – our brains evolved a moral, coalitional psychology capable of distinguishing allies from adversaries. This psychological mechanism attributes to groups specific intentions, values, status, and prerogatives.[5] Consequently, we instinctively identify with and defend our group's interests, interpreting the world through an "us versus them" lens. Importantly, moral reasoning and emotions play a crucial role in reinforcing these group boundaries. Moral intuitions, such as loyalty to the in-group and condemnation of perceived threats, serve to maintain group cohesion by fostering trust and cooperation within the group while justifying hostility toward outsiders. While these coalitional instincts were once advantageous for survival, in modern society they contribute to social divisions, including racial biases. By understanding how morality is intertwined with group dynamics, we can begin to recognize and challenge the ways in which moral judgments reinforce racial and social hierarchies.

Development of race as groupness in childhood

Growing up in Türkiye, my family moved frequently, due to my parents' public sector jobs. In fact, by the time I started high school, I had lived in seven different cities. One of the biggest challenges of this constant relocation was having to make new friends in every neighborhood and school. When I was younger, before starting elementary school, I remember feeling a bit shy about approaching new children. My parents, however, had a simple yet effective strategy: they would walk me over to a group of kids playing in the street and directly ask, "Can Rengin play with you?" The result was almost always immediate and effortless – I would naturally blend into the group and begin playing. I never recall having trouble finding playmates until I started school. Simply arriving with the intention to play and make friends seemed to be enough to be accepted into this new *coalition.*

Research on infants and their social preferences supports this anecdotal experience, suggesting that young children rely more on behavioral cues than on static features like race or clothing when forming social alliances.[6] Infants exhibit coalitional thinking as an innate evolutionary adaptation that helps them navigate social interactions. From distinguishing friends from foes to choosing play partners, they demonstrate a remarkable ability to perceive and react to group dynamics from an early age. Studies show that infants prefer individuals who cooperate with one another, and they tend to ignore or even reject those who hinder others.

A now-classic study by psychologists Kiley Hamlin, Karen Wynn, and Paul Bloom illustrates this phenomenon in an innovative way.[7] In the experiment, six- and ten-month-old infants watched a puppet show featuring simple wooden shapes with large googly eyes. In the show, a blue circle attempted to climb a hill but struggled and began to slide backward. A triangle or a square either helped by pushing the circle up or hindered its progress by pushing it down. When the infants were later asked to choose between the helper and the hinderer, both age groups overwhelmingly preferred the helper, suggesting that even at just six months old, human infants can track coalitional intentions through behavioral cues.

Interestingly, when the same puppets appeared without the glued-on eyes, the infants no longer showed a preference between the helper and the hinderer. This suggests that the presence of eyes signaled important social cues, allowing infants to categorize the puppets as intentional social agents. A key implication of this finding is that infants first categorize objects as animate or inanimate – agents with intentions versus those without – before evaluating their cooperative behaviors. This early ability to distinguish social agents and assess their interactions lays the foundation for more complex social categorization and coalition building later in life.

While identities based on physical characteristics have not yet developed in early childhood, the fundamental components of coalitional thinking and morality begin to emerge during this stage.[8] As demonstrated in the previous example, infants can distinguish between cooperators and those who defect from coalitions. By fifteen months of age, they are capable of making fairness judgments – such as recognizing unequal distributions of prized possessions like toys or candy.[9] Furthermore, infants around this age begin to categorize race differently depending on the social context. For instance, in a research study, 14-month-old infants were primed with collaborative interactions (i.e., with a video where two individuals collaborated to build a Lego train) versus competitive interactions (i.e., with a video where two individuals competed over the Lego pieces) and then asked to categorize images of Black and white men and women separately.[10] The infants' looking time and the direction of their gaze (standard measures of categorization in infants) were used as measures of categorization. When infants were primed with the collaboration video, they were better able to distinguish between Black and white women. On the other hand, when they were primed with the competition video, they were better able to distinguish between Black and white men. Accordingly, "collaboration" enhanced racial categorization of women while "competition" facilitated the same for men, likely because of the evolutionary and social association of women with nurturing and cooperative roles and men with conflict and intergroup competition.[11] These findings suggest that infants are not only sensitive to coalitional cues before they fully understand group structures but also that they use this information to guide their social categorization.

However, coalition-based racial preferences, moving beyond categorization, do not fully emerge until after two and a half years of age, when children enter the toddler stage. Research on fairness judgments in children reveals a developmental shift in racial bias over time. In one study, two-and-a-half-year-old white toddlers displayed a tendency to attribute fair resource distributions to Black distributors, whereas seven-year-olds exhibited a pro-white bias.[12] This finding suggests that early social categorization does not inherently favor one's racial in-group but instead evolves with social exposure and learned biases.

These developmental changes in group perceptions and judgments coincide with the maturation of moral evaluations, particularly moral emotional processing in children.

A study examining the neurodevelopmental origins of moral sensitivity analyzed 126 participants ranging from four years old to 37 years old.[13] Participants were presented with visual scenarios depicting moral (harm directed at people) versus non-moral (harm affecting objects) situations, with actions categorized as either intentional (e.g., hitting someone on purpose) or unintentional (e.g., accidentally knocking someone over). Across all age groups, individuals exhibited more intense emotional responses to intentional moral harm, with heightened activity in brain regions associated with emotion processing, such as the amygdala and the insula. However, these emotional responses were strongest among younger children, who showed little to no activation in the prefrontal cortex, the region responsible for higher-order reasoning and self-regulation. With age, activation in the vmPFC – a key brain region for socio-moral emotional regulation – increased and exhibited stronger connectivity with the amygdala, suggesting a developmental shift toward more regulated moral reasoning.

From what I recollect, the dynamics of friendships and social groups became more complex as I grew older, particularly around visible markers of status – such as the shoes we wore or the type of pencil box we had – which started playing a role in determining popularity. While I still made friends easily, I was not as popular as some of my peers. My birthday parties, which usually consisted of a homemade cake and pastries prepared by my mother, had no elaborate decorations or entertaining games – typical for an average Turkish family. As a result, they were usually attended by only a handful of peers. I don't recall ever having large birthday celebrations. Looking back, I had a small but close-knit group of friends, most of whom came from families with a similar socioeconomic background. This is interesting, considering that Turkish public schools at the time were quite socioeconomically diverse. In hindsight, I might call this a kind of coalition.

Research supports the idea that young children become attuned to social class cues, which often signal resource ownership and allocation. A study observing children from the ages of three to eleven found that younger white children – about the age of three – tended to allocate more resources to white peers, whom they also perceived as wealthy.[14] However, when asked to explain their reasoning, they primarily gave personal, subjective explanations, such as "Cuz I like him more." As they grew older, children's justifications evolved to incorporate social category knowledge, with statements like, "He is better because he has a bigger house." Interestingly, while children aged five and six showed a clear preference for wealthier peers, regardless of race, by the time they reached nine years old, they began to express a dislike for rich peers and favored a more equitable distribution of resources. Although young children can categorize racial groups and associate social class characteristics like wealth with these categories, it is not until later in childhood that they begin to develop racial preferences or in-group affiliations that resemble those of adults.[15] As they grow, their understanding of morality, fairness, and group identity becomes more nuanced and socially informed, integrating these concepts in ways that shape their social perceptions. My personal experiences align with these scientific findings.

By the time I started middle school, at about the age of eleven or twelve, my family was still relocating frequently, and my interactions with peers continued to evolve. While visible status markers, such as clothing, remained important, non-visible factors – such as music preferences or knowledge of "cool" cultural references – began to play a larger role in social dynamics. Despite being a book nerd, I started to gain more popularity, partly due to my older brother, who was in college and well-connected. Through him and his friends, I was exposed to new music, fashion trends, and food preferences that made me more socially adaptable.

However, middle school was also when I first began to experience direct ridicule based on my skin color. My complexion is considered relatively dark in Türkiye, though in the United States it is often perceived as light brown or olive-toned. Around the age of eleven or twelve, I started hearing jokes from classmates about my darker skin tone. This was not the first time I had encountered racialized nicknames or comments – throughout my childhood, family, friends, and even strangers would casually refer to me as "the Black girl" (referring to color rather than race) or "the Arab girl," terms commonly used for Turkish people with darker skin. Occasionally, an older relative or acquaintance would make a corny joke about whether my mother had consumed too much coffee while pregnant with me.

Although such remarks were frequent even at earlier ages, I don't recall consciously registering them as significant until middle school. Before then, I had simply observed that lighter-skinned children were often favored for lead roles in school plays, public speeches, and other high-visibility activities. *Snow White* was a particularly popular school play across Türkiye during my childhood, and, predictably, the "fairest" girl in class was chosen as the princess, while darker-skinned children, like myself, were relegated to roles such as one of the seven dwarves. I remember playing a dwarf in one of these plays, but I never dwelled on it or felt particularly upset at the time.

That changed in middle school when my classmates gave me the nickname "Friday," referencing a Turkish caricature of Robinson Crusoe and Friday from Daniel Defoe's novel. In this caricature, Friday was portrayed in a heavily racial-ized manner, depicted as a Black man with exaggerated facial features – large lips and a bald head. This nickname not only ridiculed my darker complexion but also masculinized me, as it was based on the caricature of a fictional Black man. Research in the United States has found that Black women are often perceived as more masculine and less attractive.[16] My experience suggests that skin color plays a similar role in shaping gender perceptions in different cultural contexts.

Thankfully, racialized bullying was not a constant in my daily life – it was sporadic, surfacing intermittently in inter-actions with classmates. Moreover, I was fortunate to have a strong circle of friends who supported me and pushed back against ridicule. Despite these experiences, growing up in Türkiye, I had no explicit understanding of racial differ-ences in the way they are conceptualized in the United States because ethnic divisions – such as those between Turks, Kurds, Armenians, and others – were far more salient. I did not possess a defined racial identity or sense of belonging tied to race. However, I was acutely aware of my skin color and what it signified – that it was different and, in many social contexts, less desirable.

As I entered late childhood, around age ten to twelve, I became increasingly aware of the social significance of race

– not just in terms of how I was perceived by others, but also in the ways race and social belonging shaped broader group dynamics. My personal experiences of racialized teasing and the subtle (and sometimes overt) social hierarchies based on skin tone made me more conscious of how physical appearance, status markers, and social identity intersected. This period of growing awareness aligns with psychological research showing that by late childhood, children begin to develop a more nuanced understanding of their racial identities, including the societal implications of belonging to a racial group – whether in terms of discrimination or privilege.[17]

A key factor in shaping children's racial identities is parental ethnic and racial socialization. During early childhood, parents often emphasize cultural pride and heritage, fostering a positive racial identity by engaging their children in traditions, language, food, music, and customs.[18] As children grow, parents introduce discussions about racial bias, helping them recognize and prepare for racial discrimination while equipping them with coping strategies.[19]

The process of racial identity formation intensifies during adolescence, particularly when children encounter racism firsthand. Experiences of discrimination often prompt deeper reflection on racial identity, leading adolescents to actively explore their racial group membership and its broader societal significance.[20] By this stage, exposure to diverse perspectives from peers, media representations, and school curricula further shapes their understanding of race and racial dynamics in society.[21]

A strong and positive racial identity – developed through cultural pride, awareness of bias, and adaptive coping strategies – acts as a protective factor against discrimination and negative social influences. Research has shown that such an identity can boost self-esteem, academic motivation, and overall well-being among youth.[22] Moreover, racial identity development is closely intertwined with moral growth, as children and adolescents engage in discussions about fairness, social justice, and ethical decision making within their racial and social contexts. Parental socialization naturally involves moral dimensions, such as instilling a sense of moral pride in one's racial group, teaching cultural values and norms, or encouraging assimilation into mainstream moral ideologies.[23]

As this discussion illustrates, groupness and morality are inherently linked and co-develop throughout childhood. Our evolutionary adaptations as social animals have selected for cognitive mechanisms that support coalitional strategies such as cooperation, coordination, and group-based interactions. Because of this, morality and groupness are processed together in the brain, forming an essential foundation for racial cognition. In the following sections, we will explore how morality enables the processing of race – specifically – as groupness, shaping our everyday behaviors, racialized emotions, and the neural mechanisms that underlie these processes.

Morality and social life

Morality is an abstract system of norms, values, and principles that guides behaviors, emotions, and judgments. Rather than being a singular, universal concept, morality exists in multiple forms – *moralities* – that vary across historical and cultural contexts. These evaluative cultural codes help distinguish between what is considered *good* versus *bad*, *moral* versus *immoral*, or *right* versus *wrong*. While moral frameworks are shaped by cultural and societal influences, they are also biologically grounded, as our brains mediate how we perceive, evaluate, and act upon moral issues.

Research suggests that certain core moral values are shared universally among humans, shaped by both our evolutionary history and social organization. For example, Jonathan Haidt's moral foundations theory identifies six fundamental moral foundations that all human societies emphasize to varying degrees: care, fairness, loyalty, authority, sanctity, and liberty.[24] Similarly, the Schwartz theory of basic values,[25] a widely studied cross-cultural model of social values, identifies ten basic human values: universalism, benevolence, hedonism, self-direction, stimulation, achievement, power, conformity, security, and tradition. According to both theories, while societies may prioritize these values differently, the presence of common moral inclinations across cultures suggests that morality is not purely a cultural construct but is also deeply rooted in human nature.

As a highly social species, humans have always depended on cooperation and coordinated action for survival. This shared evolutionary and genetic heritage explains why values such as care, loyalty, and benevolence are emphasized across cultures – these traits provide essential advantages for fostering social cohesion and collective well-being. In essence, morality serves as an adaptive mechanism that strengthens group bonds, regulates behavior, and ensures the stability of social structures.

Morality is not just a collection of universal values that everyone shares in the same way. While humans may have evolved with certain basic moral instincts, the way these values are prioritized and expressed can vary widely across cultures and social contexts. In other words, morality is not set in stone – it is shaped by history, culture, and personal experiences. Take loyalty, for example. Loyalty is an important value for many people, but it can take different forms. Some people feel a strong sense of loyalty to their family, while others are more loyal to their country or even their favorite sports team. However, the level of commitment people show depends on the type of loyalty in question. Someone might be willing to move across the country to be closer to their family, but very few would uproot their lives to follow their favorite sports team from game to game. People have fought and died for their countries, and many endure dangerous migrations for the sake of their families – but how many would make extreme sacrifices for a sports team? This highlights how moral values, even when shared, are shaped by context and circumstance.

From a sociological perspective (which looks at how society shapes human behavior), morality can be thought of as an "ideal model" – a set of shared values influenced by historical events, economic conditions, and social structures. However, in everyday life, morality is not just about broad societal ideals; it is shaped by personal experiences and environments. The values a person holds are influenced by the family they grow up in, the schools they attend, the communities they belong to, and even the country they live in.[26]

Accordingly, morality is not a fixed set of abstract rules that exist independently of human experience. Instead, morality is something we actively "do" and "feel" – it is embodied and constantly shaped through our interactions with the world. People do not simply follow moral principles in a detached way.[27] For example, imagine seeing someone cut in line at a café or litter in a public park. You might immediately feel annoyed or disapprove of their behavior. Even if you don't consciously think about fairness or responsibility in that moment, your reaction reflects an underlying moral judgment – one shaped by social expectations and cultural norms. This process often happens unconsciously, shaping how we perceive and respond to the world around us.

The process by which macro-level moral ideals, or broader moral frameworks, are carried into our daily lives is referred to as "doing morality." Every time we judge an action, an event, or even our own thoughts and emotions as *right* or *wrong*, *good* or *bad*, we are engaging in morality – not just as a concept but as something we actively practice. The idea of "doing morality" is similar to well-known sociological concepts such as "doing gender"[28] and "doing race."[29] These theories argue that gender and race are not fixed, biologically determined traits but are instead socially constructed through our actions and interactions. Society has expectations about how people should behave based on their gender or racial identity, and individuals perform these roles – sometimes consciously, but often without even realizing it. In the same way, morality is not just a static set of rules; it is continuously created and reinforced through social interactions and lived experiences.

Our shared human history has shaped and favored certain fundamental social tendencies – sometimes competing ones – such as cooperation, loyalty, self-direction, and power. However, we can think of these as empty buckets that each person possesses. What fills these buckets – *who* we choose to cooperate with, *how* we express loyalty, or *under what circumstances* we exert power – is shaped by our personal experiences within cultural and social contexts.

At the same time, humans are both biological and social beings. Our thoughts, emotions, and behaviors are influenced not only by our social environment but also by the biological machinery of our brains and bodies. As we will see later in this chapter, decades of research have shown that the "hot" emotion- and intuition-driven areas of the brain are just as crucial – if not more – than the "cold" rational and cognitive processing regions when it comes to making moral judgments. What this means is that moral decisions are not the result of a purely logical, moral calculus ranking the most objectively moral actions. Instead, they are visceral and intuitive, shaped by gut reactions and emotions.

To give an example, let's return to that earlier café example. Imagine you stop by your favorite coffee shop on your way to work and get in line for your usual morning order – a simple medium black coffee. The person in front of you, however, takes their time asking about different non-dairy milk options and, after a long back and forth, finally orders a large, salted caramel oat milk mocha Frappuccino with five pumps of caramel, four pumps of mocha, three pumps of toffee nut syrup, extra whipped cream, and a caramel drizzle. As you watch this order unfold, you suppress a sneer, trying to hide your disdain – not just for the overly complicated, sugar-loaded drink but also for the fact that this person doesn't even tip the barista who patiently took their order. You glance at the barista, hoping to make eye contact in a shared moment of silent frustration – maybe with a subtle eye roll. This reaction happens in just a few seconds, almost automatically. There is no moral rule ranking coffee orders in a hierarchy of superiority, nor is there a universal expectation to tip on a to-go coffee order. Yet your reaction – your disapproval, your subtle judgment, and even your facial expressions – are shaped by your personal history, cultural background, and social values. What seems like a trivial moment actually reveals a moral judgment rooted in emotion rather than rational calculation.

This is a simple yet clear example of how we "do" morality in our everyday lives. We don't just think about morality in abstract terms – we embody it, react to it, and express it through our interactions. So, how is it that moral boundaries become racial boundaries?

What is "moral" about racism?

Social systems are inherently moral systems – they regulate behavior through both explicit rules (such as laws and formal policies) and implicit norms (such as social expectations, customs, and everyday practices). Morality not only provides guidance for how people should act but also serves as a way to compare oneself to others, often leading to a sense of superiority. When individuals judge others' behaviors and moral standards against their own, they reinforce social hierarchies based on perceived virtue.

For example, in the United States, moral values like hard work and honesty – which are deeply tied to meritocratic ideals – play a central role in how people evaluate one another.[30] Many Americans feel morally superior to those they perceive as having a weaker work ethic or lacking integrity. This reinforces the idea that group distinctions are based on *earned* behaviors and achievements rather than inherent group characteristics. People tend to assign idealized moral traits to their in-group while viewing out-groups as morally deficient.

These meritocratic ideals – such as individualism, work ethic, and obedience – often become justifications for discriminatory beliefs and racial prejudices.[31] For instance, in an ethnographic study of American working-class men, sociologist Michèle Lamont[32] found that white workers frequently viewed Black workers as lacking discipline, while Black workers saw white workers as domineering and indifferent to their struggles. Lamont calls this process moral boundary making – the practice of using morality to draw symbolic distinctions between social groups.

Moral boundary making is a specific form of "doing morality" – where moral judgments are not just about individual behaviors but about shaping group identities and reinforcing social divisions. In the United States, this process plays a key role in sustaining racial bias and inequality. By tying morality to race, many individuals and institutions justify racial boundaries through the lens of moral righteousness, making discrimination appear not only acceptable but even morally justified. These moral boundaries do not only apply to work ethic or individualism. Across different social contexts, various moralized contrasts are used to justify group distinctions. For example, people may be perceived as hardworking or lazy, self-sufficient or dependent, disciplined or irresponsible, law-abiding or criminal, refined or uncivilized, family-oriented or neglectful, humble or entitled. These opposing traits demonstrate how moral attributes are selectively assigned to different racial and social groups, reinforcing existing biases. This pattern is evident in political discourse as well, such as in the most recent US presidential campaign where immigrants were associated with criminals or threats to national security. By moralizing immigration and linking it to crime, political leaders enforce racialized moral boundaries that shape public perception and policy, legitimizing exclusion and discrimination. Moral boundary making not only reinforces racial and social divisions but also ensures that positive traits are associated with the dominant in-group, while negative ones are used to justify racism against out-groups. This moral framing is often so deeply embedded in social narratives that racialized moral judgments seem like objective truths rather than as the result of historical and cultural bias.

Moral boundary making sustains modern racism, using moral ideologies rather than the now-discredited biological arguments about genetic superiority or inferiority. By embedding racial judgments within moral values and standards of appropriateness, this form of bias becomes more socially acceptable and operates in a more subtle yet pervasive way in American society. While it may appear race neutral, this kind of racial bias is, in reality, a structured system of beliefs that reinforces negative evaluations of many people of color.

The more individuals embrace the belief that racial discrimination no longer creates barriers to the advancement of Black people, the more likely they are to attribute disparities to personal failings rather than to systemic inequalities. If one assumes that success is purely a matter of effort, then those who struggle are seen as responsible for their own disadvantages. This belief system, often referred to as the meritocratic archetype, frames upward mobility as achievable regardless of race, ethnicity, gender, or other social factors. In doing so, racial prejudice is buried within the ideal of working hard and getting ahead, making systemic discrimination appear nonexistent while still shaping opportunities and outcomes in deeply racialized ways.[33]

Moral and racial boundary making is reflected in everyday interactions, particularly in the ways people choose to engage with or avoid certain individuals. Feelings of unease or negativity, especially in situations where responsibility is unclear, can lead individuals to withdraw from interactions with those from different racial backgrounds. This avoidance is often driven by subtle fears or discomfort rather than explicit hostility. Research conducted in experimental settings has demonstrated how these moral boundaries influence behavior in real-life situations. In one study on emergency situations where a person needed assistance, white respondents were less likely to help Black individuals when other white bystanders were present. This reluctance was attributed to diffusion of responsibility – the idea that if others are around, one's own failure to act will not be perceived as prejudiced since someone else could step in.[34] Another study explored whether this reluctance was racially motivated and found that white participants were less likely to view emergencies involving Black victims as serious enough to warrant immediate help.[35] By downplaying the severity of the situation, participants also reduced their own sense of responsibility to intervene.

This pattern extends beyond individual interactions and plays out at a systemic level, shaping public responses to large-scale crises. For example, the Flint water crisis, which began in 2014 at the predominantly Black community of Flint, Michigan, exposed this community to contaminated drinking water for years, despite growing evidence of lead poisoning and health hazards. The Flint water crisis overwhelmingly affected Black babies, leading to worse birth outcomes such as lower birth weight.[36] Insufficient response from the government and public indifference persisted for an extended period, reinforcing the idea that emergencies affecting Black communities are often perceived as less urgent and less deserving of immediate intervention.[37] Similar patterns of neglect can be seen in disaster response efforts, where predominantly Black and low-income communities tend to receive delayed or insufficient aid compared to wealthier, white-majority areas.[38] For example, wildfires in Los Angeles County in early 2025 devastated Altadena, a historically Black neighborhood, destroying nearly half of the Black households and resulting in seventeen fatalities. Residents of this neighborhood raised their concerns about delayed emergency evacuation orders and the disparity in the urgency and resources allocated to these neighborhoods compared to some of LA's most exclusive neighborhoods where numerous celebrities live.[39]

Beyond neglect, these racialized moral boundaries also shape perceptions of wrongdoing and responsibility in ways that have deadly consequences. Just as white individuals in experimental studies were more likely to minimize the severity of Black victims' emergencies, similar biases contribute to the way Black individuals are perceived in interactions with law enforcement. Research has shown that Black people, particularly Black boys and men, are more likely to be perceived as threatening and aggressive, leading police officers to respond with greater force than they would against white individuals in similar situations.[40]

On February 4, 1999, Amadou Diallo, an unarmed 23-year-old Black man, was shot at 41 times – hit 19 times – by four New York City police officers while attempting to enter his own apartment in the Bronx.[41] The officers later claimed they mistook him for a suspected serial rapist and believed he was drawing a gun, when in fact he had been reaching for his wallet to show his identification. His killing became a symbol of excessive police force and racial bias in law enforcement, sparking national outrage and protests against racial profiling and police brutality.

More than two decades later, data continues to show stark racial disparities in police interactions. In a 2017 nationally representative study conducted by the National Public Radio (NPR), the Robert Wood Johnson Foundation, and the Harvard T. H. Chan School of Public Health,[42] half of all Black Americans surveyed reported having personally experienced discrimination during interactions with police, compared to only 10% of white Americans. Additionally, 33% of Black respondents – compared to just 2% of white respondents – stated that they had avoided calling the police when in need due to fear of discrimination. These findings highlight how deeply racialized experiences with law enforcement remain a persistent reality, shaping not only public trust in policing but also individuals' willingness to seek help in moments of crisis. In this way, moral boundary making does not just manifest in subtle everyday interactions but serves as a structural force that influences who receives help, whose suffering is ignored, and who is blamed for their own misfortune. Whether in cases of public health crises, disaster response, or policing, racialized moral boundaries shape how society determines whose lives are valued and whose crises are met with indifference or aggression.

What do emotions have to do with morality?

A core aspect of moral boundary making is the role of emotions. Moral emotions such as guilt or shame often justify or rationalize racial boundaries.[43] As seen in experiments on altruistic behavior toward Black versus white victims, emotions like empathy and sympathy – or their absence – are central to avoidant and aversive behaviors toward racial groups. Humans inevitably rely on emotions when making distinctions between the "moralness" of their perceived realities, including differentiating between moral in-groups and out-groups.[44] This emotional dimension is closely tied to brain function, particularly the vmPFC, which plays a key role in both emotional processing and moral reasoning, as evidenced by its activation in fMRI studies (as we will see later in this chapter).

Emotions are subjective experiences shaped by physiological responses to stimuli. They often manifest through facial expressions or body language, such as a smile or a frown, and are labeled with cultural terms like grief, shame, or pride. A key distinction is between "primary" and "secondary" emotions. By comparing responses across different cultures, including pre-literate and isolated tribal communities in Papua New Guinea, the renowned American psychologist Paul Ekman demonstrated that certain facial expressions (like happiness, anger, sadness, fear, surprise, and disgust) are universal across all human cultures, and hence primary.[45] In contrast, secondary emotions, also known as social or moral emotions, include feelings like guilt, pride, and shame, which are more dependent on socialization and cultural context.[46] Some researchers argue that although primary emotions are innate, whereas secondary emotions are learned, distinguishing between the two is more complex than it may initially seem.[47] Although we are born with a capacity for many basic (or primary) emotions – after all, humans are born crying –

these physiological processes are also shaped by learning.[48]
For example, in Turkish, there is a specific word – *hasret* – that
describes a deep, nostalgic longing for someone or something
that may never return. This emotion is commonly expressed
in everyday conversations and literature and is often associated with the sorrow of separation. *Hasret* can also convey
the profound yearning an immigrant feels for their homeland,
capturing both personal and collective experiences of longing
and displacement. To my knowledge, there is no exact equivalent of this emotional label in other languages, highlighting
how cultural and linguistic contexts shape the way emotions
are recognized and expressed.

Ethnographic research from sociologists also shows the
importance of socialization on not only the cultural labels of
emotions but also on the ways they are experienced across
occupational sectors. For example, while most people experience feelings of fear or unease around dead bodies, mortuary
students learn to suppress these emotions through professional
training and socialization.[49] Emotional neutrality is similarly
required in many professions, such as nursing, medicine, and
the military. At the other end of the spectrum is what sociologist Arlie Hochschild[50] calls emotional labor, where workers
– especially in the service and hospitality industries – must
manage their emotions to project positivity and warmth, even
in difficult situations. Waitresses, airline attendants, and retail
workers, for example, often have to suppress negative emotions and maintain a pleasant demeanor to meet job expectations. These examples show that emotions are not only
personal experiences but also social performances that reflect
cultural norms and expectations.

Emotions also serve as signals for group membership and
moral belonging. Research by sociologist Amy Wilkins in a
university-based evangelical Christian organization found
that happiness was used as a boundary marker.[51] Members
were expected to appear happy at all times as a demon-
stration of their closeness to God and moral righteousness,
while expressions of sadness or frustration were seen as
moral failings. A more extreme but not uncommon way in
which moral emotions shape group distinctions is through
infra-humanization or dehumanization. Infra-humanization
refers to the tendency to deny out-group members uniquely

human, secondary emotions such as pride, love, or hope, as well as moral emotions like guilt or embarrassment.[52] While in-group members are perceived as fully human and capable of complex emotional experiences, out-group members are often viewed as more animal-like and unworthy of empathy or concern.[53] This psychological process is strongly linked to a reluctance to extend altruism or assistance to out-groups, particularly in times of crisis, war, or disaster.

For instance, social psychologist Amy Cuddy and colleagues[54] conducted a study following Hurricane Katrina to examine how people's emotional responses influenced their willingness to help disaster victims of different racial backgrounds. The study found that participants believed out-group racial members were less capable of experiencing secondary emotions like grief or mourning, leading to a lower willingness to provide aid. This process of infra-humanization was reflected in media coverage as well. Many news outlets described Black survivors as "looters" while referring to white survivors as "victims," reinforcing racialized moral boundaries and shaping public perceptions of who was *deserving* of help.[55]

Similarly, infra-humanization and dehumanization also shape people's perceptions of killing and torture during war. One of the most infamous examples of war crimes, etched in public memory through graphic images released in the media, is the torture of prisoners at Abu Ghraib prison. The images depicting US soldiers physically and psychologically abusing Iraqi detainees – through acts such as hooding, water torture, forcing them into humiliating positions, and even coercing them into sexual acts – sparked international condemnation and outrage. However, understanding how such extreme brutality was normalized in the first place requires examining the psychological mechanisms that enable moral disengagement.

To explore these mechanisms, psychologist Bernhard Leidner and colleagues conducted a series of experiments in the United States and the United Kingdom.[56] Participants were shown identical news articles (based on real incidents, with names changed) describing the torture and killing of Iraqi prisoners near Baghdad. The only difference was whether the perpetrators were identified as American or Iraqi soldiers.

The study found that participants who strongly believed in the superiority of their own nationality – what the researchers termed in-group glorification – were significantly less likely to demand justice for the victims. They were less likely to support consequences for the perpetrators, such as being fired from the army, facing jail time, or providing compensation and an official apology to the victims' families.

Additionally, in-group glorification was linked to two key moral disengagement strategies that further reduced participants' demand for justice: emotional minimization and dehumanization. Emotional minimization involved suppressing sympathy and reducing emotional sensitivity toward the victims, while dehumanization led participants to perceive the victims as less than human. These psychological mechanisms serve as strategies to justify violence against outgroups while also alleviating the discomfort, or cognitive dissonance, which might arise from witnessing actions that violate moral norms.

This process is yet another example of "doing morality," as discussed earlier. Rather than morality functioning as a fixed set of principles, it is actively constructed and negotiated in ways that can justify or excuse harm. Through moral disengagement, individuals and societies can rationalize acts of violence and brutality, especially when committed against those deemed outside their moral community. Crucially, these moral judgments and justifications are not abstract; they are actively mediated by the brain. Brain regions like the vmPFC and the amygdala play key roles in shaping how individuals perceive in-groups and out-groups, assigning moral worth and regulating emotional responses to others.

Moral emotional infrastructure of the brain

While it is well understood by researchers today that *doing morality* involves a significant amount of emotional processing, the idea that emotions play a crucial role in moral judgments and behavior was considered unconventional before the 1980s. Until then, moral evaluations were primarily thought to result from rational, calculative cognitive processes that developed over time as an individual matured. This perspective was most prominently advanced by developmental psychologists[57] and Lawrence Kohlberg.[58] They argued that moral cognition progresses in stages as children grow into adulthood, developing a kind of *moral calculus* – an internalized system of reasoning based on universal moral principles. According to their theories, this rational system allows individuals to make deliberate, *cold* calculations when faced with moral dilemmas.[59]

However, beginning in the 1980s, new developments in neuroscience, psychology, and clinical practice led to a shift in how researchers understood morality. Advances in brain-imaging technologies, such as fMRI, enabled scientists to observe brain activity in real time. Simultaneously, critiques of the dominant cognitive-centered models, the rise of the *positive psychology movement* (which emphasized human well-being over clinical pathology), and the growing recognition of emotional intelligence[60] fueled what has been called the *affective revolution*. This shift placed emotions, feelings, and affect at the center of psychological sciences, leading to increased research on the role of emotions in decision making, behavior, and mental health. Cognitive behavioral therapy (CBT), for instance, began integrating emotional experiences as key factors in shaping human thought patterns and psychological well-being.

One of the most influential theories emerging from this period was the somatic marker hypothesis.[61] Neuroscientist Antonio Damasio and his colleagues at the University of Iowa studied how the brain contributes to social and moral decision making by observing patients with brain damage in specific regions. Through a series of experiments designed to simulate real-life choices, they explored how emotions guide decision making, even before conscious reasoning takes place. One of their most well-known experiments was the Iowa gambling task.[62] In this task, participants choose cards from four decks to maximize monetary rewards. Two of the decks offer high rewards but also carry high risks, often leading to large monetary losses. The other two decks provide smaller but more consistent returns. Over time, healthy participants learn to avoid the risky decks and opt for the safer, more reliable options. However, patients with damage to their vmPFC – a region deep in the frontal lobe associated with social value and reward processing – continue choosing from the high-risk decks, failing to adjust their strategy.

Psychophysiological measures, such as skin conductance responses (which track autonomic nervous system arousal), revealed that when making poor decisions, the bodies of healthy participants reacted *before* they consciously recognized the risk. This automatic bodily response – what Damasio termed *somatic markers* – was absent in patients with vmPFC damage (see Figure 2.1 for vmPFC and associate regions).[63] These findings suggest that our bodies generate intuitive signals that help guide decision making through emotional arousal, often in ways that operate beneath conscious awareness. This research fundamentally changed how scientists view moral reasoning. Instead of morality being purely a product of rational deliberation, it is now understood as a process deeply intertwined with emotions, physiological responses, and gut feelings. These insights reinforce the idea that *doing morality* is not merely an abstract cognitive exercise but a deeply embodied experience that influences human behavior at both conscious and unconscious levels.

The role of intuition and bodily feelings in social decision making is further emphasized by moral psychologist Jonathan Haidt, who expands on the idea that moral judgments are primarily driven by fast, affective, and largely unconscious intuitions, rather than slow, rational deliberation.[64] According to Haidt, these intuitions subtly nudge us toward certain behaviors, often without our conscious awareness. To illustrate the relationship between emotions and logic, Haidt introduces the elephant and the rider metaphor.[65] In this analogy, our logical reasoning is the small rider attempting to guide a massive elephant, which represents our emotions and gut instincts. While the rider may believe they are in control, the elephant – driven by strong emotions and ingrained intuitions – determines the direction. The rider can attempt to steer, but if the elephant is determined to move in a particular direction, the rider's efforts are largely futile. This metaphor highlights how emotions and intuitive reactions shape moral decision making, often overriding rational thought. Although conscious reasoning can sometimes override emotional instincts, doing so is particularly difficult when deep-seated emotions are involved.

A provocative example of this phenomenon comes from Haidt's research on moral dilemmas, specifically one that

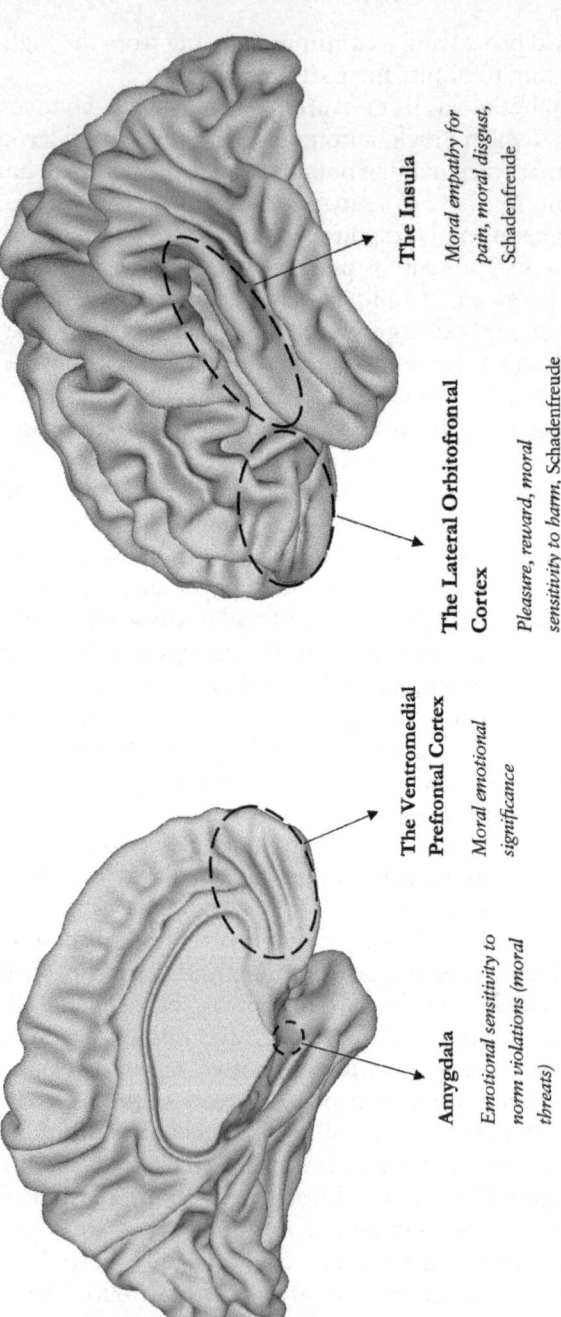

Figure 2.1 Neuroanatomy of the racial group processing regions of the brain

Source: Adapted from the Harvard–Oxford atlas developed at the Center for Morphometric Analysis (CMA) and distributed with the FMRIB Software Library (FSL) (Bakker, Tiesinga, and Kötter 2015); 3D Surface View (Majka et al. 2012)

explores people's reactions to incest.[66] In this dilemma, participants are told a fictional story about Julie and Mark, two siblings who decide to engage in consensual sex just once. Across cultures, incest is a widely recognized taboo, and when asked about the morality of Julie and Mark's actions, most participants instinctively declare it to be wrong. However, when asked to explain *why* they believe it is wrong, participants typically provide rational justifications, such as the risk of genetic abnormalities in offspring or potential social stigma if others were to find out.

Haidt's study challenges these justifications by adding conditions to the scenario: Julie and Mark use both a condom and birth control pills to eliminate the risk of pregnancy, and they agree to keep their encounter a secret and never do it again. Even when these rational objections are addressed, most participants remain steadfast in their moral judgment, insisting that incest is still wrong. This reaction demonstrates what Haidt calls *moral dumbfounding* – the idea that people often have strong emotional responses to moral issues and struggle to articulate logical reasons for their judgments. In this case, the *elephant* – their deep-seated emotional reaction – overrides any rational arguments the *rider* might attempt to make. This example underscores the power of intuitive emotions in moral reasoning. While we like to believe that our moral decisions are based on careful deliberation, in reality they are often shaped by automatic emotional responses that we then attempt to justify with reasoning.

Another American psychologist, Joshua Greene, builds on this theoretical foundation and proposes a dual-network theory of morality, which suggests that moral decision making operates through two distinct cognitive processes: deontological and utilitarian reasoning.[67] Deontology, derived from the Greek word *deon*, meaning duty or obligation, is a moral framework in which judgments are made based on principles of right and wrong, independent of consequences. Deontological moral processing tends to be automatic, fast, and emotion driven, relying on gut feelings about what seems morally right or wrong. In contrast, utilitarian moral judgments focus on the outcomes of actions rather than inherent moral rules. Utilitarian thinking is slower, more deliberate, and dependent on rational analysis, as it weighs the overall consequences of a decision to maximize well-being. Greene investigates these cognitive processes through philosophical moral dilemmas, one of the most well known being the trolley problem. Imagine a trolley (tram) is headed toward five people and its brakes are not working. It is going to hit and kill these people, but there is one way to prevent this: to pull a lever that diverts the trolley onto another track, where it will kill just one person instead of five. When presented with this scenario, most people agree that pulling the lever is morally acceptable, as sacrificing one life to save five aligns with utilitarian logic. Now imagine another scenario, where the trolley is headed at five people again, but this time the only way to stop this runaway trolley is to push a larger framed stranger off a bridge into the path of the trolley. In this case, most people say they would not push the stranger. From a strictly utilitarian perspective, both scenarios are equivalent – the loss of one life to save five. However, Greene argues that the second scenario is qualitatively different because it elicits a stronger emotional reaction. Actively pushing a person to their death feels morally wrong, even though the outcome is the same.

To test this hypothesis, Greene and colleagues conducted an fMRI study, measuring brain activity while participants evaluated moral dilemmas like the trolley problem. They found that when individuals considered scenarios involving direct physical harm – such as pushing someone to their death – the emotion-processing regions of their brains, including the vmPFC (previously identified in Damasio's studies), showed significantly higher activation.[68] This finding supports the idea that emotions play a key role in shaping moral judgments, especially in cases where moral choices involve direct personal harm. Greene's research highlights the tension between automatic, emotionally driven moral instincts and deliberate, rational moral reasoning. While utilitarian judgments require cognitive effort, deontological judgments often arise instinctively, guided by deeply ingrained emotional responses. This dual-network model helps explain why people sometimes struggle with moral dilemmas – our brains are simultaneously processing moral decisions through both an emotional and a rational lens.

The vmPFC plays a crucial role in integrating descriptive information about situations with bodily and emotional states, such as gut reactions. It is also involved in creating future anticipations based on past experiences. Some of the most striking evidence of its importance in social and moral life comes from lesion studies – studies conducted with patients who had localized brain damage due to stroke, accidents and injuries, or certain diseases. Antonio Damasio and colleagues have extensively studied patients with damage to the vmPFC – those who did not have a functioning vmPFC revealing significant behavioral and emotional changes. One of the most well-known cases is EVR, a 35-year-old patient who lost his vmPFC on both sides of his brain after undergoing surgery to remove a brain tumor as a treatment for epilepsy. Despite maintaining high intelligence and reasoning abilities, he experienced drastic life disruptions, including job loss, financial bankruptcy, and failed marriages.[69] Other studies of patients with vmPFC damage have also found lasting impairments in social-emotional capacities, such as increased frustration, emotional detachment, inappropriate social behavior, and difficulties with goal-directed actions.[70] Damasio and colleagues referred to this phenomenon as acquired sociopathy, noting that the behavioral changes in these patients closely resembled developmental sociopathy or psychopathy.[71]

During my graduate studies, I had the unique opportunity to work with patient EVR in one of my own experiments. My initial impressions of him were that he was highly intelligent, pleasant in his disposition, and quite polite. As part of my research, I was collecting data from both patients with brain damage and adults without any neurological conditions to serve as a comparison group. The experiment involved rating pictures of different social class and racial group members emotionally on a computer screen. The participants would complete their ratings without interruption, while I periodically checked in to ensure they were comfortable and understood the task. During my session with EVR, I entered the room to check on him, and he mentioned that he was feeling cold. He stood up, and we attempted to adjust the thermostat. Despite expressing discomfort, he remained cheerful and in good spirits. About twenty minutes later, when I returned to check in again, he repeated that he was still cold. Then, unexpectedly, he reached out and touched my cheek with his hands for a few seconds, saying, "See how cold I am?!" I was caught off guard. It was a subtle social interaction – not a major moral violation, but unusual enough to make me feel awkward and unsure of how to react. No other participant had ever touched my face during my sessions with approximately fifty participants in that experiment. I hesitated for a moment, then tried to smile and respond neutrally, saying, "Yes, you are cold," before quickly redirecting the session back to the experiment. This moment stood out to me because, while seemingly minor, it highlighted the effects of EVR's brain damage in ways that were difficult to fully articulate. He was not aggressive, inappropriate, or even consciously breaking a social rule, yet the interaction felt markedly different from any other I had experienced as a researcher. It was a reminder that beyond cognitive impairments, damage to brain regions like the vmPFC could subtly affect social behavior in ways that are difficult to predict – diminishing the ability to intuit unwritten social norms and gauge how one's actions might be perceived by others.

The timing of vmPFC damage also matters. When damage occurs in adulthood, patients typically retain the moral knowledge and cognitive reasoning they developed over their lifetime, but their bodies no longer produce the necessary emotional responses, disrupting their moral decision making and behavior. However, when damage occurs during childhood, the social and moral consequences are even more severe. Individuals with early-onset vmPFC damage often fail to learn appropriate social and moral rules, show little to no moral emotions like guilt or remorse, exhibit blunted affect, and frequently display antisocial or even criminal tendencies. Unlike adult-onset patients, they also seem unable to recognize that their behavior is problematic.[72] This research highlights the vmPFC's fundamental role in integrating emotions into moral reasoning and decision making.

How does the vmPFC enter into racial evaluations that are moral in their nature then? The vmPFC also plays a key role in assigning personal significance to information, determining how relevant or important a piece of information is to an individual.[73] Moral information, such as deciding whether something is right or wrong, is personally relevant and deeply tied to group identity. Brain-imaging studies confirm that the vmPFC is particularly active when processing morally significant information, including judgments about social groups. Research shows that the vmPFC exhibits greater activation in response to faces associated with higher moral status.[74] Since moral values, norms, and codes are learned through socialization within our in-groups – including family, peers, and culturally curated media exposure – people tend to attribute higher moral status to their own group while evaluating out-groups differently.

My own research further supports these findings. In a previous research study, I collected fMRI data from white adult participants in Iowa as they viewed images of white and Black individuals across different social class backgrounds. These images included poor individuals, such as homeless people, middle-class individuals, such as families posing in front of a modest home, and upper-class individuals, such as people in luxury clothing on yachts or private jets. The results showed that the vmPFC was activated in response to all social class groups of white people, with the largest activation cluster (which suggests a more extensive and robust neural response)[75] for middle-class white people, which may suggest that the participants are implicitly associating the highest moral status with the white middle-class group. For pictures of Black people in different social class groups, on the other hand, there was only significant activation for upper-class Black individuals, and the size of the activation cluster was much smaller, almost equivalent to the activation cluster size of the white lower class.[76] This finding implies that the participants might only recognize and evaluate Black individuals in higher social positions as deserving of moral consideration, reflecting broader patterns of group-based prejudice. This pattern of vmPFC activation also suggests that moral evaluations are deeply intertwined with social group perceptions, reinforcing in-group favoritism and out-group differentiation at the neural level. Since the vmPFC plays a crucial role in assigning personal significance and moral worth, its differential activation across race and class groups indicates that participants may be implicitly relying on socially learned hierarchies when making group-based evaluations.

While the vmPFC plays a crucial role in processing the moral status of in-group members, other brain regions also contribute to racial moral evaluations. The orbitofrontal cortex (OFC), particularly the lateral OFC (lOFC), is responsible for processing socially relevant information about external factors, including out-groups.[77] The OFC is located on the ventral surface of the frontal lobes, just above the eye sockets. Although it shares anatomical connections with the vmPFC, there are important distinctions between these two regions. The vmPFC, which sits slightly higher in the brain, is connected to both limbic structures, such as the amygdala, which processes emotions, and autonomic structures, such as the hypothalamus, which regulates involuntary bodily functions. The OFC, on the other hand, is located lower in the brain, closer to the eye sockets, and has strong connections with sensory processing regions, including those responsible for smell.[78] This structural distinction suggests that while the vmPFC is more involved in self-referential processes and moral evaluations of in-groups, the OFC, particularly the lateral OFC, is engaged in processing moral judgments about out-groups and other socially relevant external cues. Together, these brain regions help shape racial and moral evaluations by integrating emotional responses, past experiences, and socially learned biases into real-time decision making.

The orbitofrontal cortex (OFC) plays a key role in processing emotional and reward-related information, integrating these signals into decision-making processes.[79] Studies have shown that the OFC is activated in response to pleasurable stimuli such as smells, tastes, music, and even attractive faces.[80] Beyond processing individual pleasure and reward, brain-imaging research suggests that the OFC is also involved in group-related moral evaluations, particularly when witnessing harm inflicted on an in-group member by an out-group member.[81] For example, psychologist Pascal Molenberghs and colleagues conducted an fMRI study in which participants viewed images of individuals from their own university (in-group) or a different university (out-group) engaging in acts of physical aggression toward either an in-group or an out-group individual.[82] The results showed that moral sensitivity was highest when an out-group member attacked an in-group member, and this response was associated with greater activation in the lOFC.

Similarly, in a weapon bias study measuring implicit bias against Muslims, participants inside an fMRI scanner played the role of a police officer and were required to make rapid "shoot" or "don't shoot" decisions when presented with images of Muslim (out-group) or non-Muslim (in-group) individuals holding either a gun (threatening) or a non-lethal object (neutral).[83] The study found that participants reported less guilt when shooting an armed Muslim target than when shooting an armed non-Muslim target, and that lateral OFC activity was significantly higher when participants shot a Muslim target. Psychologists Pascal Molenberghs and Winnifred Louis explain this heightened OFC response with the German concept of *Schadenfreude*, the feeling of pleasure derived from witnessing another person's failure or suffering.[84] Think about watching a soccer (football) game. You might feel happiness and joy not only when your team scores a goal against the opposite team but also when the opposite team perhaps misses a penalty shot. So, if the vmPFC is involved in the joy from witnessing your team win, lOFC might be active during the loss of the other team.

Beyond the prefrontal cortex, other brain regions, particularly those associated with emotional processing, also play a significant role in how race is perceived as a group distinction. One of these key regions is the amygdala, which, as discussed in chapter 1, is involved in both categorical and group-based racial evaluations. The amygdala detects emotionally salient external information, including racial stereotypes and moral group dynamics. Research has consistently demonstrated that the amygdala exhibits differential activation when individuals perceive members of their own group versus an external group. Studies using fMRI have shown that out-group faces tend to elicit heightened amygdala responses compared to in-group faces, indicating an automatic vigilance or heightened sensitivity toward perceived outsiders.[85]

In 2012, political psychologist Darren Schreiber and neuroscientist Marco Iacoboni conducted an experiment in which white participants viewed images of Black or white individuals depicted in norm-conforming (e.g., families, doctors, students) or norm-violating (e.g., criminals, homeless people) situations.[86] Their findings showed that the amygdala was particularly sensitive to norm violators, regardless of race, suggesting that it plays a key role in detecting adherence to or violations of moral and social norms. Similarly, in my own research, which I previously discussed in relation to the vmPFC, I found that the right amygdala responded more strongly to images of poor Black individuals compared to poor white individuals, suggesting a heightened vigilance or threat response specifically to Black poverty.[87] These findings suggest that the amygdala rapidly evaluates and categorizes social and moral information, responding to racialized external cues such as appearance and behavior in ways that reflect learned biases and social conditioning.

While the amygdala is involved in processing external emotional stimuli, another key region, the insula, is responsible for internally focused bodily sensations and emotional experiences.[88] The insula is buried inside the lateral sulcus, which separates the frontal and temporal lobes, and it has been widely studied in relation to pain perception[89] and negative emotions such as disgust.[90] Neuroimaging studies have demonstrated that the insula becomes active when individuals react to facial expressions of disgust in others, as well as when they experience disgust themselves, such as when exposed to foul odors or disturbing images.[91]

In social cognition, the insula shows greater activation to pictures of socially stigmatized people, such as homeless people or drug abusers,[92] as well as to racial out-group members.[93] However, its role in race-related moral evaluations is complex. The insula does not just show unilaterally increased activation in response to out-groups. The insula, particularly the anterior insula, also responds to feeling pain oneself and observing the pain of others.[94] For example, the insula responds more strongly when people feel empathy with the pain of loved ones or racial in-group members and less intensely to out-group members.[95] The anterior insula also responds selectively to out-group members. In an fMRI study, the anterior insula showed less activation (less empathy) when an everyday misfortune (like having a stomach ache or sitting on chewing gum on a bench) happened to a disgust-eliciting out-group member (e.g., criminals or drug addicts) compared to a pity- or sympathy-eliciting one (e.g., elderly people).[96] Interestingly, when positive events like finding money on the street happened to out-group members who people envied (e.g., wealthy, high-status people), the anterior insula showed greater activation, suggesting a counter-empathic response or *Schadenfreude* (i.e., discomfort or resentment rather than shared happiness). These findings suggest that the insula plays a nuanced role in social and racial group evaluations by integrating visceral bodily sensations with conscious emotional awareness. It is involved in processing disgust, social pain, and *Schadenfreude*, shaping how individuals experience and react to moral and social distinctions between groups. Together, these brain regions – the vmPFC, lOFC, amygdala, and insula – contribute to the ways race is processed in moral and social contexts, influencing group-based attitudes and behaviors in profound and often implicit ways.

Summary

The research presented in this chapter highlights that racial group perceptions in the brain are fundamentally moral and emotional rather than innate or automatic. Rather than having a built-in racial cognition, the human brain evaluates the moral significance of social groups, shaping emotions such as empathy, bias, and social attitudes, which in turn influence decision making and behavior. These evaluations are deeply intertwined with coalitional psychology, a framework from evolutionary anthropology that explains how humans form alliances for social and survival advantages.[97] Our ability to make rapid moral judgments about allies and outsiders likely provided advantages in prehistoric environments where competition for resources was fierce. Over time, these processes have evolved into more complex moral systems that reward or punish coalitional allegiances based on social cues such as identity, behavior, and emotional norms. Under historical and economic inequalities, race has become one such coalitional cue in modern society.

Importantly, biological races do not exist – humans are a single species. Encounters between physically and ancestrally different human groups are a relatively recent phenomenon in evolutionary history. Early humans interacted primarily with those in close geographical proximity,[98] meaning that the human brain could not have evolved specifically to detect or categorize racial groups. Instead, the brain is adapted to encode social alliances through fast and intuitive processing of physical, verbal, and behavioral cues. The legacy of slavery, segregation, and racial oppression in societies such as the United States has transformed race into a dominant coalitional marker, shaping social and moral perceptions. The next chapter will explore this two-way process – how historical and structural forces (such as economic hierarchies and group privilege) interact with individual cognitive and emotional mechanisms to construct racial boundaries.

Moral boundary making is an embodied and interactive process. We "do" morality through our lived social experiences, intuitively making moral judgments that are deeply tied to emotions. These moral emotions drive racially biased interactions in two key ways: (1) feelings of moral superiority, where individuals view certain racial groups as lower in status or power, and (2) moral apathy and dehumanization, where racial out-groups are perceived as less deserving of empathy or moral concern. These biases can manifest in hostile emotions such as disgust or contempt, moral ambivalence such as reluctance to help racial out-groups, or moral detachment and dehumanization, where certain racial groups are not seen as fully human.

The human brain processes in-group and out-group dynamics through a network of moral and emotional signaling regions, including structures such as the amygdala, which plays a key role in racial categorization and moral evaluation. The brain is highly interconnected, with different neural regions working together constantly to process social and moral cues. This research on morality and racial boundary making aligns with evolutionary theories of coalitional psychology, which suggest that racial cognition is not an innate biological adaptation but rather a byproduct of cognitive mechanisms evolved for coalition formation.[99] Racial categories and biases emerge from historical processes that positioned race as a marker of group difference and social hierarchy.

The next chapter will further examine these historical and structural forces, outlining how economic and social conditions have shaped race as a group position over time.

3

Race in the Making

The previous chapters have demonstrated that race is not a category pre-coded or wired into our brains but a dynamic construct that emerges at the intersection of cognition, emotion, and social structure. We explored how our brains categorize race as part of an automatic cognitive process and also examined race as a form of group belonging – one that is deeply tied to moral appraisals. This dual process of race as both a perceptual category and a group position underscores its fluidity and socially constructed nature.

Building on these foundations, this chapter explores the "making of race" as a two-way process between social-structural forces – such as economic relationships and group privilege – and individual cognitive and emotional mechanisms of race. On one level, race is collectively constructed through historical events that define and reinforce group positions, where dominant racial groups maintain their status by contrasting themselves against subordinate groups.[1] These social positions are sustained across generations, fostering antagonistic emotions that deepen racial boundaries. However, race is also reinforced by the brain's inherent capacity for schemas – cognitive structures or "blueprints" that help us process new information quickly – as well as by emotion processing, which makes racialized perceptions and biases appear intuitive and self-relevant.[2] The vmPFC, in conjunction with memory and emotion-processing regions, plays a crucial role in activating schema processing[3] and potentially racial schemas, influencing everything from social interactions to policy decisions.

The emotional and cognitive mechanisms that sustain racial hierarchies, fueling biases and stereotypes, are not merely abstract ideas – they are encoded in our daily interactions, shaping how we see, feel, and respond to different racial groups. Media portrayals, for example, play a crucial role in this process. During Hurricane Katrina, which struck the Southern United States in August 2005, Black survivors were frequently depicted as "looters" rather than victims, while white survivors were described as "evacuees" in need of assistance.[4] These differences in wording evoked emotions like fear, disgust, and contempt toward Black communities, reinforcing preexisting biases and reducing empathy. Research conducted in the aftermath of Katrina found that white Americans were significantly less likely to attribute the inadequate government response to systemic racism, highlighting the role of racialized cognition and emotion in shaping public perceptions of crisis and injustice.[5]

A more recent example is the differential treatment of Syrian and Ukrainian refugees in recent years. In 2015, political crises erupted in several European countries over the number of refugees fleeing civil war in Syria, seeking routes into Europe. For example, thousands of Polish people marched in Warsaw with the slogan "Today refugees, tomorrow terrorists!"[6] Polish president Andrzej Duda opposed welcoming refugees from the Middle East and North Africa because they might threaten the financial and physical security of Polish citizens as well as their health through potential epidemics.[7] Yet this same president, a few years later, signed a bill extending the legal stay in Poland of Ukrainian refugees fleeing Russia's invasion of Ukraine, as well as ensuring continued access to Ukrainian refugees' "health, family, and social benefits."[8] This differential treatment reveals an underlying moral hierarchy intertwined with racial ideologies. Ukrainian refugees are perceived as more deserving of state protection and support, while Syrian refugees are stigmatized as potential threats. This division reflects not only political or security concerns but also moral judgments about who is worthy of compassion and rights. Morality becomes a lens to evaluate and justify the treatment of different groups, revealing that what might appear as neutral policy decisions are deeply imbued with moral judgments about worth, safety, and belonging.

What a neurosociological approach reveals is that racialized emotions and cognition are not only learned but also biologically encoded as schemas – patterns of neural activity that shape our automatic reactions.[9] By examining the interplay between social structure and mind, this chapter underscores the ways in which racial categories are not just imposed from the outside but are internalized and reproduced through everyday thought and emotion.

Yet, if race is so readily processed and enacted through our brains, one might wonder whether it does indeed have any solid biological grounding. Before proceeding further, we take up this critical question: do human races exist in a biological sense?

Do human races exist?

While race is deeply embedded in human perception and institutions, it does not exist as a natural or essential category outside of those perceptions and institutions. In traditional biological research on non-human animals, the term "race" is often equated with "subspecies." According to molecular geneticist Alan R. Templeton, a subspecies is a population that has lived in geographic isolation long enough to evolve distinct morphological and genetic traits.[10] By one definition, a population qualifies as a subspecies if at least 25% of individuals from one group can be correctly classified as belonging to that population (and not another) based on observable genetic differences. Another definition of race or subspecies refers to populations sharing the same ancestral lineage, with historical splits over time resulting in the formation of distinct species.

Using these criteria, research shows that chimpanzees – humans' closest evolutionary relatives – have races or subspecies. At least three distinct chimpanzee subspecies exist, separated by geographic boundaries: Upper Guinea, Gulf of

Guinea, and the combined equatorial African populations.[11] These groups have accumulated significant genetic differentiation due to geographic isolation (albeit still within the African continent). In contrast, while human populations exhibit genetic variation across different regions spread across the globe, they do *not* meet the criteria for biological races. Templeton identifies five broad human population clusters: (1) sub-Saharan Africans; (2) Europeans, Near and Middle Easterners, and Central Asians; (3) East Asians; (4) Pacific populations; and (5) Amerindians. However, genetic differences between these socially defined racial groups account for only about 4% of human genetic variation, compared to 30% among chimpanzee subspecies. Almost all genetic variation in humans – approximately 93% – exists *within* populations rather than between them, whereas in chimpanzees, within-population variation is lower at 64%. Moreover, there are no clear genetic boundaries between human groups: genetic variation exists along a continuum rather than as discrete racial divisions. (It is also important to note that even in research in non-human animals, the concept of "subspecies" is criticized with the arguments that the boundaries between subspecies are fuzzy at best and the methods to quantify them are inexact.[12])

Thus, humans do not have races in the biological sense. Instead, race, as it is commonly understood, is a social reality, not a biological one. While racial categories do not reflect essential genetic differences, they exert powerful influence over social life, shaping opportunities, inequalities, and group identities. Race exists as a social construct, continually being redefined through historical struggles over power, privilege, and domination. Recognizing race as a social and symbolic system, rather than a biological fact, is crucial for understanding how racialized perceptions, emotions, and hierarchies persist in society.

Race as a socially constructed symbolic category

The American Psychological Association defines race as a socially constructed categorization of people based on their physical traits, whereas ethnicity is understood as a categorization based on shared culture such as music, food, and language, along with ancestry and history.[13] While these definitions often overlap, they are not always easily distinguishable. Individuals living in the same geographical region – whether a continent, country, or city – may share similar physical traits, cultural practices, and historical narratives.

The term *race* originated as early as the 1500s in Europe, where it referred to groups of people connected by kinship or other associations.[14] In contrast, the concept of *ethnicity* was introduced by sociologist Max Weber in his 1922 work *Economy and Society* (Weber 1978 [1922]) where he used it to describe collections of people with shared cultural and historical characteristics.[15] Given the overlapping nature of these terms, one may ask: if ethnicity better captures the social and cultural nature of group divisions, why not use ethnicity instead of race?

The answer lies in the unique function of race as a powerful analytical tool that ties superficial, arbitrary, and outwardly observable differences – such as skin tone, hair texture, facial features, or accents – to entrenched social hierarchies. Unlike ethnicity, which emphasizes cultural affiliation, race has historically been used to establish and justify moral distinctions between groups, legitimizing the unequal distribution of resources and power. While race is not a biological category, it is a symbolic category, socially constructed through historical struggles for domination. This process involves drawing upon elements of ancestry, phenotypical traits, and, most importantly, the legacy of systemic inequalities.[16]

Over time, these symbolic racial categories become "naturalized" or perceived as objective realities. Political, economic, and social distinctions – initially created through power struggles – are reinforced and normalized through institutional structures, media representations, and everyday interactions. As a result, race is not only a classification system but also a mechanism through which privilege, discrimination, and moral boundaries are inscribed onto the social world. Understanding race as a historically constructed system, rather than a biologically determined reality, is essential for challenging the assumptions that sustain racial hierarchies. As we explored in the previous chapter, the perception

of race as tied to moral superiority has played a crucial role
in shaping social attitudes and institutional structures, further
entrenching racial disparities in contemporary society.

Institutional racism:
race as a structural category

Institutions play a pivotal role in reinforcing racial hierarchies. The racial wealth gap, disparities in college completion
rates, and inequities in homeownership are not just individual
outcomes but are embedded in systemic policies and practices
that advantage (whether directly or indirectly) certain racial
groups over others. These disparities highlight how race functions as a structural category, shaping access to resources and
opportunities through institutionalized mechanisms.

The Civil Rights Act of 1964 formally outlawed discrimination based on race, color, religion, sex, or national origin
in the United States. However, persistent racial and ethnic
disparities in education, wealth, healthcare, and the criminal
justice system suggest that legal protections alone have not
eradicated structural inequities. According to the latest US
Census data, the percentage of adults over age twenty-five
who have completed a college degree increased from 2012
to 2022.[17] Yet racial gaps remain stark. While approximately
59% of Asian Americans and 42% of non-Hispanic white
Americans hold college degrees, only about 28% of Black
Americans and 21% of Hispanic Americans do.

Racial wealth disparities are even more pronounced.
According to the Census Bureau's 2021 Survey of Income and
Program Participation, white households had ten times the
median wealth of Black households. While the median wealth
of white households stood at US$250,400, Black households
had a median wealth of just US$24,520. Homeownership,
a key driver of wealth accumulation, also reflects these disparities: approximately 70% of white Americans own their
homes, compared to only 39% of Black Americans.[18] These
statistics reveal that racial inequality is not merely an issue
of personal achievement or effort but is deeply rooted in systemic advantages and disadvantages that have been historically reinforced over time.

Race as an institutionalized system

The persistence of racial disparities in wealth, education, and opportunity underscores the ways in which race functions at both the structural and individual levels. At the macro level, systemic racism preserves a racial order that privileges white Americans through legal, educational, political, and economic institutions. At the individual level, racism manifests both through explicit discriminatory actions – sometimes referred to as "old-school racism" – and through unconscious, implicit biases that shape everyday interactions.[19] Together, these forces create what sociologist Eduardo Bonilla-Silva[20] describes as a "racialized social system," where racial hierarchies influence social, economic, and political outcomes.

Viewing racism solely as an issue of personal bias – a perspective that sociologists Matthew Desmond and Mustafa Emirbayer[21] call the "individualistic fallacy" – ignores the deeply embedded, institutionalized nature of racial inequality. Racism is not merely a collection of harmful thoughts or isolated acts of discrimination; it is a system of power that operates at multiple levels. While this book primarily focuses on interpersonal and brain-level mechanisms that create and reinforce racial inequalities, these processes are inseparable from broader institutional and cultural structures. One clear example of how race operates at both the structural and individual symbolic levels is the case of Richard and Mildred Loving, an interracial couple who were arrested in Virginia in 1958 for violating the state's anti-miscegenation laws.[22] Their personal experience of racial persecution – being forcibly removed from their home and sentenced to a year in prison – was not just the result of individual prejudice but was legally sanctioned by the state through institutionalized racial segregation in marriage laws. The Lovings were forced to leave Virginia under threat of imprisonment, a punishment that reflected broader efforts to enforce racial hierarchy through legal means.[23] Although their case, *Loving v. Virginia* (1967),[24] ultimately led to the US Supreme Court striking down laws banning interracial marriage, this example is still very revealing about how racial inequality was upheld through both personal discrimination and codified legal structures. These codified legal structures were reinforced by state and federal institutions, including the US Census, which historically categorized individuals by race in ways that upheld segregationist policies. By codifying racial distinctions, the Census contributed to the maintenance of racial boundaries that anti-miscegenation laws sought to protect.

Racial formation and the evolution of race in the US Census

The process by which socioeconomic, political, and historical forces shape racial categories is what sociologists Michael Omi and Howard Winant[25] describe as racial formation. This process is dynamic rather than fixed; racial categories evolve in response to changing social and political conditions. For example, the racial category "Black" as it exists today did not emerge until the late seventeenth century when multiple African ethnic groups were consolidated into a single racial identity under an ideology of slavery, exploitation, and racial dominance. Over time, laws and policies codified these distinctions, reinforcing the economic and social subjugation of Black individuals.

The US Census has played a significant role in shaping and reinforcing racial classification (see Figure 3.1 for examples of how Census race questions have changed over time). Since 1790, the Census has categorized racial groups in ways that reflect the dominant racial ideologies of each era.[26] In the 1850 Census, the recorders were required to categorize Black individuals separately as Black, "mulatto" (mixed Black or "colored"), enslaved Black and enslaved mulatto. In 1890, the one-fourth ("quadroon") and one-eighth ("octoroon") rules were introduced, distinguishing people with a quarter (one of the grandparents) and one-eighth (one of the great-grandparents) Black ancestry. In 1900, the word "negro or negro descents" (in lower case) was added to the US Census next to "Black."[27]

In 1910, the question was worded as "color or race," calling out attention to the skin tone of the respondents. By 1930, in response to the state of Virginia's 1924 Racial Integrity Act, the Census adopted the "one-drop rule," categorizing any person with only one drop of Black "blood" or a trace of ancestry as Black (they were referred to as "Negro" with the "N" capitalized at this time). This meant individuals could not be classified as both white and Black or as mixed race – any known Black ancestry resulted in classification as Black. These racial categories determined fundamental aspects of life, including who could marry whom, who could own land and property, and where people were allowed to live.

Over time, racial classification in the Census continued to evolve. Until 1960, Census takers assigned racial classifications rather than allowing individuals to self-identify. The question remained labeled "color or race" until 1980. It was not until the 2000 Census that individuals were allowed to select more than one racial category, acknowledging multiracial identities for the first time.[28]

As a side note, it was not until the 2010 Census that the word "Negro" was dropped from the US Census, a word that had long been a subject of controversy[29] and has deep historical ties to slavery and Jim Crow-era racism. I recall an experience in an undergraduate classroom at Georgia State University in Atlanta, one of the most racially diverse college campuses in the United States. The class had an almost equal Black and white presence. While discussing the history of racial categorization, I displayed statistics from the 2010 Census on racial demographics. A young Black student, looking both surprised and unsettled, raised his hand and asked why the term "Negro" appeared on the Census breakdown on the screen. It was an uncomfortable moment as I, a non-Black professor, tried to explain that this was the official language still in use by the federal government and the Census Bureau. It was clear that the term felt outdated and contentious, sparking a conversation about the politics of racial terminology. At the time, I was unaware that the Obama administration would later take steps to address this issue. Toward the end of 2015, a bill was signed to remove the words *Negro* and *Oriental* – the latter still used in some official documents for people of Asian origin – from all federal documents and surveys.[30] As a result, the term "Negro" was officially removed from the US Census, beginning with the 2020 Census.

The fluid and contested nature of racial categories extends beyond Black and white classifications. For example, from 1850 to 1920, the US Census categorized Mexicans as white, a classification that emerged immediately after the Mexican American War (1846–8). However, while Mexicans were

3.1a 1850

DESCRIPTION.		White. Color: { black, or mulatto.
Age.	Sex.	
4	**5**	**6**
3	f	
18	f	
42	fw	

3.1b 1890

	INQUIRIES.
1	Christian name in full, and initial of middle name.
	Surname.
2	Whether a soldier, sailor, or marine during the civil war (U.S. or Conf.), or widow of such person.
3	Relationship to head of family.
4	Whether white, black, mulatto, quadroon, octoroon, Chinese, Japanese, or Indian.

3.1c 1930

PERSONAL DESCRIPTION				
Sex	Color or race	Age at last birthday	Marital condition	Age at first marriage
11	**12**	**13**	**14**	**15**
M	W	72	S	
M	W	51	M	20
F	W	52	M	20
F	W	30	S	
M	W	25	S	
M	W	23		

3.1d 1960

Is this person—
White
Negro
American Indian
Japanese
Chinese
Filipino
Hawaiian
Part Hawaiian
Aleut
Eskimo
(etc.)?

(P5)

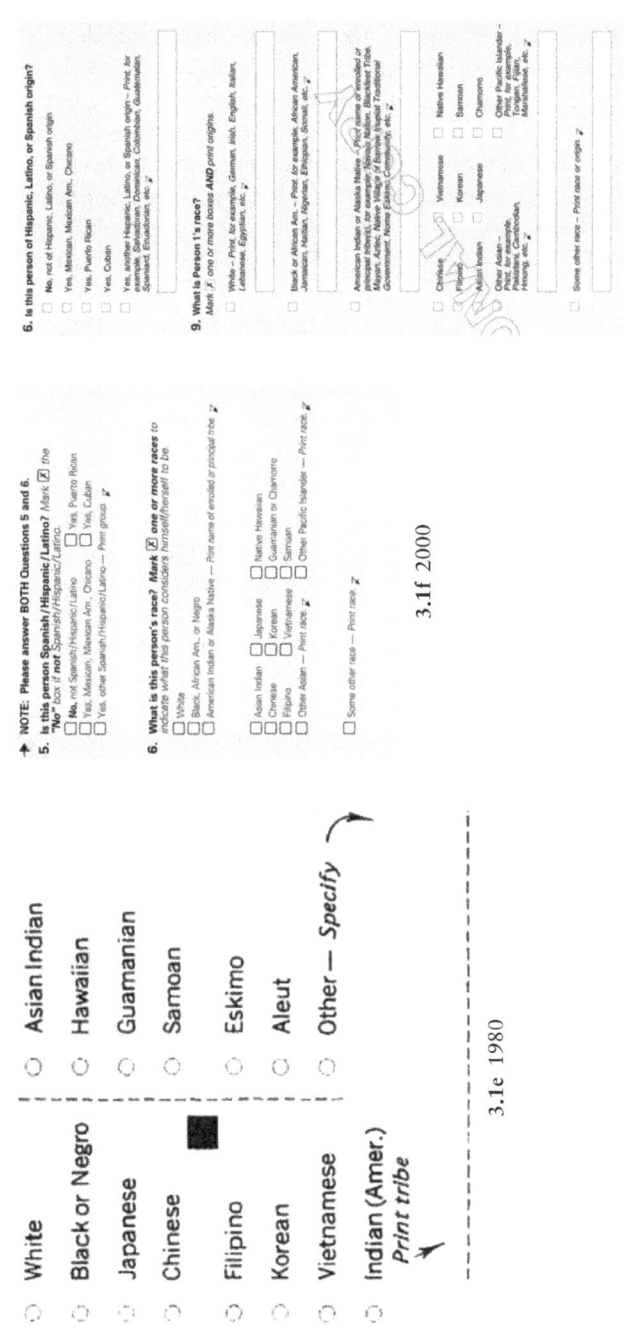

Figure 3.1 Samples of enumerator-recorded and self-recorded race questions on the US Census across time

Source: US Census Bureau History (census.gov/about/history.html)

legally recognized as white, they were often regarded as non-white in social status and by local, state, and federal officials.[31] In response to political pressures surrounding naturalization and citizenship, the 1930 Census introduced a separate "Mexican" category, formally distinguishing Mexicans from the white category. However, due to lobbying efforts and political advocacy from the Mexican American community, the "Mexican" category was eliminated from the Census in 1940.

By 1970, the Census began to explore a broader categorization for individuals of Latin American descent, including "Mexican, Puerto Rican, Cuban, Central or South American, or other Spanish origin." In 1980, the Census formally implemented the separate "Spanish/Hispanic origin" question, distinguishing ethnicity from race. In 2000, the term "Latino" was added. However, many people of Hispanic origin found this classification system confusing, often skipping the race question altogether or selecting "some other race."[32]

This confusion also applied to people of Middle Eastern and North African (MENA) descent, including myself. Most Hispanic or Middle Eastern individuals did not identify as white, yet the race question did not offer specific options for their identities. In 2010, the Census conducted research on combining the ethnicity (Hispanic origin) and race questions and explored the addition of a Middle Eastern/North African (MENA) category. The revised version performed better in capturing racial and ethnic identities.[33] However, despite these findings, the Census Bureau did not introduce the new format in the 2010 Census, delaying its implementation until March 2024. Looking ahead, the 2030 Census will include the updated, combined race/ethnicity question with Middle Eastern/North African as a response option.[34]

Race is not a fixed biological reality but a fluid and historically constructed system shaped by political and institutional forces. The evolution of racial categories in the Census illustrates how race is both symbolic and yet also consequential, influencing legal rights, economic opportunities, and social status.

Understanding race as both a category and a group: insights from sociological research

Despite reaching many official milestones for equality, persistent bias and discrimination has led sociologists to focus on "newer" and more subtle forms of racial prejudice. Modern racial prejudice is less overt and hostile, manifesting instead more typically through covert avoidance behaviors. Research on racial prejudice, particularly in the United States, gained momentum in the 1970s following the end of the Jim Crow era. Although the Civil Rights Act of 1964, the Voting Rights Act of 1965, and the Fair Housing Act of 1968 officially ended segregation in public and private spaces, racial discrimination remained widespread. This was evident in various life outcomes, such as disparities in employment rates, income levels, and incarceration rates.

A major body of research, including field experiments or audit studies, has demonstrated that racial discrimination in housing and employment persists despite legal protections.[35] In these studies, researchers send out two or more fictitious applicants who are identical in all aspects except for one social characteristic under study, such as race, class, or gender. If one group systematically faces disadvantages – such as being denied a job callback or a rental opportunity – this differential treatment is attributed to discrimination.

For example, in the widely cited study "Are Emily and Greg More Employable than Lakisha and Jamal?," economists Marianne Bertrand and Sendhil Mullainathan sent out fictitious résumés with either stereotypically Black- or white-sounding names to real job postings in Boston and Chicago newspapers.[36] They found significant racial disparities in callback rates, which were even more pronounced for résumés with higher qualifications. White-sounding names received callbacks 50% more often than equally qualified Black-sounding names – equivalent to an additional eight years of work experience.

Harvard sociologist and W. E. B. Du Bois scholar Lawrence D. Bobo refers to this modern-day racism, somewhat tongue in cheek, as a "kinder, gentler" racism.[37] While explicit support for Jim Crow-era segregation, state-sanctioned discrimination, and beliefs in Black biological inferiority have declined, this shift has not been replaced by an active commitment to dismantling the inequalities created by slavery and segregation. Instead, a form of "laissez-faire racism" has taken hold, which frames Black–white disparities as the result of individual ambition, work ethic, or effort rather than structural barriers.[38] Sociologist Eduardo Bonilla-Silva expands on this idea, arguing that colorblind racism has emerged as the dominant racial ideology in the United States.[39] This seemingly race-neutral ideology allows institutional and individual practices to perpetuate racial inequality while at the same time hiding it under the veil of a meritocratic "American dream" where seemingly anyone who works hard can achieve better life outcomes.[40]

While critical race scholars like Eduardo Bonilla-Silva[41] argue that race – despite not being an objective biological reality – remains a fundamental pillar of social relations, other sociologists, like Loïc Wacquant, Mara Loveman, and Rogers Brubaker,[42] have proposed a revisionist critique[43] that calls for abandoning race as an analytical category altogether. These scholars contend that the current concept of race – as studied from the lenses of critical race scholars like Bonilla-Silva – conflates "groups" with "categories" (treats a dynamic and group-based phenomena as if it is an essential category), reifies and essentializes "race," and separates race from ethnicity arbitrarily without using any objectively empirical criteria.[44] They argue that much of the literature on race fails to distinguish between "folk" and "analytical" concepts of race, reinforcing commonsense racial assumptions rather than dismantling them.[45] For instance, studies that examine racial differences in intelligence often rely on socially constructed racial categories – such as Black, white, or Asian – as if they represent biologically distinct groups, inadvertently giving legitimacy to these racial categories.[46]

Although I recognize the merit in some revisionist critiques, including the need for an integrated approach to race, ethnicity, and nationality, I argue that race remains an essential analytical tool. As demonstrated in earlier chapters, race functions both as a category *and* as a form of group belonging. Race acts as a cognitive category through which people perceive and respond to one another, influencing interactions via stereotypes, biases, and implicit social schemas. This categorization, however, is not static or essential, but dynamic and context dependent.

Race is also a sense of "groupness," as articulated in sociologist Herbert Blumer's theory of group position.[47] According to Blumer, racial categories gain meaning through historical processes in which groups define themselves relationally. This concept also aligns with Karl Marx's distinction between a group in itself and a group for itself, referring to the transition from mere categorization based on shared conditions (group *in* itself) to collective awareness and social consciousness (group *for* itself).[48] W. E. B. Du Bois famously applied this concept of group consciousness through his notion of "double consciousness."[49] Double consciousness refers to the identity divide and the tensions between staying true to one's Black culture and origins while also trying to keep up with the predominantly white American societal norms. Du Bois calls double consciousness "a peculiar sensation" of feeling "twoness" – an American and a Black person, or the feelings of being both an insider and an outsider.

This framework extends beyond Black Americans. Sociologist Neda Maghbouleh,[50] in *The Limits of Whiteness*, explores how Iranian Americans experience racialization in their daily lives – whether in school, peer interactions, or airport screenings – while simultaneously being classified as white in official census records until 2024, or in other words, "whitewashed."[51] Sociologists Tiffany Joseph and Tanya Golash-Boza[52] similarly apply the concept of double consciousness to undocumented Latinx immigrants, arguing that racialized barriers shape their immigration experiences and marginalization. Joseph and Golash-Boza argue that immigrants who are not of European descent and have darker skin have greater barriers to immigration to the United States; and, once they arrive, are racialized and marginalized. Both Du Bois's original framework and these contemporary extensions suggest that being American is often equated with being white, creating a dual racialized group position for immigrants and citizens of color alike.

Psychological research also underscores the important role of group identity in racial categorization. Social psychologists Henri Tajfel and John Turner's social identity theory explains how people categorize themselves and others into in-groups ("us") and out-groups ("them"), forming the basis of prejudice and group cohesion.[53] This process, known as depersonalization, leads individuals to perceive others primarily as representatives of their group rather than as unique individuals, reinforcing group boundaries.[54] However, this same mechanism can also be harnessed to cultivate a positive sense of racial identity. Campaigns like "Dark is Beautiful" in India illustrate how marginalized groups can creatively redefine their identities in empowering ways, leading to greater self-esteem and collective pride.[55]

Political scientists have also explored race as a group position, particularly in analyzing Black political participation in the United States.[56] Research shows that Black Americans from lower socioeconomic backgrounds are often more politically engaged than their white counterparts, driven by an acute awareness of their marginalized social position.[57] This racialized double consciousness shapes levels of trust in government, perceptions of political efficacy, and voter participation. Similarly, research connects racial consciousness and identity to positive self-esteem and well-being among Black people in the United States,[58] suggesting that a strong sense of racial identity – like that encouraged in social movements – can serve as a source of resilience against discrimination. Just as depersonalization reinforces racial divisions, the reclaiming of racial identity can empower marginalized communities, fueling both individual self-worth and collective political action. This dynamic where identity consciousness fosters liberation struggles is evident in social movements ranging from Black Lives Matter to activism in India, which fights against discrimination faced by the Dalit caste (formerly known as "Untouchables").

It's important to note, however, that race as group identity does not imply a homogenous or unified racial consciousness. Factors such as social class, political ideology, geography, cultural background, and personal experiences all shape how individuals understand and experience race; therefore, racial consciousness remains an ongoing process of collective construction.[59] Nonetheless, race remains a superseding hierarchical social category, influencing access to wealth, education, and political power.[60] The dominant salience of race can be seen, for instance, in those examples where ethnicity and nationality, though distinct from race, often become racialized when they are tied to moralized social, political, and economic inequalities on a global scale. Recognizing race's dual role as both a cognitive category and a socially constructed form of group belonging allows for a more nuanced understanding of its impact on contemporary society.

The moral and emotional construction of race

Race can function as both a category and groupness, tying outward physical differences to moralized power inequalities, influencing resource distribution and social status. This dual perspective allows for understanding how race as a category can affect various aspects of life such as education, finance, healthcare, and interactions with law enforcement, while at the same time race as groupness can create a protective racial consciousness within marginalized communities, influencing political engagement and identity formation.

The example of Jeremy Meeks and the subsequent viral "mugshawtys" – a portmanteau of "mug shot" and "shawty" (a catcall) – phenomenon illustrates how race operates as both a category and a groupness via racial and gender-based moral judgments embedded in public reactions to criminality. On June 18, 2014, Jeremy Meeks, a light-skinned, mixed-race man with blue eyes, was arrested during a gang sweep in Stockton, California. His mug shot, which was posted the same day on the Stockton Police Department's website, went viral with over 15,000 "likes" and comments in just about 24 hours because of his looks, giving him the nickname "hot felon." Upon his release from prison in 2016, Jeremy went on to become a fashion model. In 2015, a Twitter (now X) account named "mugshawtys" started posting mug shots of attractive female felons. Within a few years, this account went viral and now racks up over 491,000 subscribers, along with an Instagram account boasting over 1.9 million followers. It has also released two editions of a photo book featuring curated mug shots.

Analyzing comments left on a popular public "mug shot website,'" sociologists Danielle Dirks, Caroline Heldman, and Emma Zack[61] found that conventionally attractive, white female offenders are seen as less guilty and criminal and more redeemable. The public fascination with the penal system and criminal justice, what sociologist Michelle Brown has called "penal spectatorship," is a social phenomenon where punishment – especially criminal punishment – is turned into a spectacle for public consumption.[62] Today, living in the digital age, we have digital penal spectatorship, where the public engages with criminal justice issues from a distance, often through digital platforms.[63] True crime shows, court dramas, prison reality TV, dedicated social media posts, or accounts like the "mugshawtys" are all examples of this digital phenomenon. Digital penal spectatorship is racialized and gendered, with people's varying judgments on offenders and their guilt being shaped by those offenders' race and gender. It functions as a tool of white supremacy, reinforcing the idea that whiteness/light skin color is inherently good and redeemable, while non-whiteness/dark skin color is associated with criminality.[64] This phenomenon, also exposed by Dirks and colleagues in their research, is called "white protectionism" – a type of privilege that protects whites but not other racial groups from criminal designations. White protectionism can be described as a form of racial, moral boundary making[65] that we may – or may not – be aware of.

This example highlights how contemporary society processes criminality through both moral and racial lenses. On the one hand, the public's reaction – celebrating a light-skinned, conventionally attractive offender like Meeks with "likes" and a nickname such as "hot felon," while similarly portraying attractive white female offenders as less guilty and more redeemable – reveals how moral judgments are unevenly distributed. This selective empathy (white protectionism) serves as a form of moral boundary making. In this view, certain bodies are deemed inherently more worthy of compassion and redemption, reinforcing a moral hierarchy where whiteness and conventional attractiveness equate with moral virtue. On the other hand, the phenomenon underscores how race operates both as a category and as a group identity. As a category, race is processed through visible markers – light skin, blue eyes, and other features – that trigger immediate, fixed assumptions about an individual's character and criminality. Simultaneously, the collective response to these individuals reveals race as a group dynamic: whiteness, as a shared identity, is imbued with an implicit promise of redeemability and protection, a dynamic that influences broader social perceptions of guilt and innocence, and the associated emotions.

These dual-direction processes of delineating racial group belonging and reaffirming racial hierarchies occur through racialized cognition and racialized emotions.[66] American psychologist Carroll Izard's concept of "emotion schemas" can help us understand how racialized cognition and emotions enter our daily lives by shaping social interactions and relationships, resulting in "felt" social outcomes such as feelings of exclusion and marginalization. Emotion schemas are complex, dynamic cognitive-affective structures that represent integrated experiences shaped by learning, culture, and individual history.[67] Emotion schemas significantly influence motivation by providing an affective charge to cognitive interpretations, driving people toward or away from certain behaviors or groups – in other words patterning our felt emotions.[68] They reflect both momentary states and more stable, trait-like personality characteristics that profoundly shape thoughts, motivations, and behaviors in daily life.[69]

Processing of emotion schemas in the brain involves complex cognitive-affective structures formed through the interaction of basic emotional responses and higher-order cognitive processes, including memory, belief, and evaluation.[70] The formation and activation of these schemas rely heavily on neural circuits involving the emotion and moral emotion regions of the brain, like the vmPFC and the amygdala, as well as memory-processing regions like the hippocampus.[71] According to recent neuroscientific research, emotion schemas are encoded and consolidated through interactions primarily between the vmPFC and the posterior brain regions, such as the hippocampus and amygdala, which provide emotional memory and appraisal context.[72] As you may remember from chapter 2, the vmPFC plays a key role in incorporating emotions into moral decision making through attributing personal meaning and significance to information, and it is primarily involved in processing of race as groupness in our brains. The amygdala, on the other hand, evaluates and responds to emotional salience (including threats and norm violations) from the external environment and is associated with the processing of race both as a category and as groupness. These interactions between these brain regions integrate emotional significance with personal meanings and conceptual knowledge, shaping the frameworks through which experiences are perceived, interpreted, and recalled.[73]

Specifically, the vmPFC plays a critical role in emotion schemas, acting as a neural hub that integrates emotional valence and cognitive content to reinforce or diminish schema-congruent memories and responses.[74] For example, neurostimulation studies have shown that inhibiting vmPFC activity significantly reduces the recall of negatively biased emotional memories, highlighting its essential role in maintaining emotionally congruent schema processing.[75] Additionally, vmPFC lesions lead to profound deficits in schema reinstatement, causing patients to misapply schemas, even in contexts where these schemas are no longer relevant, suggesting a vital role for the vmPFC in appropriately activating and utilizing schemas in real-time interactions.[76] For example, imagine you are at a funeral. Multiple cues in that environment – such as somber music, the sight of grieving individuals, and cultural rituals surrounding death – can trigger pre-established emotional frameworks such as feelings of sadness and grief. If a person has previously experienced loss or has strong cultural associations with mourning, the funeral setting might automatically activate a schema. This activation can lead to predictable responses like sadness, introspection, or even anxiety about one's own mortality. We can argue that the vmPFC works with the hippocampus and the amygdala to retrieve contextually congruent memories, such as prior experiences of loss or culturally learned funeral norms, reinforcing the emotional responses appropriate to the occasion.[77] Now imagine, a person is laughing during a funeral or wearing bright colorful clothes. For most western funeral rituals, these behaviors would be incongruent with the funeral schemas.

Emotion schemas are central to how individuals navigate their daily lives and social environments, influencing motivation, decision making, and behavior. They form through repeated emotional experiences that become associated with specific thoughts or cognitive interpretations. Over time, these schemas become ingrained patterns influencing how people interpret and respond emotionally and cognitively to situations and interactions. Emotion schemas thus significantly shape social behavior and relational dynamics.[78] In the context of racial processing, emotion schemas can reinforce categorical distinctions by encoding emotional associations with racial categories. For example, emotional memory schemas facilitated by vmPFC-amygdala-hippocampal networks[79] may strengthen the automatic association of negative or positive valence to racial categories through repeated cultural exposure or personal experiences. When these schemas are activated, the visual cortex contributes significantly by encoding emotional category information directly from sensory input, rapidly guiding emotional categorization and potentially reinforcing racial stereotypes based on perceptual features.[80] This process occurs even at early stages of sensory perception, indicating a deep embedding of emotional schema processing within visual systems themselves.[81]

The repeated pairing of specific emotions (such as fear, disgust, or contempt) with particular racialized groups through cultural, historical, or social narratives creates powerful emotion schemas. For example, media portrayals or societal narratives associating a particular racial group with threat or criminality can activate emotion schemas of fear or disgust when encountering or even thinking about members of that group. These schemas then serve as cognitive and emotional frameworks guiding judgments and interactions, often at a non-conscious or implicit level. This helps explain the findings of experiments like the IAT discussed in chapter 1, where participants demonstrated faster associations between white faces and positive words, but slower associations between Black faces and positive words. These reaction-time differences revealed the automatic nature of racialized emotion schemas. Similarly, the weapon bias study demonstrated how these emotion schemas can influence real-world decisions – participants were more likely to mistakenly "shoot" an unarmed Black person than an unarmed white person in a simulated task, highlighting the power of racialized fear schemas shaping high-stakes judgments. In this way, emotion schemas and racialized emotions significantly shape how these racial categories are cognitively internalized and morally justified. Individuals internalize complex emotions and cognitive beliefs through cultural narratives, which define racial categories as morally laden distinctions between "us" and "them."[82]

Sociologist Eduardo Bonilla-Silva's concept of "racialized emotions" also complements this perspective by emphasizing that emotions related to race are not merely individual experiences but collective phenomena embedded in structural racism – or the making of race as groupness. Emotions are central to racial identities and interactions, as dominant and subordinate groups develop distinct emotional repertoires reflecting their positions within a racial hierarchy.[83] For instance, white individuals often exhibit emotions such as fear, disgust, or anxiety toward racial minorities, reflecting and reinforcing racial boundaries. Conversely, members of marginalized groups may experience collective emotions of anger, grief, and frustration due to experiences of racial oppression and discrimination, further delineating racial boundaries. Emotion schemas carry motivational informational and regulatory information and shape group identities by structuring emotional reactions into culturally meaningful patterns that affirm shared experiences, solidify group membership, and define moral boundaries between groups.[84]

Emotion schemas play a critical role in group identification and boundary making through collective emotional experiences, especially when considering race as a social group rather than merely a category. The vmPFC's integration of emotional and contextual knowledge aids in the rapid evaluation of social interactions, aligning individuals emotionally and cognitively with their perceived group identity and strengthening emotional boundaries against perceived out-groups. For instance, schemas involving fear or threat may become activated in interracial contexts due to historically constructed social narratives, with brain mechanisms reinforcing these schemas through interactions between the amygdala (emotion), hippocampus (contextual memory), and the vmPFC (emotion integration and evaluation),[85] resulting in intensified group-based emotional responses and racial biases. In this way, the brain mechanisms underlying emotion schemas deeply influence racial processing, functioning simultaneously at the categorical level – structuring how emotional valence is associated with racial perceptions – and at the group level – informing collective emotional experiences and solidifying intergroup moral and emotional boundaries.

Summary

If men define situations as real, they are real in their consequences.

W. I. Thomas, *The Child in America*, 1928

Race is one of the first things we notice about a person and in fact it gives us uneasiness when we cannot make out what someone's race is. Race is a ubiquitous yet confusing and sometimes mystified concept. Race is socially constructed yet influences real-life outcomes. Race is perceived as a category, yet it is also a fluid process of groupness. All these issues are issues about the ontology or the existence of race. That is how we define race. As can be seen from the debates in sociology (between critical race theory and its revisionist critiques), there is no single or unified theory on the ontology of race. There is still much to be studied and learned. However, as is clear, racism persists in modern societies, affecting various aspects of life such as education, finance, healthcare, and interactions with law enforcement. Racial disparities are perpetuated at both individual and institutional levels, maintaining racial hierarchies.

Race operates simultaneously both at broader structural and global levels, upheld by historical and contemporary power dynamics, and at individual levels, enacted through our racialized brains. Racial hierarchies continue to influence who is seen as worthy of compassion and opportunity, often manifesting as colorism or selective empathy toward lighter-skinned individuals. Institutions – from the US Census to educational and economic systems – have codified these hierarchies, perpetuating racial disparities in wealth, home-ownership, and higher education.

Central to this process is the moral and emotional dimension of race. Consciously or not, societies routinely assign worth and legitimacy along racial lines, creating and reinforcing a hierarchy of "deservingness." Whether in the contrasting depictions of Black and white survivors during

Hurricane Katrina or the public fascination with "attractive" felons, race-based moral and emotional judgments fuel the cycle of stigma and privilege. These judgments, in turn, are reinforced through everyday language, media portrayals, and policy decisions, continually fortifying the symbolic and institutional boundaries of race.

Racialized emotions and cognition are learned schemas corresponding to patterns of neural activity, *racializing* our brains. The brain architecture and the connectivity between the vmPFC and emotion and memory regions of the brain support racial schema activation.[86] There are two important implications from this argument. First, these schemas result in "felt" social outcomes, such as feelings of exclusion and marginalization, as if it is physical pain[87] as I elaborate on in the next chapter. Second, these "learned" patterns of neural activity can be "unlearned," as discussed in chapter 5.

4

The Aftermath of Race

In her essay titled "Notes from a Trip to Russia," American intersectional feminist writer and activist Audre Lorde, who describes herself as "a Black, lesbian, feminist, socialist, poet, mother of two,"[1] describes a dream that she had upon returning from her trip to Russia in 1976.[2] In this dream, Lorde is making love to a lover who is ill and needs a kidney and a brain scan. When she fears these will not be provided, she realizes that she is in Russia, where "medicine and doctor bills and all of the rest of that are free." This moment of realization highlights how access to healthcare – often viewed as an individual burden in the United States – is structured differently across societies. After the Bolshevik Revolution in 1917, Russia established a universal, state-controlled healthcare system – a model that, for many Americans, remains a distant dream. The US healthcare system is the most expensive in the world, with Americans paying significantly more while receiving less care than residents of other developed nations.[3]

The structure of US healthcare is one social factor that facilitates and contributes to stark contrasts between health outcomes for different social groups in the United States, not least health disparities between different racial groups. These health inequalities underscore how race functions both as a category and as groupness in shaping life outcomes. While race as a category structures differential access to healthcare through legal and institutional frameworks – such as health insurance disparities, residential segregation, and employer-based health benefits – race as groupness shapes how different racial communities experience and respond to healthcare inequalities. The recent killing of the CEO of a major US health insurance company by a young man, 26-year-old Luigi Mangione, allegedly driven by frustration with the American healthcare system, reflects how deep-seated inequities provoke not only financial hardship but also emotional and psychological distress.

The classification of healthcare systems – ranging from universal coverage models to private insurance schemes – impacts the distribution of health resources and services, influencing how inequalities manifest and persist across nations.[4] While the Soviet model represents an idealized vision of universal care, it was not without flaws. The Soviet healthcare system also suffered from chronic underfunding,[5] deteriorating infrastructure, inadequate medical supplies, and poorly paid health workers, leading to low morale and declining health outcomes compared to the West.[6] There were visible inequalities, affecting health outcomes in Soviet Russia. For example, life expectancy data from 1958 to 1960 show significant disparities across ethnic groups, with Chechens (a Sunni Muslim group) and the Tuvian people of Siberia (a Turkic ethnic group) having the lowest lifespan with an average of 50 years and Latvians (a Baltic ethnic group) living up to 73 years.[7] These disparities reveal that while race and ethnicity were not formally institutionalized in Soviet medical policy, group-based inequities persisted, reflecting how health outcomes are shaped not only by state policies but also by sociohistorical group relations.

Globally, health disparities remain striking, particularly between nations in the Global North and Global South. Childhood mortality rates in sub-Saharan Africa and Afghanistan exceed 200 deaths per 1,000 births, compared to just 20 per 1,000 in industrialized nations.[8] These inequalities are not merely categorical (differences between countries) but also reflect group-based historical relationships of colonialism and resource extraction. The enduring impact of colonial rule on healthcare infrastructure, economic development, and environmental conditions means that many nations in the

Global South still struggle with extreme poverty, inadequate healthcare access, and low sanitation coverage.

In the United States, race as both a category and a form of groupness shapes health inequalities. Public health research consistently finds that Black, Indigenous, and Latinx populations experience worse health outcomes than white Americans. For instance, Black Americans report lower levels of well-being[9] and experience higher rates of obesity,[10] hypertension,[11] and mortality compared to white Americans.[12] While the debate on the role of genetics in racial health disparities[13] will be briefly covered here, the main argument of this chapter is that these disparities persist not because of genetic variation but because of existing racial inequalities. Race as a category (used in medical research, census data, and clinical guidelines) often reifies differences as if they are innate, while race as groupness reflects the shared historical and structural conditions that produce those differences.

This chapter connects the social science literature on health disparities with the neuroscience of exclusion and stress to illustrate how racial discrimination affects the brain, the role of genetics and epigenetics, intergenerational transmission of racism and trauma, and finally some of the "paradoxes" in the literature and protective factors. As will be discussed in this chapter, neuroscience studies broaden our eyes to the ways race gets "under our skin" or "within our brains." However, neuroscience research also offers very promising insights and tools into the ways we can rewire our brains to combat racism, which are discussed in the following chapter.

Fundamental causes of health inequalities

When COVID-19 hit the United States in March 2020, I was teaching at UC Riverside while living in Pasadena. At first, I didn't grasp the virus's severity, but within weeks in-person classes were canceled. Fortunately, UCR's quarterly system allowed me to quickly move final exams online, and the university swiftly transitioned to remote learning, providing faculty with professional Zoom accounts and other resources. I adapted by setting up a home recording space and researching effective asynchronous teaching methods. While the rapid shift was stressful, I was fortunate to have the flexibility to work safely from home, a privilege that became even more apparent as the pandemic exposed deep social inequalities.

As COVID-19 spread, it became clear that its impact was deeply tied to American racial and economic disparities. Black, Hispanic, and Asian communities faced disproportionately higher infection rates, ICU admissions, and deaths.[14] While the slogan "We are all in this together" echoed across social media and political speeches, the reality was far from equal. The ability to work from home, access healthcare, order groceries online, and avoid public spaces became a form of privilege – one that insulated people like me from the harshest consequences of the pandemic. In contrast, frontline and essential workers, disproportionately from communities of color, were unable to retreat into the safety of remote work. They faced increased exposure to the virus, often without the luxury of paid sick leave, stable healthcare, or financial security. In this context, my struggles with online teaching felt trivial compared to the systemic inequalities that left so many vulnerable. My initial concerns over transitioning to online teaching, while real in their own right, were ultimately a reflection of privilege and access to what American sociologists Bruce Link and Jo Phelan call "flexible resources," resources that come with money, power, and knowledge tied to economic status (SES – income, education, and wealth).

Flexible resources are social and economic advantages that enable individuals to avoid health risks and access protective measures.[15] These resources are considered "flexible" because they can be applied across different health conditions and changing circumstances, continuously shaping health outcomes over time. Flexible resources can be understood through the lens of race as both a category and a group experience. As a category, race structures the distribution of resources through institutional policies that create disparities in wealth, education, and employment – each of which influences health outcomes. As a form of groupness, race shapes how different communities experience and respond to systemic inequalities. The pandemic illustrated this distinction clearly: while Black and Hispanic workers were disproportionately employed in high-exposure essential jobs, their ability to mobilize community networks for support reflected a shared racialized experience of navigating exclusion and survival strategies.

Fundamental cause theory (FCT), introduced by Bruce Link and Jo Phelan (1995), argues that, despite new progress in medicine and treatment of diseases, deep-rooted social conditions (e.g., SES, systemic racism, social class) are "fundamental causes" that create and sustain health inequalities through the unequal distribution of flexible resources.[16] As one of the most widely researched theories focusing on social determinants (as opposed to biological determinants) of health, this theory has also been applied to the distribution of the COVID-19-related health outcomes. Interestingly, this research has found that while higher SES was associated with earlier COVID exposure, likely due to greater likelihood of global travel and passing through the airports or vacation spots, lower SES was related to increased incidence and mortality rates.[17] Communities of color, who are more represented in low-wage and essential workforce on the front lines and thus have less of these flexible resources, were more likely to be negatively affected by the COVID-19 virus. They were not able to take sick days or work remotely when the COVID-19 pandemic hit and thus were more likely to be exposed to the virus.

In December 2020, at the height of the second COVID-19 surge in the United States, Bruce Link and I launched an online study to investigate racial disparities in pandemic-related outcomes. Using availability quota sampling with a well-known panel survey company, we collected data from approximately 1,880 respondents, ensuring our sample reflected the racial, age, gender, and income distributions of the US population. Our sample included 20% white, 6% Asian, 12% Black, 17% Hispanic, and about 4% multi-racial or other racial groups. We used the Census's updated racial classification system (which will be implemented in 2030) that combines Hispanic identity with racial categories and includes a Middle Eastern category.

As can be seen from Table 4.1, our findings aligned with FCT's predictions: Black, Hispanic, and multi-racial respondents were significantly more likely to experience job loss, financial hardship, and barriers to healthcare access than their white and Asian counterparts. For example, Black and

Table 4.1 COVID-19-Related Outcomes by Race – December 2020 Survey

	COVID-19-Related Job and Health Outcomes by Race			
	Lost job due to the COVID-19 pandemic (% yes)	Working less hours due to the COVID-19 pandemic (% yes)	Diagnosed with COVID-19 (% yes)	Hospitalized due to COVID-19 (% yes)
Asian	11%	17%	5%	4%
Black	19%	23%	11%	12%
Hispanic	23%	28%	14%	10%
White	12%	21%	8%	6%
Other/Multi-race	45%	41%	24%	21%

	Economic Stress-Related to the COVID-19 Pandemic by Race			
	Been concerned about losing job (% fairly often & very often combined)	Been concerned about going into financial hardship (% fairly often & very often combined)	Been concerned about not being able to pay rent (% fairly often & very often combined)	Been concerned about not being able to buy essential items like groceries (% fairly often & very often combined)
Asian	21%	25%	24%	24%
Black	28%	38%	37%	36%
Hispanic	33%	43%	41%	40%
White	19%	26%	20%	23%
Other/Multi-race	40%	46%	55%	49%

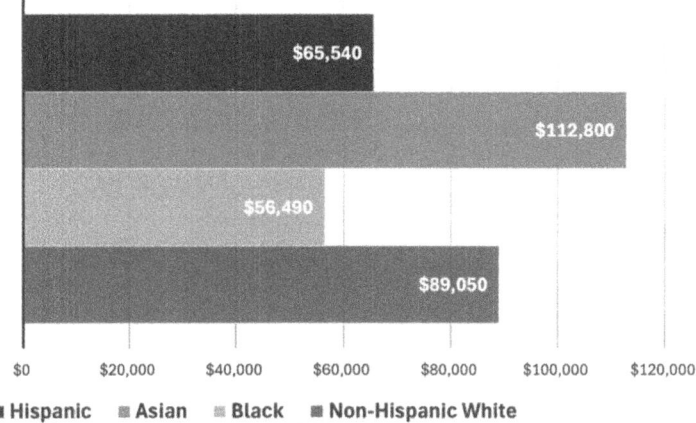

$65,540

$112,800

$56,490

$89,050

$0 $20,000 $40,000 $60,000 $80,000 $100,000 $120,000

■ Hispanic   ▪ Asian   ▪ Black   ■ Non-Hispanic White

Figure 4.1 Median household income by race, 2023

Source: Data from US Census Current Population Survey Annual Social and Economic Supplements

Hispanic respondents were almost twice as likely – and multi-racial respondents nearly four times as likely – to report job loss due to the pandemic. These groups were also significantly more likely to report concerns about financial instability, struggling to pay rent, or affording groceries. Health disparities mirrored these economic inequalities: Black, Hispanic, and multi-racial respondents were twice as likely to report being diagnosed with COVID-19 or being hospitalized compared to white and Asian respondents.

These findings highlight how race operates both as a systemic category that structures access to resources and as a group experience that shapes lived realities. The racial wealth gap – one of the most persistent forms of structural inequality – exacerbates health disparities by limiting access to stable employment, quality healthcare, and safe living conditions. The stark income and wealth inequalities of race in the United States are evident in Figures 4.1 and 4.2. According to the data from the US Census's Current Population Survey, the median income for Black households is nearly half that of Asian households,[18] and Black families are three times more likely to have zero or negative net worth than white families.[19] Homeownership and retirement savings also show stark racial gaps: only 39% of Black households own homes, compared

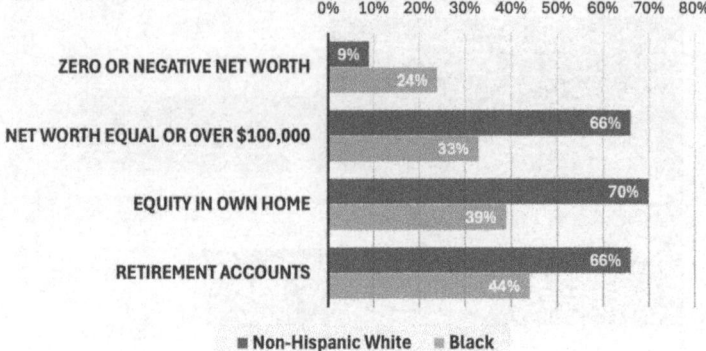

Figure 4.2 Household wealth by Black and white race, 2021
Source: Data from US Census Survey of Income and Program Participation

to 70% of white households. These disparities illustrate how wealth – accumulated through generations of racial exclusion – translates into health advantages or disadvantages.[20]

Discrimination and health

While material resources play a crucial role in predicting health outcomes, socioeconomic factors alone do not fully explain racial health disparities.[21] For example, Black mothers and their babies are significantly more likely to die during or shortly after childbirth compared to their white counterparts, a disparity that persists across income levels.[22] Even among high-income Black mothers, maternal and infant mortality rates remain as high as those of low-income white mothers. This suggests that racial disparities in health are not simply a function of economic class but rather reflect deeply embedded structural and systemic inequities that operate independently of wealth or education.

Tennis superstar Serena Williams's experience illustrates this phenomenon. In a *Vogue* cover interview, Williams recounted how, shortly after giving birth to her daughter Olympia, her concerns about shortness of breath were dismissed by medical staff, who attributed them to post-surgical pain medication.[23] With a history of pulmonary embolisms, Williams persisted in advocating for a CT scan, which revealed several small blood clots in her lungs. Had she not insisted on being taken seriously, her life could have been in danger. Williams's experience is far from unique – many Black women report feeling dismissed or unheard by medical professionals, regardless of socioeconomic status.[24] This persistence of racial health inequalities across class lines reflects how race functions both as a structural category and as a form of group experience. As a category, race structures medical interactions, healthcare access, and resource allocation – as seen in the historical exclusion of Black individuals from medical research and the ongoing racial biases in clinical decision making. As a group experience, race shapes how individuals interpret, internalize, and respond to these disparities, including through medical mistrust, coping strategies, and communal resilience.

Mechanisms of racism and health disparities

Harvard public health scholar David R. Williams and his colleagues identify three primary mechanisms through which racism creates health inequalities: cultural racism, institutional racism, and individual discrimination.[25]

Cultural racism and internalized racism

Cultural racism refers to the ideological system that normalizes racial hierarchies through stereotypes, stigma, and biases. One of the most insidious manifestations of cultural racism is internalized racism, where individuals adopt negative stereotypes about their own racial group. This occurs when marginalized individuals come to see their own group through the lens of the dominant racial order, leading to self-doubt, reduced self-worth, and harmful coping behaviors.[26] Believing that one's own racial group and oneself is not as desirable or beautiful, not as smart or intelligent or hardworking, are all examples of internalized racism.

The impact of internalized racism on health is profound. In a study of Afro-Caribbean women aged 18 to 55 in Dominica, internalized racism was linked to higher fasting glucose levels and increased abdominal fat, both risk factors for diabetes and obesity.[27] While the exact physiological mechanisms remain unclear, researchers speculate that internalized racism contributes to chronic stress, disruptions in cortisol regulation, and unhealthy lifestyle choices, such as increased alcohol consumption. Despite its significance, internalized racism remains an underexplored topic, largely due to the concern that studying internalized racism may reinforce victim blaming rather than expose systemic racial oppression.[28] That is why there are few longitudinal studies[29] exploring the causal links between internalized racism and health outcomes. While these studies provide strong statistical associations, the question of causal mechanisms remains complex. Some research[30] attempts to theorize pathways – such as stress-related physiological responses or identity-related cognitive distortions – but empirical evidence on specific mechanisms remains limited. Further research is needed to uncover its full impact and develop effective interventions.

Institutional racism and residential segregation

Institutional racism refers to race-neutral policies that, in practice, systematically disadvantage Black, Indigenous, and other marginalized communities. One of the most significant examples of institutional racism affecting health is residential segregation, which continues to shape health disparities in the United States. Despite the passage of the Fair Housing Act in 1968, which made housing discrimination illegal, racial segregation persists and has worsened in many cities. A 2019 study by the University of California, Berkeley's Othering and Belonging Institute[31] found that 81% of metropolitan areas in the United States became more segregated from 1990 to 2019, with cities like Detroit, Cleveland, and Philadelphia experiencing some of the highest levels of racial isolation. Segregated neighborhoods are disproportionately affected by concentrated poverty, lower educational opportunities, reduced access to quality healthcare, higher crime rates, and environmental hazards – all of which contribute to poorer health outcomes.[32] Indigenous communities experience similar structural disadvantages. American Indian reservations suffer from chronic underfunding and limited healthcare infrastructure, with the Indian Health Service (IHS) struggling to meet the needs of Indigenous populations.[33] The persistent lack of medical services, economic investment, and access to clean water on reservations underscores how institutional neglect and policy decisions sustain health inequities.

Individual discrimination and medical bias

The third mechanism through which racism influences health is individual discrimination, particularly in healthcare settings. Discrimination at the individual level occurs both through direct interactions with medical professionals and through the physiological stress responses triggered by racial bias. A significant barrier for Black, Indigenous, and Latinx patients is the dismissal of their symptoms by healthcare providers, which results in delayed diagnoses and inadequate treatment.[34] Studies report that members of communities of color face medical discrimination such as not receiving quality care or respect from the medical staff (e.g., nurses, doctors, or receptionists), not having enough time with the doctor, not being included in the medical decision-making process as much, in turn leading to medical mistrust, underutilization of medical services, and as a consequence an increased risk of health complications.[35]

A personal experience highlights these issues. A few years ago, a pea-sized, rubbery bump appeared on my left shoulder after an inflamed acne breakout. Over several months, the bump grew harder and more prominent. Concerned, I visited my primary care physician, a white doctor, who could not diagnose it. She referred me to a dermatologist, also white, who was similarly uncertain but suggested it might be a keloid. However, she could not provide clear information on treatment options or prognosis. I was a bit shocked with this lack of information and treatment options and quite annoyed with this big bump on my shoulder. After months of back-and-forth discussions, I was prescribed cortisol injections, which I paid for out of pocket since my insurance refused to cover the treatment. To my frustration, the injections had no effect on the bump. Later, a Black friend casually identified it as a keloid, noting that they are common among darker-skinned individuals. Embarrassed by my lack of knowledge, I began researching and discovered that Black and Brown people are disproportionately affected by keloids,[36] yet medical education often lacks sufficient training in dermatology for darker skin tones.[37] Additionally, insurance companies often do not cover keloid treatment, reinforcing racial inequities in dermatological care.[38]

This example illustrates how racial biases in medical education, insurance coverage, and treatment protocols reinforce structural disparities in healthcare. The absence of adequate medical imagery and research on darker skin tones leads to frequent misdiagnoses and substandard care for Black and Brown patients.

Discrimination, social exclusion, and stress

While race is often treated categorically in medical research and healthcare policy, the lived experience of racialized individuals reveals that race functions not just as a classification system but as a deeply embodied group identity that shapes social interactions, stress responses, and access to care. The cumulative effects of chronic discrimination, structural barriers, and cultural racism manifest in heightened stress responses, increased cortisol levels, and elevated risk for chronic illnesses.[39] These heightened stress reactions are not just transient; they can have long-term health consequences. The body's ability to respond to stress is governed by a system known as the hypothalamic–pituitary–adrenal (HPA) axis, which regulates the release of the hormones cortisol (see Figure 4.3). The HPA axis is a neuroendocrine feedback system where the hypothalamus in our brain responds to a stressor by releasing corticotropin-releasing hormone (CRH), which then prompts the pituitary gland (a pea-shaped structure under the hypothalamus) to release adrenocorticotropic hormone to be relayed to the adrenal gland (on top of our kidney) to secrete cortisol (which in turn signals the hypothalamus to stop producing CRH, creating a negative feedback loop). Under normal circumstances, the HPA axis helps the body manage acute stress by triggering a series of physiological responses that prepare an individual to either confront or flee from a threat. However, chronic exposure to stressors like discrimination can lead to dysregulation of the HPA axis,

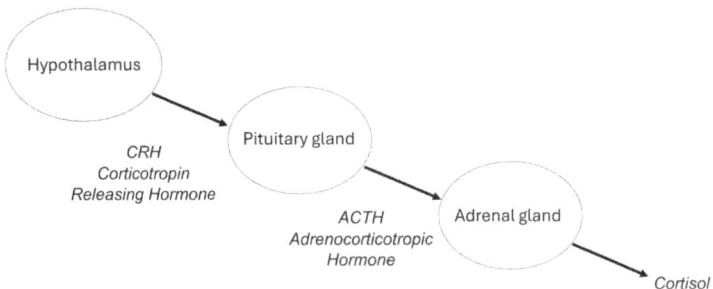

Figure 4.3 The hypothalamic–pituitary–adrenal (HPA) axis

resulting in prolonged or exaggerated responses that place strain on the body.

Repeated experiences of discrimination, as well as negative inter-ethnic encounters, can contribute to what is known as allostatic load – the cumulative wear and tear on the body due to the constant need to adapt to stress. Allostatic load reflects the long-term consequences of repeated activation of the body's stress-response systems, including not only the HPA axis but also the sympathetic nervous system. Over time, this load can overwhelm the body's capacity to maintain balance, or homeostasis, leading to a host of negative health outcomes. For example, sustained high blood pressure, chronically elevated cortisol levels, and increased heart rate can impair cardiovascular function and increase the risk of chronic diseases such as hypertension, heart disease, and diabetes.[40]

The relationship between discrimination and allostatic load highlights the complex, bidirectional link between stress and physical health. Chronic activation of stress pathways can also impair immune function, increase inflammation, and contribute to mental health disorders, further compounding the negative effects of discrimination. Ultimately, the cumulative burden of discrimination-induced stress not only disrupts the normal functioning of the HPA axis but also accelerates the physiological wear and tear that increases vulnerability to a range of diseases and health disparities.[41] For example, Deepa Purushothaman, herself a former senior executive, conducted interviews with 500 women-of-color executive leaders and found that two out of three women that she interviewed felt physically sick due to workplace

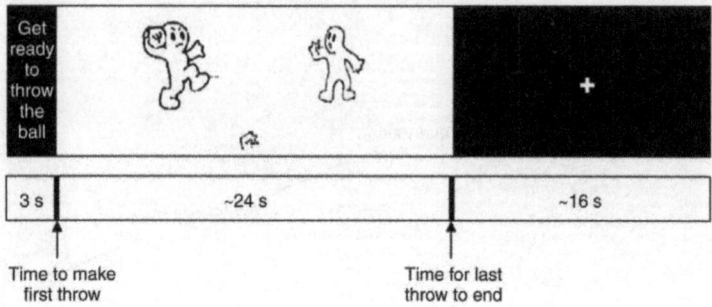

Figure 4.4 Cyberball game within the fMRI

microaggressions and toxicity – a phenomenon she calls the "tox-sick pattern."[42]

Another way social exclusion and potential discrimination affect our bodies and our brains is through activating the social distress network in the brain. A 2003 brain-imaging study by neuroscientists Naomi Eisenberger, Matthew Lieberman, and Kipling Williams used a virtual ball-tossing game, called Cyberball, which simulated social exclusion and found that brain regions related to physical pain (dorsal anterior cingulate cortex) responded to social exclusion.[43] So, social rejection is experienced in our brains as if it is physically hurting us. Later on, it was suggested that social exclusion relied on a larger network of social distress that also includes the frontal cortex (particularly the orbitofrontal cortex).[44]

I have personally used the same Cyberball experimental paradigm in a brain-imaging study (see Figure 4.4). In this experiment, participants were led to believe they were playing an online ball-tossing game with two other players. At some point, the other players stopped passing the ball to the participant, continuing to play among themselves. This unexpected exclusion triggered strong emotional reactions – so much so that one participant stopped the experiment mid-scan to protest that they were being ignored. My study also showed activation of the anterior cingulate cortex in response to social exclusion, supporting previous findings.[45] In another study, Black emerging adults who were excluded by white peers in a Cyberball game exhibited increased cortisol release, indicating heightened HPA axis activation in response to social

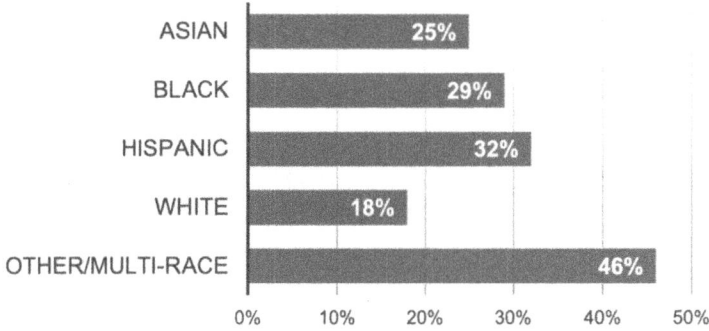

Figure 4.5 Respondents who reported experiencing racial exclusion by race in our 2020 survey

rejection.[46] This suggests that racialized social exclusion not only affects the brain's pain centers but also triggers a physiological stress response, further contributing to cumulative health disparities.

Looking back at the survey we conducted in 2020, during the early stages of the COVID-19 pandemic, we explored whether racial exclusion and its effects were exacerbated by the crisis. When COVID-19 first emerged, it was frequently referred to in the media as the "Wuhan Virus" or the "Chinese Virus," contributing to a rise in hate crimes against Asian Americans.[47] Given this context, our survey included questions about racial discrimination and exclusion. To assess racial exclusion, one key question we asked participants was whether people acted as if they wanted nothing to do with members of their racial or ethnic group because of COVID-19. When we combined responses from those who reported experiencing this "sometimes" or "often" (as opposed to "never" or "rarely"), we found that Asian, Black, Hispanic, and other/multi-racial groups all experienced heightened levels of racial exclusion due to COVID-19 (Figure 4.5). Interestingly, Black, Hispanic, and other/multi-racial respondents reported even greater levels of racial exclusion than both Asian and white Americans in our sample. Nearly one-third of Black (29%) and Hispanic (32%) respondents, along with almost half of other/multi-race respondents (46%), indicated experiencing racial exclusion. In comparison, 18% of white and 25% of Asian respondents reported similar experiences.

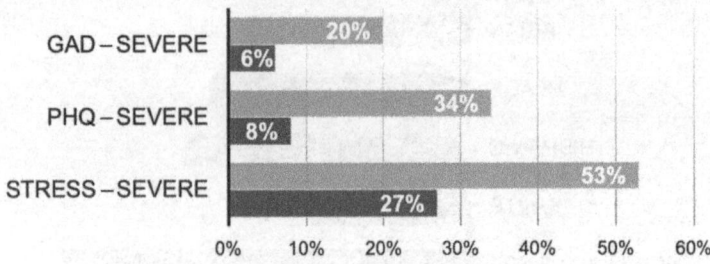

Figure 4.6 Mental health outcomes for respondents who reported experiencing racial exclusion by race in our 2020 survey

Overall, 23% of our total sample reported experiencing racial exclusion at least "sometimes."

When we look at stress and mental health outcomes among those who have reported experiencing racial exclusion versus those who have not, these adverse outcomes are also strikingly elevated. We measured stress using a question adapted from Cohen's Perceived Stress Scale,[48] asking participants how often they had felt nervous and stressed since the outbreak of COVID-19 in March 2020. To identify individuals experiencing severe stress, we grouped responses indicating stress "fairly often" or "very often." Depression and generalized anxiety were assessed using two widely recognized measures: the Patient Health Questionnaire (PHQ-8)[49] and the Generalized Anxiety Disorder Scale (GAD-7).[50] These scales evaluate how frequently, over the previous two weeks, participants had experienced symptoms of depression (e.g., feeling down, fatigue, poor appetite or overeating, moving or speaking slowly) or anxiety (e.g., excessive worrying, trouble relaxing, irritability). Severity scores for PHQ-8 and GAD-7 were calculated by summing item responses, yielding total scores ranging from 0 to 24 for PHQ-8 and 0 to 21 for GAD-7. Severe symptoms were defined using a standard cutoff score of 15 or higher.[51] Our findings reveal that individuals who reported experiencing racial exclusion "sometimes" or "often" were more than three times as likely to report severe anxiety, more than four times as likely to report severe depression, and nearly twice as likely to report severe stress (Figure 4.6). Although the cross-sectional nature of our data prevents us from establishing causality between racial exclusion and poor mental health outcomes, the strong association is telling. These findings underscore the profound psychological burden experienced by individuals facing racial exclusion due to COVID-19.

How about genes?

The relationship between race, genetics, and health disparities has long been a subject of inquiry, controversy, and evolving understanding in science and medicine. A central debate is whether race should be used as a genetic classification or understood primarily as a social construct with lived consequences. This debate reflects the broader distinction between race as a category – a system of classification often used in biomedical research – and race as groupness – a shared social experience that shapes health outcomes through structural inequities, discrimination, and intergenerational stress.

Biomedical researchers have historically used racial categories as proxies for genetic variation. Proponents argue that these classifications can help identify genetic markers that influence disease risk and treatment response. For example, studies have shown that Black Americans may respond differently to certain antihypertensive medications due to variations in drug metabolism genes.[52] However, using race as a biological variable, rather than a socially constructed one, reinforces stereotypes and diverts attention from addressing systemic inequities.[53] Using race as a proxy for genetic differences oversimplifies the complex interplay of genetic, environmental, and social factors that shape health outcomes. Instead of using race as a fixed biological category, researchers advocate for a focus on genetic ancestry, which offers a more precise understanding of population-level genetic variation without reinforcing racial essentialism.[54]

To understand the role of genetics in health disparities, we need to distinguish between genotype, phenotype, and ancestry. The genotype refers to an individual's full set of genes inherited from both parents. Phenotype includes the observable traits – such as height, skin color, eye color, and proneness to diseases – that result from the interaction of genes and environmental factors.[55] Genetic ancestry, on the other hand, is the biological tracing of a person's lineage based on inherited deoxyribonucleic acid (DNA), often linked to geographic regions. Oftentimes, the phenotype – people's observable traits – are what we use to categorize others into racial groups. While genotype – our genetic makeup – can determine some of these inherited traits, there are no clear-cut genetic boundaries that define racial categories. Geographic genetic ancestry provides a more precise lens for studying health disparities. It identifies genetic variation patterns linked to specific regions of the world. For example, specific genetic markers associated with conditions like sickle cell anemia or Tay–Sachs disease are more prevalent in populations from malaria-endemic regions or Ashkenazi Jewish communities, respectively.[56]

The Human Genome Project (HGP), completed in 2003, revolutionized our understanding of human genetics. By sequencing the entire human genome, the project revealed that humans share approximately 99.9% of their DNA, with the remaining 0.1% accounting for individual and population-level genetic variation.[57] Crucially, the HGP demonstrated that genetic differences between so-called racial groups are minimal compared to the variation within them, debunking the notion of biologically distinct human races.[58] The HGP also introduced tools to study genetic ancestry at a granular level. Unlike race, which is a social construct reflecting historical and cultural identities, genetic ancestry provides a scientific framework to trace the geographic origins of an individual's ancestors. For instance, the APOE4 allele, associated with a higher risk of Alzheimer's disease, is more common in certain European populations. Similarly, variants in the PCSK9 gene, which influence cholesterol levels, are more prevalent among individuals of West African descent.[59] These genetic variations, however, do not align neatly with socially constructed racial categories, highlighting the limitations of using race as a proxy for genetic differences. These findings underscore that race is an inadequate category in genetic research – race does not map neatly onto human genetic diversity. However, despite progress in dismantling these overtly racist frameworks, race continues to be conflated with biology in modern biomedical research. This legacy has shaped how health disparities are framed and addressed, often attributing them to genetic differences rather than systemic inequities.[60]

While race as a category does not align with genetic reality, race as groupness profoundly shapes health through social, economic, and political conditions. The emerging field of epigenetics helps explain how racial disparities in health are perpetuated not through genetic inheritance, but through the biological embedding of social experiences. Epigenetics studies heritable changes in gene expression that occur without alterations to the DNA sequence. Stressors such as racial discrimination, socioeconomic inequality, and adverse childhood experiences can trigger epigenetic modifications, affecting how genes regulate bodily processes like inflammation, stress responses, and immune function.[61] One prominent example is cardiovascular disease, which disproportionately affects Black Americans.[62] Research indicates that early-life stress and adverse maternal conditions, influenced by systemic discrimination and economic inequities, play a significant role in this disparity.[63] Epigenetic changes during fetal development, such as modifications to gene expression related to stress and inflammation, connect maternal experiences to adult-onset conditions like hypertension and diabetes.[64] These findings underscore how early-life environmental factors become biologically embedded through social experiences, influencing long-term health outcomes.[65]

Similarly, chronic pain disparities illustrate how race as groupness interacts with biology. Chronic pain is another area where racial disparities are evident.[66] Black Americans experience more frequent, severe, and disabling chronic pain compared to non-Hispanic whites.[67] This disparity has been linked to DNA methylation changes in genes associated with stress response and inflammation. Chronic stress, economic hardship, and racial discrimination amplify these epigenetic changes, exacerbating the pain experience and reducing the efficacy of coping mechanisms. These findings suggest that racial health disparities are shaped by lived social experiences rather than innate genetic differences.

The effects of race as groupness extend beyond individuals to intergenerational health outcomes. Chronic exposure to racial discrimination alters stress-regulation systems (like the HPA axis discussed previously), leading to a phenomenon known as weathering – the premature aging of Black and marginalized bodies due to sustained physiological stress.[68] These epigenetic effects are also evident in the brain. Pregnant mothers who experience racism and chronic stress can biologically transmit these effects to their babies. Newborns of mothers with high exposure to racial discrimination exhibit stronger connectivity between the amygdala and hippocampus regions associated with threat detection and memory.[69] These heightened connections may predispose infants to higher vigilance, anxiety, and stress reactivity, illustrating how social conditions become biologically embedded across generations.

Intergenerational trauma also involves how the brain responds to chronic stress. For instance, children growing up in poverty or under constant stress show heightened activity in their amygdala and reduced activity in the prefrontal cortex.[70] This pattern mirrors the effects of trauma seen in their parents and creates a cycle where stress responses are amplified, making it harder to recover from or adapt to challenges. Over time, this can lead to ongoing mental health struggles and even physical health issues, such as heart disease or immune system problems.[71]

While genetics can offer insights into population-level disease risks, racial disparities in health cannot be fully explained by biology. A holistic approach to health disparities must integrate genetic insights with social determinants of health. For instance, while genetic studies have identified the BRCA1 and BRCA2 mutations as significant risk factors for breast and ovarian cancer in Ashkenazi Jewish populations, these findings must be contextualized within broader factors, such as access to genetic testing and preventive care.[72] Similarly, the prevalence of sickle cell anemia among individuals of African descent highlights the importance of considering both genetic and environmental factors. The sickle cell trait evolved as an adaptive response to malaria, yet the disease's impact today is exacerbated by inadequate healthcare infrastructure in many affected regions.[73]

We need systemic interventions to combat racism, reduce chronic stress, and improve early-life care and incorporate both social and biological approaches, recognizing the interplay of lived experiences and their epigenetic consequences. This comprehensive perspective calls for targeted strategies to break the cycle of racism and inequality and to promote health equity.[74]

Paradoxes

Despite having lower socioeconomic status, lack of access to healthcare resources, and experiences with discrimination, some racial groups also have better health status. Often called epidemiological paradoxes, the most well-known examples of this phenomenon are the Black–white mental health paradox and the Hispanic health paradox. The Black–white mental health paradox highlights the surprising finding that Black Americans often report similar or better mental health outcomes compared to white Americans, despite enduring greater exposure to socioeconomic disadvantages and systemic racism. For instance, studies consistently show lower rates of mood, anxiety, and substance-use disorders among Black Americans.[75] The Black–white mental health paradox spreads across lifetime, predicting mood, anxiety, and substance-use disorders across ages and genders, with the exception of middle-aged Black men (ages 45–64), who have higher odds of lifetime substance-use disorder compared to their white male peers.[76] The mental health advantage of Black Americans persisted even during the COVID-19 pandemic, with lower levels of distress and somatic symptoms, depression, and anxiety.[77]

The Hispanic health paradox refers to the counterintuitive finding that Hispanic individuals in the United States often exhibit comparable or better health outcomes than non-Hispanic whites. This phenomenon, evident in their higher life expectancy, lower infant mortality rates, and reduced prevalence of chronic conditions like cardiovascular disease,[78] suggests that health outcomes cannot be fully understood through categorical racial classifications alone. For example, in 2019, Hispanic individuals had a life expectancy advantage of 3.0 years over non-Hispanic white people and 7.1 years over non-Hispanic Black people.[79] Similar trends are observed in Europe, where first- and second-generation Turkish immigrants in Germany have lower mortality rates than their German counterparts, despite experiencing structural disadvantages.[80] However, this paradox is not universal – Puerto Rican and Cuban immigrants do not always exhibit the same health advantages as Mexican-born immigrants,[81] highlighting the fluidity of racial categories and the role of group-based experiences in shaping health outcomes.

Traditional explanations for the paradox, such as the "salmon bias" (where ill immigrants return to their home countries) and the "healthy immigrant effect" (where selective migration favors healthier individuals),[82] often treat race as a static category, failing to account for the ways in which racial groupness interacts with health. Over time, exposure to systemic racism, restrictive immigration policies, and acculturative stress erodes these initial health advantages, demonstrating how group-based social positioning impacts long-term well-being. For example, after the 2016 US presidential election and during Trump's second presidency, heightened anti-immigrant rhetoric increased stress and reduced healthcare access among Hispanic immigrants, worsening both mental and physical health outcomes.[83] This reflects how race as a category (legal and social classifications) intersects with race as groupness (shared lived experiences of exclusion and discrimination).

At the same time, the resilience of racialized groups plays a crucial role in shaping these paradoxes. Cultural mechanisms such as *familismo* in Hispanic communities – characterized by strong family interconnectedness, shared resources, and collective problem solving – demonstrate the importance of race as groupness in fostering emotional well-being and buffering against stress.[84] Similarly, Black Americans rely on extended family networks and religious communities.[85] For both Black and Hispanic Americans, religious communities often serve as a source of social integration and emotional support, offering opportunities to build resilience through shared values and collective rituals and fostering a sense of hope and purpose.[86] These support systems illustrate how racialized groups develop protective mechanisms not as inherent traits of racial categories but as responses to historical and structural inequalities.

Psychological coping resources, such as self-esteem and cultural pride, further illustrate how racial groupness influences health resilience. Despite systemic discrimination, Black

Americans often exhibit higher levels of self-esteem than white Americans, a phenomenon linked to a historical legacy of collective struggle and identity formation.[87] Historical experiences of navigating and resisting systemic barriers have fostered a collective sense of identity and resilience, enabling many Black individuals to reframe adversity and maintain positive mental health.[88] This suggests that while race is often perceived categorically – as a set of fixed biological or legal classifications – it functions socially as a dynamic form of group belonging. However, this resilience coexists with persistent disparities in access to mental healthcare, as systemic inequities limit Black Americans' ability to receive culturally appropriate support.[89] Understanding these paradoxes requires moving beyond racial categories to examine the ways in which race as a social group shapes collective resilience, coping mechanisms, and responses to structural inequities. By integrating both perspectives, we can better analyze the complex interplay between health outcomes, cultural strengths, and systemic barriers.

Summary

This chapter explored the intersection of race, health disparities, and systemic inequalities. As I outlined here, and throughout the book, race functions both as a category and as groupness. As a category, race is often used in medical research to classify differences in health outcomes, yet this framing risks biologizing racial disparities instead of addressing their structural and lived social roots. In contrast, understanding race as groupness – as a set of shared social, historical, and lived experiences – helps explain how social experiences, structural racism, and intergenerational stress responses shape health outcomes, even at a biological level (e.g., epigenetics and brain development).

As a form of groupness, race and racism operate as fundamental causes of health disparities, depleting flexible resources that might be used to facilitate the uptake of protective measures, and as predictors for exposure to social exclusion and stress.[90] These mechanisms of racialized health disparities were evident during the COVID-19 pandemic, disproportionately affecting communities due to structural inequities in resources and access to healthcare. An important mechanism carrying over the effects of macro-level racial inequality to the individual is the stress processes.[91] Discrimination and exclusion heighten stress responses in the body, including blood pressure, heart rate, and cardiovascular reactivity.[92] Similarly, neuroimaging studies have also shown that brain regions related to feeling physical pain, that is, the dorsal anterior cingulate cortex (dACC), are activated in response to social exclusion.[93] Cumulative exposure to negative inter-ethnic interactions over time overload the body's allostatic load – the capacity to react and adjust to challenges and stress through physiological responses such as blood pressure, cortisol activity, and cardiac output.[94]

Exposure to chronic and early-life adversities like poverty or experiences with racial discrimination not only affects the functioning of brain regions crucial for emotion regulation in oneself but also in one's offspring.[95] Racism and chronic stress cause epigenetic changes, perpetuating health disparities across generations by biologically embedding social inequalities. However, racial disparities in health and well-being persist not because of genetic variation but because of existing racial inequalities. Despite these challenges, certain epidemiological paradoxes, such as the Black–white mental health paradox and the Hispanic health paradox, reveal unexpected resilience in marginalized groups. Cultural strengths like family support, religious involvement, and strong self-esteem contribute to better mental health outcomes for some racial minorities, despite systemic inequities. These findings highlight the role of cultural strengths and community support in fostering resilience against systemic challenges.

Neuroscience research broadens our eyes to the ways racial inequalities get "under our skin." While neuroscience reveals the damaging effects of racism on health, it also suggests ways to combat racial bias and mitigate its consequences, which are explored in the following chapter.

5

Rewiring Our Brains

The human brain is often thought of as a fixed structure, with its functions predetermined by genetics and early development. However, groundbreaking research in neuroscience has revealed that the brain is far more adaptable than previously believed. This phenomenon, known as neuroplasticity, allows the brain to rewire itself in response to experience, learning, and even injury. It is this capacity for change that enables people to acquire new skills, recover from trauma, and, perhaps most intriguingly, reshape deeply ingrained thought patterns and biases.

But can neuroplasticity extend beyond individual learning and recovery to address larger societal challenges, such as racial bias and systemic discrimination? Many efforts to combat prejudice have focused on education and awareness, yet research suggests that cognitive knowledge alone is not enough to produce lasting behavioral change. Neurosociology, at the intersection of neuroscience, psychology, and social science, offers a promising path forward – one that moves beyond surface-level interventions to target the underlying neural mechanisms of bias and decision making. However, for meaningful change to occur, it is essential to recognize that biases and prejudices are not just cognitive habits but are deeply embedded within structural and systemic inequalities. These biases are reinforced through institutional policies, historical narratives, and social hierarchies that shape the distribution of power and opportunity. This chapter explores how neuroplasticity influences not only personal growth but also social transformation. It delves into the brain's ability to change through structured interventions, such as empathy training, empowerment strategies, and the fostering of equal-status interactions. Yet lasting change requires more than just individual rewiring; it demands systemic interventions that address the root causes of inequality. By understanding how biases are formed and reinforced both in the brain and in society, we can develop more effective ways to challenge and ultimately dismantle them. If neurons that fire together wire together, what would it take to rewire the brain – and by extension, society – for a more just and inclusive future?

To achieve this, in this chapter I propose the 3E framework, an integrated approach combining insights from neuroscience and the social sciences. This framework emphasizes three key components: (1) empathy: expanding our moral and social in-groups by enhancing neural and emotional responses to out-group members through structured interventions like perspective-taking and compassion training; (2) empowerment: equipping individuals and communities with the agency and tools to actively challenge bias and discrimination, shifting from passive bias suppression to proactive bias reduction; and (3) equality: creating systemic conditions that promote equal-status interactions and reduce structural inequities, reinforcing positive social learning and intergroup contact through policy-driven change.

By leveraging neuroplasticity in conjunction with institutional reform, the 3E framework offers a scientifically grounded, action-oriented pathway to dismantling racism and fostering a more equitable society.

Neuroplasticity

While inside her mother's womb as an unborn baby, Mora Leeb had a stroke, which damaged most of her left brain and left her with seizures when she was only three months old. After doing an MRI, the doctors found that Mora had almost no activity in the left side of her brain resulting in whatever neurons remaining on this side causing the epileptic seizures.[1] To cure Mora of her seizures, when she was only nine months old, the doctors removed the left side of her brain entirely with a procedure known as a hemispherectomy.

The human brain has two hemispheres, left and right, divided by a sheet of fibers known as the corpus collosum that allow for communication between the two. The left hemisphere of our brains controls the right side of our bodies, and the right side of our brains controls the left side, a phenomenon known as the lateralization of the brain. For example, when someone has a stroke on the right side of their brains, they lose control of the left side of their face and body. Also, different hemispheres of our brain are specialized in different functions. Language processing and speech production are two such important capacities that are located on the left side of our brains (among right-handed people, which is roughly about 90% of the human population).[2]

Given this, having her left side of the brain completely removed, little Mora then would have been unlikely to control movements on the right side of her body and not be able to speak at all. However, this was not the case. Over time, Mora has slowly gained the ability to use the right side of her body and understand and produce speech. In fact, at her bat mitzvah, Mora was even able to give a short speech and described herself as a "glass half-full" type of girl. While her speech ability and movement on the right side of her body is still limited compared to a teen at her age with two intact hemispheres of the brain, Mora Leeb's case is a remarkable example of neuroplasticity – the brain's ability to adapt and rewire itself.

Neuroplasticity allows us to learn new skills by making new neural connections in our brains. While during critical periods in our childhood, our brains might be more open to being rewired (especially when learning a new language or how to play a musical instrument), adults still show impressive reorganizing and learning in their brains. For example, a research study comparing the brains of London taxi drivers to a control group that did not drive taxis found that a part of the hippocampus storing geographical representations from the environment was larger among taxi drivers, correlating positively with the years spent as a taxi driver.[3] What is more is that changes in our brain can happen rather quickly, without having to wait for years. In one experiment, adult participants underwent training that taught them new names for shades of blue and green with only a two-hour session spread over a span of three days. Scanning their brains before and after this training revealed that their gray matter volume in a region of their visual cortex responsible for color vision had increased significantly.[4] This research shows that our brains can adapt rapidly through learning and exposure.

Can we rewire our brains to unlearn bias?

Given what we know about the neuroplasticity of our brains, can we rewire our brains to unlearn racism or reduce the stress caused by discrimination? After the discoveries in implicit bias and the brain, unconscious bias training was created. Unconscious bias training became one of the most widely used diversity, equity, and inclusion (DEI) initiatives, designed to reduce prejudice by making individuals aware of their implicit biases. These programs often include interventions such as counter-stereotyping (offering counter-narratives to challenge stereotypes) and negation (rejecting stereotype-consistent associations during IAT-like exercises). However, research suggests these interventions have little long-term impact on actual behavior.

A meta-analysis by Forscher and colleagues[5] found that while unconscious bias training can lead to small shifts in implicit attitudes, these changes do not translate into meaningful behavioral shifts or sustained reductions in discrimination. Worse, some studies indicate that bias training may even backfire, reinforcing stereotypes rather than dismantling them.[6] When individuals are told they hold biases they were previously unaware of, they may respond defensively or feel that bias is an inevitable trait rather than a changeable habit.

Corporate bias training also often relies on outdated or reductive cultural narratives. For example, I once took "diversity and cultural competence" training that included scripted scenarios meant to depict intercultural interactions. One sketch showed a Russian man attempting to kiss a coworker on the mouth, implying that Russian culture inherently promotes unprofessional behavior. Another scene depicted a Muslim man refusing to shake hands with female colleagues, reinforcing rigid stereotypes rather than promoting nuanced understanding. Such superficial portrayals fail to account for the diversity within cultures and instead reduce identity to rigid behavioral scripts.

Going back to our initial question of whether or not we can rewire the brain to unlearn bias, the answer lies at the intersection of neuroscience and social structures. Racial bias and systemic inequality are not merely individual attitudes but deeply embedded neural and social processes reinforced by institutionalized discrimination. From early childhood, social environments shape how the brain encodes and categorizes race, making certain biases feel automatic and intuitive. However, just as the brain adapts to new physical and cognitive challenges, it can also be trained to overcome ingrained biases.

Executive control of bias in our brains

Most unconscious bias training focuses on trying to change implicit and often emotional biases with explicit and cognitive techniques, which activate the cognitive control-related regions of our brains, such as the dorsolateral prefrontal cortex (dlPFC). The dlPFC acts almost like a "brake" for the brain, playing a central role in top-down control, goal maintenance, and emotion regulation, helping individuals align their behaviors with egalitarian intentions. It facilitates the suppression of automatic biases when individuals consciously strive to act in non-prejudicial ways.[7] The dlPFC is part of a neural network, together with the anterior cingulate cortex (ACC), governing the suppression of automatic, stereotype-driven responses and facilitating alignment with explicit goals, such as egalitarian behavior.[8] During tasks like the IAT, the dlPFC is activated to override automatic associations between social groups and stereotypes, ensuring that behavior adheres to socially endorsed norms.

Neuroimaging and behavioral studies show that the dlPFC is actively involved in reducing prejudice. For instance, when individuals encounter racial stimuli – such as faces, symbols, or language associated with different racial groups – the dlPFC and the anterior cingulate cortex (ACC) work together to suppress automatic, stereotype-driven responses. The ACC monitors for conflict between automatic biases and conscious egalitarian goals, while the dlPFC implements strategies to override these biases. These mechanisms are activated during tasks like the IAT, where incongruent responses (e.g., associating Black faces with positive attributes) demand higher dlPFC engagement to suppress stereotypes.[9] When the dlPFC is involved in executive control and suppressing bias during intergroup interactions, however, it also depletes cognitive resources – in other words, it is mentally exhausting.

For example, in a research study by American psychologist Jennifer Richeson and colleagues, white participants completed a race IAT and then interacted with a Black experimenter.[10] After this interracial interaction, they completed a well-known psychological test called the Stroop color-naming test, which measures cognitive inhibition, and also underwent fMRI testing while viewing faces of unfamiliar Black people. In the Stroop test, words naming colors are printed on the screen with either congruent names (e.g., the word "red" appears in the color red) or incongruent ones (the word "red" appears in the color blue). The test measures how long it takes the participants to name the color and whether or not they name it correctly (e.g., the participant should respond with "blue" when they see the word "red" written in blue). What they found was that after interacting with a Black person, individuals with higher levels of racial bias showed greater activation in their dlPFC (indicating a great effort in top-down control of their bias) and performed worse on the Stroop test (depletion of cognitive resources).[11] This suggests that regulating prejudice taxes the dlPFC, temporarily impairing its capacity for other cognitive tasks.[12]

As we learned in previous chapters, one of the key findings of neuroscience research is that racial bias operates implicitly through the activation of emotion-processing neural structures like the amygdala (that process threats automatically) to which the dlPFC has no connection.[13] However, most unconscious bias training and interventions rely on explicit and deliberative processes (e.g., presenting evidence for why racism is harmful, discussion of case studies, and so on), therefore targeting the executive regions of our brain rather than the subcortical, emotional regions or the socio-moral emotional regulation regions like the vmPFC (as discussed in chapter 2). Unconscious bias training tries to control the behavioral expression of implicit bias rather than the sources of it.[14] These types of training offer individuals an external motivation (standards, conventions, norms, and rules) to modify their prejudiced views, while research shows that internal motivations (personal values and goals) play a more effective role in modulating bias.[15] When external pressures (such as the approval of others) disappear, externally motivated individuals no longer have a reason to suppress their prejudices. However, when egalitarian values are internalized and merged with one's self-concept, internal motivations continue to fight against prejudice, even in the absence of external pressures.

Moreover, much unconscious bias training focuses on individual attitudes rather than structural barriers. Bias is not just a cognitive issue; it is reinforced by institutional policies, workplace cultures, and systemic inequities. Without addressing the broader social and structural factors that perpetuate discrimination, unconscious bias training fails to produce sustained, meaningful change. The failure of unconscious bias training underscores the need for alternative approaches that integrate emotions (rather than solely cognitive suppression) with systemic change. Instead of relying solely on awareness-based interventions, organizations must invest in structural reforms, inclusive policies, and long-term strategies that foster equity beyond individual training sessions. In the following sections, I explore how the 3E framework (Figure 5.1) – empathy, empowerment, and equality – offers a more effective model for reducing bias and fostering lasting change.

The 3E framework

Empathy

We have learned in previous chapters that the historical conditions that fostered racially unequal societies have caused race to become an automatic trigger in our brains. In chapter 3, we

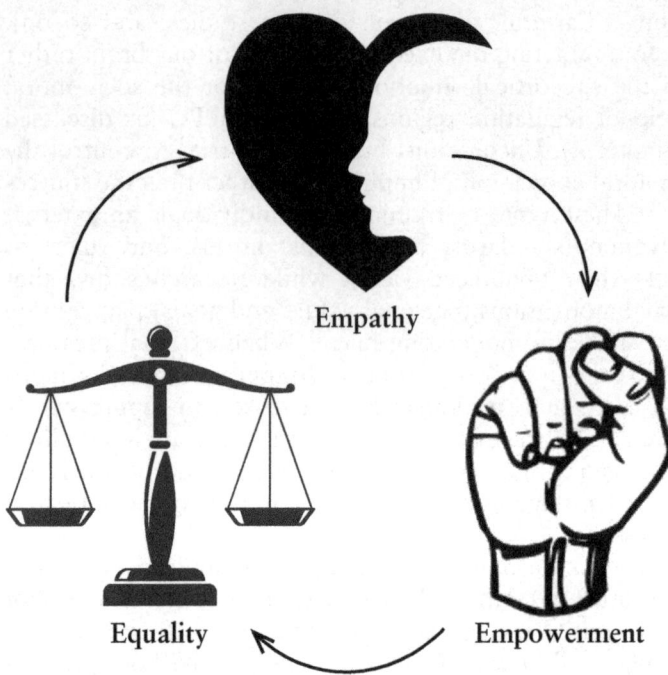

Empathy

Equality   Empowerment

Figure 5.1 The 3E framework

unpacked how the brain's moral and emotional framework tends to instinctively reinforce racial distinctions and racism in societies structured around race, unless actively challenged by anti-racist initiatives. One of the powerful ways to rewire our brains to expand our moral in-groups that encompasses changing our internal motivations is through expanding the bounds of our empathy.[16] Empathy is a multifaceted psychological construct that includes the ability to understand and respond to others' mental states and emotions. It is broadly categorized into cognitive and affective dimensions. Cognitive empathy refers to the ability to understand another person's perspective, thoughts, and emotions.[17] It involves "mentalizing" or adopting another's viewpoint to comprehend their mental state without necessarily sharing their feelings. This perspective-taking aspect of empathy is also referred to as the "theory of mind" and engages brain regions associated with higher-order cognition, such as the medial prefrontal cortex and temporo-parietal junction.[18] Affective empathy involves sharing or resonating with the emotions of others. It is tied to emotional contagion or the mirroring of feelings and relies on neural systems associated with shared emotional experiences.[19] Although distinct, cognitive and affective empathy often interact. For example, cognitive processes can modulate affective responses, ensuring empathy is contextually appropriate. Neuroimaging studies reveal both processes involve separate but sometimes overlapping neural mechanisms, indicating their interconnected yet independent roles in social understanding.[20]

Research shows that, unfortunately, racial bias influences empathy in our brains. When we experience empathy for the pain and suffering of others, the anterior insula of our brains gets activated (see chapter 2 for more on the insula).[21] One of the common ways to measure empathy for pain neurologically is via an experimental protocol. People inside a scanner are shown images of faces being pricked with a needle or tapped with a cotton swab. When presented with images of own (e.g., white) versus other (e.g., Asian) faces being pricked with the needle, people show greater activation in their anterior insula to racial in-groups compared to racial out-groups.[22] That is, they feel more pain when they see people from their own race in pain. Neural and emotional biases in empathy translate into observable behaviors, such as reduced helping, increased harm endorsement, and dehumanization of out-group members. Recent neuroscience research finds that mindfulness and compassion-based training programs offer very promising pathways to mitigate the impact of these biases and retrain our brains to increase empathy.[23] One such impactful neuroscience initiative is the ReSource Project. The ReSource Project, initiated by German neuroscientist Tania Singer in 2008, is a large-scale, longitudinal study designed to examine the trainability of mental capacities such as mindfulness, compassion, and perspective taking. Conducted between 2013 and 2016 with over 300 participants, this nine-month longitudinal training investigated how distinct contemplative practices impacted empathy, mental and physical health, brain plasticity, and social behaviors. The program was divided into three distinct three-month modules: the Presence Module, which focused on cultivating mindfulness and attention; the Affect Module aimed at enhancing social intelligence, compassion, and empathy; and the Perspective Module designed to improve perspective-taking abilities.[24]

Tania Singer and her colleagues have published the results from their longitudinal research into these trainings and brain plasticity in over forty publications. What they primarily found was that these different contemplative practices led to improvement in distinct mental capacities. Present-based mindfulness training emphasized awareness of the present moment, including thoughts, emotions, and bodily sensations, without judgment. These practices primarily targeted attentional regulation and emotional resilience via techniques like breathing meditation and body scan (awareness of different parts of one's body – aka interoceptive awareness).[25] Present-based mindfulness training enhanced functioning in brain areas involved in attentional control, such as the dlPFC and the posterior cingulate cortex (PCC), helped reduce stress through improved regulation of the HPA axis and reduction in emotional reactivity, and increased present-moment awareness by reducing mind-wandering and emotional reactivity.[26]

Perspective-taking training was designed to enhance socio-cognitive abilities, focusing on meta-cognition (understanding and reflecting on one's own thought processes) and perspective-taking (understanding others' viewpoints).[27] This module integrated practices to improve the ability to infer the mental states, beliefs, and intentions of others ("mentalize") and foster self-awareness through practices like observing thoughts meditation (observing thoughts as they arise and fall) or the perspective dyad (a partner-based practice alternating between speaker and listener roles to encourage cognitive perspective taking). Perspective-taking training improved the ability to understand oneself and others (theory of mind) and was linked to increased activation and structural changes in brain regions associated with perspective taking, such as the temporoparietal junction (TPJ) and the dmPFC.[28]

Compassion-based mindfulness training centers on developing socio-affective qualities, such as empathy, kindness, altruism, and the ability to care for oneself and others.[29] These practices often aim to foster emotional connections and promote prosocial behaviors with techniques like loving-kindness meditation (cultivating positive feelings of warmth, care, and kindness first toward oneself and gradually extending to others), compassion training (structured exercises to enhance compassion for others' suffering), and the affect dyad (similar to the perspective dyad but focused on cultivating acceptance and empathic listening via awareness of bodily feelings and emotions).[30] Compassion-based mindfulness training increases activity and structural changes in brain areas linked to prosocial behavior and reward, such as the ACC, the anterior insula, and the vmPFC, decreases stress levels and enhances social bonds and connections. Notably, partner-based socioemotional practices, like the affect dyad, foster deeper connections by encouraging nonjudgmental listening and emotional acceptance, showing promise in boosting empathy and compassion toward others.[31]

A significant implication of the ReSource Project is the targeted neuroplasticity observed in social and emotional brain networks. For example, the Affect Module fosters changes in circuits associated with care and affiliation, regulated by systems like oxytocin (a hormone key for trust and bonding), which enhance emotional resilience, reduce empathic distress, and promote prosocial motivation. Similarly, the Perspective Module strengthens networks that support theory of mind and cognitive empathy, enabling participants to better understand and respond to others' mental states. Moreover, the project reveals the long-term benefits of mental training with measurable increases in cortical thickness in regions associated with attention, emotion, and social cognition. These anatomical changes correlate with improved cognitive flexibility, emotional stability, and resilience to stress. Such findings underscore the potential of targeted mental training to mitigate racial prejudice and bias by improving empathy and the associated mental health problems, including conditions like anxiety, depression, and stress-related disorders.

Empowerment

While many unconscious training approaches are not effective because they are not based on scientific knowledge,[32] one of the most thoroughly studied training approaches that actually works is the prejudice habit-breaking intervention by the American psychologist Patricia Devine and her colleagues.[33]

Devine and colleagues approach bias as a "habit of mind" that can be broken through empowering or equipping individuals with the understanding, tools, and agency to independently recognize, reduce, and address bias and promote inclusion.[34] The empowerment method in this context is rooted in the idea of engaging participants as active agents of change, rather than passive recipients of information. This method emphasizes the importance of intrinsic motivation to combat bias. Participants are encouraged to personally care about reducing bias rather than feeling pressured externally. This empowerment model contrasts with more traditional diversity training approaches, which often focus on compliance and can evoke defensiveness.

However, empowerment cannot be fully understood without acknowledging the structural and systemic forces that shape racial hierarchies and implicit bias. While individual efforts are crucial, lasting change requires dismantling the institutional mechanisms that sustain discrimination in workplaces, education, and social policies. Without addressing these broader structures, empowerment remains an incomplete solution, placing the burden solely on individuals rather than on the systems that create and perpetuate inequality. Furthermore, as I have laid out throughout this book, race itself operates on two interconnected levels – both as a category and as a form of groupness. As discussed in sociological and neuroscientific research, race is first processed as a cognitive category, where the brain instinctively sorts individuals based on visible traits like skin color. However, race does not stop at categorization; it also functions as groupness, forming social identities that are reinforced by historical, cultural, and institutional contexts. This distinction is critical because bias-reduction interventions that focus only on race as a category perception fail to address the deeper structural forces that solidify racial group positions in society.

The training introduces several evidence-based strategies that empower individuals to recognize and counteract implicit biases through stereotype replacement (identifying stereotypical responses and replacing them with non-stereotypical alternatives), counter-stereotypic imaging (visualizing examples of individuals who contradict stereotypes, e.g., strong Black female leaders, also shown to be an effective method in reducing implicit bias by other research[35]), individuation (focusing on the unique qualities of individuals rather than group-based assumptions), and increasing intergroup contact (creating opportunities for meaningful interactions across different groups).[36] By fostering a sense of internal control and responsibility, the training empowers individuals to not only reduce their own biases but also to act as advocates for inclusion in broader social and professional settings. As a result of this training, participants demonstrate significant, long-term reductions in implicit bias as measured by the IAT.[37] These effects last for months or even years post intervention. The intervention increases participants' awareness of their biases and concern about societal discrimination, leading to greater engagement in discussions about inclusion. Participants are also more likely to speak up against bias, engage in inclusive behaviors, and generalize the strategies they learn to address biases in contexts not explicitly covered during training.

Yet, while these personal transformations are meaningful, true systemic change requires integrating these individual-level interventions into larger institutional reforms. As research on race as groupness suggests, racial hierarchies are not simply a byproduct of implicit bias – they are actively maintained by institutions that privilege certain racial groups over others. For instance, racial wealth disparities, employment discrimination, and unequal access to education are all manifestations of how race is reinforced as a group-based hierarchy rather than just a perceptual category. Without structural interventions – such as revising hiring policies, diversifying leadership, and reforming discriminatory laws – implicit bias training alone is insufficient to challenge racial inequality at a systemic level.

The idea that empowerment enables positive change is also supported by positive psychology and sociology literatures. These literatures often focus on the concept of "agency," which refers to people's subjective feelings of control in shaping their lives.[38] Agentic orientations empower individuals by enabling them to reframe their relationships within existing constraints.[39] For example, having a sense of agency can empower people to try to think outside the box. Psychologist Albert Bandura also emphasizes agency as a cognitive capacity to help counter the adversities of life proactively using different strategies in his social cognitive theory.[40] Bandura explains how agency and self-empowerment can help individuals with the adoption of healthier habits and life choices, improving their overall health.[41] Other research also shows that people with a stronger sense of agency are better able to challenge and find ways to overcome the situational life difficulties that they face, including discrimination[42] or the stigma associated with disabilities.[43] By doing so, they can better navigate adversities and achieve their goals more effectively, and their accumulated experiences of success contribute to positive self-worth and enhance life satisfaction.[44]

However, agency does not exist in a vacuum. It is shaped by social structures that either constrain or enable individuals' ability to exercise power. As sociologist Eduardo Bonilla-Silva argues,[45] systemic racism is not just a set of individual biases but a "racialized social system" that preserves privilege through policies, laws, and institutional norms. Moreover, our sense of agency is closely linked to the way race functions as a social group rather than just a category. When race is conceptualized only as a category – a matter of perception – it ignores the ways in which racial identities are socially constructed through history, law, and economics. Empowerment must therefore extend beyond individual self-awareness to collective action that challenges the very structures that produce racial disparities.

Imagine that you are trying to open a drawer and one of your hands is constantly closing the drawer that you opened – as if it is acting on its own. Alien hand syndrome, also known as Dr. Strangelove syndrome or anarchic hand syndrome, is a rare neurological condition where a person feels that one of their hands acts independently, without their control.[46] Caused by damage to certain brain regions (like the corpus callosum, medial frontal lobes, or parietal regions), the alien hand syndrome draws our attention to the neurological origins and manifestations of a sense of agency. A sense of agency comes from a mix of brain processes involving movement, sensory feedback, and thinking.[47] In recent years, neurosciences have made great advancements in our understanding of a sense of agency. The sense of agency consists of both ownership of our body and our actions and the voluntary control of our actions with respect to how they might affect the external world.[48] Therefore, in our brains, the sense of agency often recruits both our motor cortex (for coordinating movement) and the frontal lobes (for volition and control). The sense of agency is closely related to the concept of metacognition – our understanding and control of our own cognitive processes.[49] Recent neuroscience research has shown that cognitive strategies to improve metacognition contribute to neuroplasticity and neuro-empowerment by enhancing connectivity between prefrontal and subcortical regions and increasing neural efficiency.[50]

This understanding of agency highlights the potential for cognitive and behavioral change, but it also underscores the need to extend these insights to broader social change. Neurosociological research has shown that racialized perceptions and biases are not only learned but also reinforced through societal institutions that shape laws, economic policies, and social interactions. Thus, empowerment must be conceptualized as both an individual and a structural process – where cognitive shifts are accompanied by systemic reforms that challenge exclusionary policies and practices in education, employment, and criminal justice.

In sum, while individual empowerment is a critical step in addressing bias and fostering inclusion, it must be paired with systemic change to dismantle the social structures that perpetuate inequality. True empowerment goes beyond self-awareness and behavioral shifts; it requires collective action that challenges discriminatory policies, restructures institutions, and promotes equity on a societal level. Without this broader lens, efforts to reduce bias risk being superficial and ineffective in tackling the deeply ingrained racial hierarchies that shape access to opportunity and social mobility. By integrating personal empowerment with institutional transformation, we can move toward meaningful and lasting change.

Equality

The third dimension that I would like to talk about is equality – or rather equal status in building diverse coalitions as a mechanism for reducing racial bias and challenging systemic inequities. The evolution of coalitional cognition is deeply rooted in human history, shaped by the adaptive challenges of living in complex social environments. Our human ancestors, navigating the dangers of intergroup conflict and resource competition, developed cognitive mechanisms to manage alliances effectively. These mechanisms underlie complex systems of human morality and racial categorization as both a cognitive category and a social position (as discussed in chapter 3). Ancestral human environments, characterized by limited mobility and localized interactions, did not require or promote race-based distinctions as a core cognitive function. Instead, race as a category emerged from the brain's general ability to classify social groups, and only later did it become racialized through historical and structural forces (as also explained in chapter 2). Rather than race being a biologically fixed category, humans evolved to prioritize markers of cooperation and shared interests that predicted alliances, such as shared language, behavior, and cultural practices.[51] This is why race operates as both an individual-level perception and a social-level group construct – our brains categorize race instinctively, but societal institutions reinforce racial groupness through laws, policies, and economic disparities.

Empirical studies also suggest that when race is removed as a marker of coalitional membership (e.g., when group affiliation is cued by markers like sports team jerseys rather than race), its perceptual salience is reduced, suggesting racism's malleability under shifting social contexts.[52] This finding aligns with the idea that racial bias is not purely an automatic brain function but is instead reinforced by social systems that dictate which group categories matter. Cognitive and evolutionary anthropologist Pascal Boyer and colleagues describe these mechanisms through a "coalitional safety index," which is a regulatory variable that evaluates perceived support and threat within and between groups.[53] This evolved capacity to detect coalitional threats interacts with modern institutional structures, where racialized perceptions are shaped by historical narratives, systemic inequities, and legal frameworks that maintain social stratification. These coalitional processes influence modern societies, especially in diverse social settings. Ethnic and racial diversity often correlates with reduced social trust and well-being due to perceived threats to coalitional safety (seeing out-group members as a threat to our in-group coalitions). This perception arises from historically constructed racial hierarchies that reinforce the association of out-groups with danger or economic threat, rather than from any innate evolutionary bias. However, intergroup contact, particularly under equal-status conditions, can modulate these effects, offering potential pathways to mitigate intergroup tensions and improve well-being in diverse surroundings.[54]

Intergroup contact is a widely researched phenomenon in social psychology. First proposed by psychologist Gordon Allport in his 1954 book *The Nature of Prejudice*, the "contact hypothesis" suggests that under the right conditions, intergroup contact can promote understanding, reduce hostility, and foster more harmonious relations between diverse groups.[55] These right conditions included equal status, common goals, cooperation, and support from authorities, laws, or customs.[56] The individuals involved in contact must perceive themselves as equals during the interaction. If there is a power imbalance, the benefits of contact are less likely to materialize. Collaborative efforts, such as solving a problem or achieving a mutual goal, can also reduce tensions and highlight commonalities. This is why racial bias interventions that focus solely on individual-level bias reduction without addressing structural inequalities often fail to produce meaningful, long-term change. Institutions must actively create environments that support equal-status interactions, whether in schools, workplaces, or social policies.

The common goal is also one of the mostly used science-fiction movie tropes, where different nations of the world unite against a common enemy, the alien. However, in real-world social settings, the "common enemy" is often systemic inequity itself – inequalities in wealth, education, and opportunity that disproportionately impact marginalized groups. Structural interventions must ensure that intergroup contact is not superficial but embedded in efforts to dismantle the racial group hierarchies that prevent true coalition building. The intergroup interaction to reduce prejudice should also involve cooperation rather than competition. Working together fosters positive relationships and reduces intergroup hostility. And finally, the intergroup contact should be supported by institutions or social systems in order to create a safe environment for individuals to engage positively with each other. If interracial contact is accompanied by colorblind policies that ignore structural inequalities, it can reinforce disparities rather than reduce them. "Diversity" without systemic change merely sustains the status quo.

Neuroscience research also supports intergroup contact theory, particularly when this contact is under equal shared status conditions. Frequent contact with other-race individuals (e.g., having them as friends, hanging out with them socially, or working with them on shared tasks) modulates early neural processes associated with face perception, improving recognition of other-race faces.[57] This is an example of how race, as a perceptual category, is not fixed in the brain but is shaped by experience and environment. Similarly, increased intergroup contact reduces racial biases in neural empathic responses, as seen in brain regions like ACC, which mediate empathy for the observed pain of others.[58] Lifetime interracial contact (having friends from other racial groups both at childhood and throughout life) also reduces racial bias in mentalizing tasks (in cognitive empathy).

In one study, psychologists Grace Handley, Jennifer Kubota, and Jasmin Cloutier use the Reading the Mind in the Eyes test, a well-known test for theory of mind or cognitive empathy. This measures a person's ability to interpret the emotions and mental states of others based solely on looking at pictures of people's eyes to investigate if interracial contact improves brains' performance for reading the mental states of racial out-groups.[59] This research aligns with broader findings in sociology, which show that exposure to diverse social environments helps break down rigid racial group boundaries and encourages cross-group solidarity. They found that white participants with lower levels of lifetime interracial contact exhibited higher superior temporal sulcus (STS, a brain region involved in cognitive empathy) activation in response to white people's eyes. White participants with high levels of lifetime interracial contact, on the other hand, showed similar activation in their STS in response to both Black and white eyes, indicating the importance of interracial contact for neuroplasticity of empathy – a finding that supports the idea that racial perception is not innate but socially conditioned and therefore malleable.

Interracial friendships also reduce intergroup anxiety, stress, and depression, diminishing their psychosomatic symptoms (e.g., fatigue, insomnia) or the cortisol hormone.[60] For example, psychologist Elizabeth Page-Gould and colleagues[61] randomly assigned white and Latinx undergraduate students to same or cross-race dyads and had them complete structured friendship-building tasks over three weekly meetings. They found that while participants with higher implicit prejudice or rejection anxiety from racial out-groups before the experiment showed elevated cortisol levels, this hormonal stress response decreased over time as friendships formed, demonstrating that intergroup coalitions are not only socially beneficial but also biologically transformative. Furthermore, these effects carried forward to other settings. In the weeks after this experiment, individuals who were initially implicitly more prejudiced started to seek out more cross-racial friends and adjusted better to the diverse university environment. This highlights the broader role of institutions in structuring intergroup interactions: when schools, workplaces, and communities promote equitable, inclusive environments, they create conditions for reducing bias at both individual and systemic levels.

Ultimately, for diverse coalitions to be effective in reducing bias and fostering equality, they must be structured in ways that challenge the racialized systems that define group membership. Race is not just an issue of personal perception; it is embedded in the legal, economic, and political structures that shape power and opportunity. Equal-status interactions – whether in education, workplaces, or broader social policies – must be actively facilitated to dismantle the institutional barriers that reinforce racial group boundaries. By fostering meaningful, equitable intergroup contact, we can begin to undo the deep-seated structures of racial inequality, moving from categorization to coalition and from division to transformation.

"Neurons that fire together, wire together"

The Hebb's rule, which is a principle of neuroplasticity proposed by Donald Hebb in 1949,[62] is often summarized by the mantra, "neurons that fire together, wire together." This suggests that when two neurons are repeatedly active at the same time, the connection (synapse) between them is strengthened.

In other words, the co-activation of neurons, even with seemingly unrelated functions, leads to stronger associations between them. This principle underpins mechanisms of learning, memory, and plasticity and offers profound insights into the neuroscience of racial perception, bias, empathy, and intergroup relations.

For example, when a person who has never played the piano listens to piano music, the auditory cortex of their brain gets activated. However, when this person takes piano lessons, so that hearing the piano music is coupled with playing, their motor cortex (responsible for finger movements) starts firing simultaneously with the auditory cortex, forming stronger neural connections.[63] Similarly, when individuals repeatedly associate race with particular attributes – whether through media representations, personal experiences, or societal narratives – these neural pathways become deeply engrained. Learning rewires our brains, but so do social experiences that reinforce group boundaries and stereotypes.

I suggest that the Hebb's rule can be applied to the three Es: empathy, empowerment, and equality. Empathy involves understanding and sharing the feelings of others. As Hebb's rule guides the association between observed actions and executed actions, they are also thought to underpin mirror neuron activation in the brain. Mirror neurons, first discovered in the premotor cortex (F5) and parietal lobe (PF) of monkeys, activate both when an individual performs an action and when they observe someone else performing the same action.[64] Because neurons in sensory and motor regions fire together during repeated social interactions, the connections between these regions strengthen, forming mirror-like properties. Observing others' emotions (e.g., pain, happiness) activates corresponding regions in the observer's brain, forming a neural basis for empathy.[65] However, race as a social category complicates this process, as biases shape how much empathy people feel for in-group versus out-group members. Neuroscientific studies show that people exhibit stronger empathic responses toward those they perceive as belonging to their racial in-group, reinforcing racial groupness as a barrier to empathy.

These mirror-like responses likely arise through associative learning during social interactions. When individuals frequently observe or engage in acts that elicit shared emotions across group boundaries (e.g., witnessing out-group members in distress and offering support), the shared emotional states that fire together lead to strengthened connections between the out-group and empathetic responses. Over time, these repeated empathetic interactions can override racial group distinctions, fostering a greater sense of shared humanity. In contrast, if individuals rarely interact with out-group members in emotionally significant ways, the neural circuits that link racial out-groups to indifference or even fear remain dominant. This highlights the importance of institutional structures that encourage meaningful, positive intergroup contact rather than reinforcing racial segregation in neighborhoods, schools, and workplaces.

If past negative interactions with a group created strong neural connections between the out-group and fear, distrust, or hostility, systemic interventions that promote equal-status collaboration can help rewire these associations. New positive and consistent interactions, through the empowerment-based techniques discussed above, can weaken these old associations (due to competitive neural plasticity) and replace them with more positive associations. For instance, social environments that provide exposure to counter-stereotypical individuals – such as Black women in leadership roles or Latino scientists – can disrupt rigid racial schemas. When neurons representing the stereotyped group fire simultaneously with neurons representing positive or diverse traits (e.g., intelligence, kindness), new associations can be formed. Minimizing exposure to environments or narratives that reinforce stereotypes can also reduce the strength of biased associations. Without co-activation, the synaptic strength of the stereotypical association diminishes over time, following principles of neural plasticity.

Additionally, empowering marginalized individuals at an institutional level to advocate for themselves and take leadership roles reinforces neural pathways associated with agency, competence, and control. Simply put, the more often individuals from historically marginalized groups are seen in positions of power, the stronger the neural links between these groups and leadership, competence, and innovation become – not only for those groups themselves but also for wider society. Offering programs that equip marginalized people with skills to take on leadership positions, ensuring they experience success and recognition in these roles, facilitating platforms where they can share powerful stories and perspectives, can break the historical neural associations that have linked racialized identities to subordination rather than leadership. This creates positive feedback loops of empowerment and acknowledgment, challenging systemic barriers that have traditionally excluded marginalized voices from positions of influence.

Repeated cooperative tasks with out-group members can also rewire associations from "threat" to "ally." When individuals from different groups have repeated positive interactions (e.g., working together on a project or sharing enjoyable experiences like going to a concert together), their neural circuits may "fire together," strengthening associations of the other group with positive emotions and reduced bias. These repeated positive contacts reinforce the neural pathways that link out-group members to feelings of safety, acceptance, and trust, demonstrating that racial bias is not an immutable trait but a malleable neural process shaped by experience and environment.

Hebbian learning depends on the repetition of co-activation to solidify neural associations. With this principle, consistent and frequent intergroup interactions must be embedded in institutional practices – whether through diverse hiring policies, equitable educational settings, or cross-racial mentorship programs – to prevent the decline of positive associations and ensure their dominance over competing negative stereotypes. Creating environments that consistently reinforce equal status, fairness, and cooperation strengthens positive neural pathways. As long as systemic inequalities persist, intergroup contact alone is insufficient – social policies must actively create conditions where intergroup cooperation is both meaningful and structurally supported.

Emotional salience can also enhance Hebbian learning by making neural connections stronger. Emotionally significant intergroup encounters – such as cross-racial friendships formed in deeply personal contexts or witnessing acts of racial justice advocacy – have the potential to create long-term shifts in perception. Fostering emotionally significant intergroup encounters encourages strong, positive emotions like joy or sympathy during intergroup contact, enhancing neural plasticity and making positive associations more enduring. For instance, social movements that amplify the lived experiences of marginalized groups, paired with meaningful policy changes, can reinforce these neural shifts in public consciousness.

Once positive associations are formed, they can create feedback loops that further enhance intergroup empathy and reduce prejudice, aligning with Hebbian reinforcement processes.[66] These loops extend beyond the individual level and into broader social change: when enough individuals undergo neural rewiring through sustained intergroup contact, societal attitudes can shift, influencing media representations, policy decisions, and legal frameworks. In this sense, bias reduction is not just a matter of individual cognition but a collective societal process that requires structural reinforcement.

In short, the principle that "neurons that fire together, wire together" offers a powerful framework for understanding how racial biases are both formed and dismantled. While neural plasticity provides a foundation for change, sustained social and institutional interventions are necessary to ensure that intergroup contact occurs under conditions that support equality, fairness, and long-term structural reform. By aligning neuroscience with systemic policy changes, we can rewire both our brains and our societies to foster a more equitable and inclusive future.

Summary

The principle that "neurons that fire together, wire together" encapsulates the transformative power of neuroplasticity, illustrating that repeated experiences and associations shape the brain's structure and function. This understanding has far-reaching implications, not only for individual learning and recovery from injury but also for societal efforts to address bias and discrimination. Unconscious bias training programs are often ineffective as they tend to target explicit, cognitive processes rather than the implicit, emotional roots of prejudice and often rely on external motivations like compliance rather than fostering internal values and motivations. This is largely because the best practices of DEI are often in fact best guesses that are not backed by scientific literature.[67]

This chapter addresses these challenges by focusing on the 3E framework – empathy, empowerment, and equality – which proposes a more holistic approach, leveraging neuroplasticity to foster meaningful intergroup understanding, equip individuals with the tools to challenge bias, and create structural conditions that support lasting change. The human brain has the remarkable capacity to adapt, change, and rewire itself. This power is called neuroplasticity and can be harnessed to combat racism and discrimination. The 3E framework provides a scientifically grounded and actionable pathway for reconfiguring racial prejudice. Empathy enables us to broaden our moral circles, empowering individuals to connect across racial and cultural divides. Neuroscience research, such as the ReSource Project by Tania Singer, demonstrates that mindfulness and compassion training can enhance empathy and reduce racial bias by promoting positive neural changes. Empowerment involves equipping individuals with the tools and strategies to actively combat bias, such as stereotype replacement, individuation, and increasing intergroup contact. Evidence from interventions like the prejudice habit-breaking training shows that empowering individuals leads to significant, long-term reductions in bias. Equality is the final component, emphasizing the importance of creating conditions for equal-status interactions. Research supports the effectiveness of intergroup contact in reducing prejudice, particularly when participants perceive themselves as equals and collaborate toward common goals.

However, true transformation requires both individual and systemic shifts. As Hebb's rule teaches us, consistent and repeated positive interactions are essential for rewiring both our neural circuits and societal norms. Just as the brain requires reinforcement to solidify new connections, society needs long-term, structural commitments to inclusion and equity. While individual bias training is a step forward, it must be paired with policies that address systemic discrimination, such as equitable hiring practices, diverse leadership representation, and inclusive educational curricula. By integrating these insights into everyday practices, from workplaces to schools, and prioritizing long-term engagement over superficial training, we can foster a more inclusive and equitable world. The science of neuroplasticity reminds us that change is possible, but it must be intentional and sustained. Our brains – and our societies – are shaped by the environments we create. By leveraging the principles of the 3E framework and aligning neuroscience with institutional reforms, we can actively rewire ourselves and the world around us for the better. This process is not merely theoretical; it is a call to action – an opportunity to build a future where bias is actively challenged, where inclusion is embedded into our institutions, and where equality is not just an aspiration but a reality.

Conclusion

As we've seen across this book, race is a core mental organizing characteristic, but it is vitally constructed and reinforced by societal forces. The journey through this book has traversed the complexities of race, the human brain, and societal structures, illuminating how deeply interconnected these domains are. While there is no biological race, racialized experiences still shape our biologies – our bodies and brains. And thus, it is only with the relatively newer neuroscience research that we can begin to observe and better understand what happens within the individual as a result of these societal forces; and that mind, self, and society[1] are fundamentally intertwined.

As such, chapter 1 explored neurological and cognitive processes underpinning racial categorization and bias, emphasizing that there is no hardwired racial cognition center. Instead, racial categorization emerges from social learning and exposure. Early in life, humans begin categorizing others based on observable traits such as skin color, a process that becomes automatic over time. Studies of infant cognition reveal that while babies initially recognize faces without racial preference, exposure to specific racial groups leads to the development of an "other-race effect," where individuals differentiate own-race faces more easily than those of other races. Race exists both as a category (enabling stereotyping) and as a group position (driving prejudice). Both processes are deeply rooted in automatic social categorization, a mechanism that simplifies complex social environments. While this cognitive shortcut has evolutionary benefits, it also reinforces hierarchical biases. Even though our brains are not hardwired for racial bias, societal structures and lived experiences engrain these patterns, making them difficult but not impossible to change.

While race functions as both a category and a social group, this book challenges the notion that one necessarily precedes the other. Instead of framing it as a "chicken and egg" dilemma, race as a group position and race as a category are mutually constitutive – each shaping and reinforcing the other. In other words, hierarchical power relations and group-based distinctions emerge together, with prejudiced perceptions and stereotypes forming alongside them. Many psychological theories suggest that an in-group requires an out-group to exist, with humans automatically categorizing outsiders. This book offers a different perspective, emphasizing that humans first identify potential allies through an evolved cognitive system attuned to coalition building. It is not merely about distinguishing threats but about recognizing social bonds and group affiliations.

Our brains' built-in system for automatic in-group categorization – rooted in coalitional psychology – relies on the "moral emotional infrastructure" of the brain, as discussed in chapter 2. Humans and other great apes have evolved in groups that cooperate and live together. Humans are different from other great apes in that we live in larger groups and have a bigger brain size. We navigate a complex social environment through moral rules and standards, which influence our feelings and behaviors toward social coordination and cooperation. In modern societies, racism becomes so difficult to change because racial evaluations are intertwined with moral appraisals. The overlap between key brain regions involved in processing morally and socially significant information and those engaged in racial boundary making suggests that racial categorization is not a separate phenomenon but a byproduct of a broader cognitive system designed to navigate complex social landscapes. Rather than prioritizing one over the other, this book argues that race as a category and race as a group position are interdependent, emerging through the same cognitive and social mechanisms.

Chapter 3 establishes that race is a socially constructed reality, with historical, political, and cultural forces shaping its definitions and hierarchies over time. While biologically human races do not exist, the social reality of race profoundly influences individuals' lives. For example, despite the formal abolition of overt racism in the United States through legislation like the Civil Rights Act of 1964, systemic racism operates across institutional and societal levels, creating disparities in education, wealth, housing and health. There is no significant genetic differentiation between racial groups. Humans have not been around (or in isolated groups) long enough to have evolved into racial groups. Instead, race functions as a "symbolic category" shaped by sociopolitical forces and institutionalized practices. The fluidity of racial categories is evident in ever-changing racial categories in historical statistics like the US Census.

As decades of sociological study of emotions have taught us, race has become one such perceptual cue for detecting alliances under historical conditions that created racially inegalitarian societies. Morality serves as a lens through which individuals and groups justify social hierarchies. Implicit biases, aversive racism, and subtle prejudice thrive under the guise of moral righteousness, perpetuating exclusion and inequity. Emotional responses, such as empathy and guilt, further reinforce in-group and out-group dynamics, creating a moral framework that often privileges dominant racial groups.

Once established, racial hierarchies not only "racialize" our brains via negative evaluations of racial out-groups (race as a category) but also through affecting our bodies and health. Chapter 4 examines how systemic racism affects physical and mental health, highlighting the link between social inequality, stress, and adverse health outcomes. Racial discrimination acts as a stressor, triggering physiological responses like elevated blood pressure and heart rate. Over time, these stressors accumulate, increasing the allostatic load and leading to chronic health problems such as hypertension, obesity, and mental health disorders among racial minorities. The COVID-19 pandemic also illustrated the rapid catastrophic effects of racial disparities. Communities of color, particularly Black,

Hispanic, and Indigenous populations, faced higher rates of infection, hospitalization, and death during the pandemic due to socioeconomic vulnerabilities and systemic barriers to healthcare. Racial disparities of health are rooted not in genetic differences but in structural inequalities, such as lower access to resources and increased exposure to stressors. What is more, the effects of racism can be passed down through intergenerational trauma causing epigenetic changes.

While racism has devastating impact on health and mental health, particularly through overloading neural mechanisms for stress, neuroscience research has the potential to identify pathways for healing and diminishing racial bias. Neuroplasticity is the brain's ability to adapt and rewire itself. Chapter 5 highlights the limitations of traditional DEI initiatives, particularly unconscious bias training, which often fail to produce lasting changes in attitudes or behaviors. I propose a novel approach to anti-racist interventions called the 3E framework, which emphasizes empathy, empowerment, and equality. This approach argues for a multidisciplinary strategy that integrates social science and neuroscience to address the root causes of racial bias. By leveraging the brain's plasticity, it posits that individuals can unlearn ingrained biases and develop more equitable ways of thinking and behaving. Empathy encourages emotional connections and understanding, empowerment provides the tools and confidence to act against biases, and equality emphasizes structural changes to dismantle systemic barriers. Compelling research on the plasticity of the brain has shown that individuals who learned entirely new skills, such as navigating complex city maps or mastering musical instruments, demonstrated significant changes in the brain's structure and functionality. Even brief, focused interventions can create measurable changes in neural pathways. Immersive experiences like compassion meditation, dyadic emotional empathy, and perspective-taking exercises can rewire our brains to increase empathy and reduce bias in just a few months. We should be creating targeted, science-based interventions focusing on empathy, empowerment, and equality to counteract ingrained racial biases.

Systemic bias in neuroscience methodologies

While this book has focused on neuroscience research and the ways the brain operates, it is not meant to read as if neuroscience is an objective and value-free science that has no embedded bias. As with many scientific methodologies, neurosciences have also suffered from biases and lack of diversity in its methodologies, samples, and its creative workforce, applying what sociologists Tukufu Zuberi and Eduardo Bonilla-Silva would call "white logic, white methods."[2] Unfortunately, when they see a picture of a brain attached to a scientific claim, many people take it as the final truth. Often viewed as the remarkable science that can look inside the black box of a brain, neuroscience findings can create this illusionary authority that goes beyond the methodologies and statistical techniques applied to it. Admittedly, I have also benefited from this illusionary authority many times. During some of the research talks or lectures I give, audience members show awe and astonishment as I uncover some sort of truth about the nature of racial cognition, even though I explain to them that fMRI studies are correlational, with small sample sizes and often low ecological validity.

From recruitment practices to technological designs, neuroscience research often excludes racially and ethnically minoritized groups. For example, advanced imaging techniques such as MRI and fNIRS are less effective for individuals with darker skin or coarse hair textures, leading to the exclusion of such participants from critical research initiatives.[3] Similarly, electroencephalography (EEG) relies on secure electrode-to-scalp contact, which is often compromised in individuals with textured hair, leading to data deemed "unusable."[4] Optical neuroimaging technologies like fNIRS are influenced by melanin's light-absorptive properties, resulting in higher "noise levels" for individuals with darker skin.[5] This systemic oversight perpetuates a cycle where diverse data are excluded, limiting the generalizability of neuroscientific findings. Recruitment for neuroscience studies also remains skewed toward western, educated, industrialized, rich, and democratic (WEIRD) populations, neglecting the demographic diversity of the global population.[6] For instance, large-scale initiatives like the Human Connectome Project and the UK Biobank heavily overrepresent white participants, compromising the global applicability of findings.[7] Within the United States, the NIH-funded studies reflect similar biases, where white participants dominate, while Hispanic and Black communities remain significantly underrepresented. These practices not only hinder scientific advancements but also exacerbate healthcare disparities, as findings fail to reflect the diverse neurobiological needs of marginalized communities.[8]

These biases also have important implications for the legal and healthcare systems. The introduction of neuroscience evidence into criminal legal systems and healthcare has been proposed as a means to increase objectivity and reduce bias. However, the complexity and perceived objectivity of neuroscientific data can obscure inherent biases, potentially reinforcing systemic inequities. For example, technologies like EEG and MRI often fail to account for the phenotypic and environmental variations that influence neural responses. As such, data derived from marginalized groups are not only underrepresented but also risk misinterpretation within contexts like risk assessment in legal trials.[9] Furthermore, the reliance on standardized brain scans to draw conclusions about "normative" brain function often fails to account for environmental stressors like systemic racism, covered in chapter 4. These factors influence neurodevelopment and mental health outcomes, creating a feedback loop where biased data perpetuate stigmatization of marginalized groups.[10] For instance, the use of neuroscience to assess risk factors in criminal trials may amplify racial disparities by relying on data derived from over-policed communities, which reflect systemic inequities rather than inherent traits.[11] In fact, many studies compare the effects of neuroscientific evidence on mock-jury decisions and find that offering evidence from the brain about the root causes of a condition (e.g., brain damage causing psychosis) mitigated sentencing decision (i.e., reduced the death penalty decision) as opposed to the same case being presented with psychological but not neuroscientific evidence.[12] These studies show the important ethical implications of neuroscience research in real-world decisions that might impact even life or death outcomes.

However, many neuroscientists are also aware of the burden of such ethical dilemmas caused by their research. Earlier in my graduate school career, I was regularly attending early morning research meetings at the Neuroscience Department at the University of Iowa, which would sometimes cover a clinical case, sometimes a student research presentation, and sometimes more well-established researchers in the field presenting their research. In one of those meetings, I remember a young but prominent neuroscientist who studied morality visiting our lab meeting. His presentation was about how he was called recently to the courtroom as an expert witness to help the jury decide on whether or not the defendant had a center of morality in their brains (with the implication being that if they did not, then they also could not be found guilty). I remember the apparent dilemma and his struggle over how to talk about this in the courtroom. While neuroscientists refer to certain brain regions playing an important role in a behavior, attitude, or feeling (or even in abstract constructs like morality, as discussed in chapter 3), the current state of neuroscience knowledge of most social behaviors is that many parts of our brains work together to help generate (or sometimes modulate or even inhibit) that behavior. There is no single morality center in the brain as there is no single racism center. An audience member in one of my talks once asked me (to my shock and surprise) if I was researching this topic to identify the brain region responsible for racism so we can take it out. I believe I tried really hard not to scream a "no" and instead calmly tried to explain to him that this is not how the human brain works and, no, that would not be ethical. We are not going back to phrenology.

In sum, although there is considerable bias in neuroscience research, there are neuroscientists who are actively and consciously thinking about the ethical implications of their research, particularly to communities they work with. There have been many calls to bring attention to systemic racism in neuroscience research by scientific journals and federal funding agencies in recent years. Researchers have been shifting their attention and energies into reducing bias in neuroscience research, or in other words trying to move beyond "white logic and white methods." Here, let me suggest three effective strategies in this pursuit for more equitable research to end systemic oppression and racism in neurosciences.

Strategy 1: Community-empowering research

Equity requires proactive outreach to historically underrepresented communities, not only in participation but in the sharing of knowledge and benefits derived from research. Community-empowering research is a participatory framework that prioritizes collaboration between researchers and the communities they study, fostering equity, diversity, and inclusion. Community-empowering research involves the active participation of communities in every stage of the research process, from design to dissemination. By engaging communities in the research process, community-empowering research ensures that the research outcomes are both scientifically robust and socially relevant. It operates on principles of equity, collaboration, and reciprocity, addressing power imbalances inherent in traditional research paradigms.[13] Empowerment is a process wherein individuals and groups gain control over decisions affecting their lives, fostering both individual agency and collective action. As we learned in chapter 5, empowerment is an important tool in combatting bias and contributing to neuroplasticity of our brains. Why not then use this tool to also bolster our research? Community-empowering research integrates the principles of empowerment into research, enabling communities to co-create knowledge that directly impacts their well-being. One key aspect of this type of research is the use of tools like community-based participatory research. Community-based participatory research actively involves community members as equal partners, ensuring their voices are central to the research process. This framework challenges traditional top-down approaches, emphasizing trust and shared ownership of outcomes.[14]

Toward the end of 2019, right before the COVID-19 pandemic began, I started a collaboration with the Kids Interaction and Neurodevelopment (KIND) Laboratory at the University of California Riverside (UCR) alongside my colleague, developmental neuropsychologist Dr. Kalina J. Michalska. KIND

Lab had been collecting longitudinal brain, physiology, and behavior data from Latina youth and their parents in the Inland Empire region of Southern California to understand the neurodevelopment of emotion regulation and mental health outcomes. This region of Southern California is primarily rural with a majority Mexican-descent population, marked by stark health disparities and underutilization of mental health services. We had received a grant from the Center for Health Disparities at the UCR School of Medicine to add a community-empowering research component to Dr. Michalska's longitudinal study, taking advantage of my background and expertise on race and culturally informed approaches to the neurosciences. We wanted to take this community-empowering approach to create a platform for open dialogue and meaningful collaboration with community members and fostering trust while also ensuring cultural sensitivity. We thought, and still think, that to understand the community – whether it be the neurodevelopmental changes in brains or social attitudes – we need to work with the community. Even more, we (the researchers) needed to be guided by the community. In order to receive this guidance and elevate the voices of our community members, we helped form a community advisory board (CAB), consisting of Latina mothers, to help inform our study. CABs serve as collaborative entities where community members and researchers co-develop research agendas, ensuring that the voices of underrepresented populations are included in every phase of the research process. They provide guidance throughout the research process, ensuring cultural relevance and ethical rigor. For instance, CABs can help design studies that accommodate cultural sensitivities, improving recruitment and retention of diverse participants.

We held regular meetings with our CAB members, talking to them about our research protocols, including language in our recruitment flyers and consent documents, our recruitment methods, any stigmas or concerns around brain imaging, and even the concepts and tools that we use in our research. In some of these meetings, our CAB members discussed the challenges of navigating racial and ethnic discrimination, immigration-related stress, and stigma surrounding mental health. Some participants highlighted the negative effects of anti-immigrant sentiment on their families' psychological well-being. These discussions informed our research team's approach to studying how sociopolitical factors influence brain development and mental health outcomes in youth. Based on the feedback, we incorporated measures to assess experiences of discrimination and ethnic-racial socialization into their data collection protocols. This is one example in demonstrating how we were able to collaborate with our community to co-create science. Co-authored with our CAB, we published a research article offering a template of a potential research strategy with practical tools to build a community-empowering neuroscience study.[15]

While community-empowering research offers significant advantages, it is not without challenges. Decades of mistrust between marginalized communities and researchers have created barriers to participation. This collaborative approach rebuilds trust, as community members see their needs and perspectives reflected in the research agenda. However, establishing trust, navigating power dynamics, and ensuring equitable participation require time, resources, and cultural competence. Community-empowering research requires researchers to actively dismantle barriers to participation. Practical measures, such as offering transportation assistance, providing childcare during study visits, and using culturally inclusive recruitment materials, can help improve community participation.[16] These efforts can mitigate logistical challenges that disproportionately affect marginalized groups. We as researchers must also critically examine our own biases and positionalities to ensure they do not inadvertently reinforce systemic inequities. By making our social positions and assumptions visible, we can foster greater accountability and inclusivity.[17] Furthermore, we must balance scientific objectives with community priorities, which may not always align. This is particularly important in neuroscience, where sensitive topics like mental health require nuanced and culturally informed approaches.

Community-empowering research represents a paradigm shift in neuroscience, addressing historical biases and fostering inclusive, impactful science. Empowerment-focused approaches can also yield tangible health benefits to address systemic health disparities. Additionally, engaging young

participants in research can inspire interest in higher education and empower them to see themselves as active contribu-
tors to scientific knowledge.

Strategy 2: Color-conscious leadership

Color-conscious leadership represents a critical framework
for addressing systemic oppression and racism within organizations, and so can be applied to scientific research and the
agencies and institutions that support it, including education
departments, funding agencies, as well as research teams. By
acknowledging and addressing the pervasive role of color
and race in shaping societal structures and individual experiences, color-conscious leaders can actively disrupt inequitable
systems. Color-conscious leadership framework drives very
valuable insights in education research. This perspective is
especially important in the current climate where critical race
theories are under attack in many states and banned from
school curricula.[18]

Color-conscious leadership emphasizes the active acknowledgment of racial identities and histories within organiza-
tional and societal contexts, which includes addressing biases
in research practices. In neurosciences, color-conscious leadership is particularly critical due to the historical and ongoing
underrepresentation of minority groups in research and clinical practice, as we mentioned above.[19] Colorblind approaches
ignore or downplay the salience of race.[20] In neuroscience
research, this can manifest as the exclusion of race as a variable in studies or the failure to examine how systemic racism
impacts brain health. By incorporating color-conscious perspectives, researchers can uncover the ways in which social
determinants of health influence neurological outcomes and
develop interventions that address these disparities.

Color-conscious leadership seeks to interrogate racial narratives and address the structural inequities that perpetuate
oppression. This framework operates at the intersection of
awareness *and* action – leaders must not only recognize systemic injustices but also implement policies and practices
to mitigate these disparities.[21] Colorblind approaches (especially in sciences), which are often adopted under the guise of

neutrality, fail to address systemic inequities by denying the relevance of race.[22] However, intergroup conflicts in diverse organizations often arise from cultural incongruities and systemic inequities. Leaders who fail to recognize and address these dynamics perpetuate exclusion and marginalization.[23] In contrast, color-conscious leadership adopts an asset-based perspective, fostering inclusive environments that value diversity and address the unique challenges faced by marginalized communities. In neuroscience, this might also mean prioritizing funding for studies that address the health disparities of certain groups and support the career advancement of underrepresented researchers.

Leaders, educators, and scientists who practice color consciousness engage in ongoing self-reflection, challenge their own biases, and create spaces for open dialogue about race and equity. Color-conscious leadership should also be culturally responsive. Leaders who integrate cultural knowledge and community engagement into their practices can address systemic barriers more effectively.[24] Culturally responsive leadership refers to the practice of incorporating the cultural identities, histories, and experiences of individuals and communities into leadership philosophies, policies, and practices. In neurosciences, community-empowering approaches that I described in the previous pages are one such way of ensuring that research is relevant and beneficial to the populations it seeks to serve.

Of course, color-conscious leadership also faces many obstacles, including resistance to change, lack of awareness, and institutional barriers.[25] There is a certain amount of discomfort with addressing race explicitly and a reluctance to acknowledge systemic inequities in many institutions, leading to resistance to change and a preference for maintaining the status quo.[26] There is also a pervasive lack of awareness (especially in seemingly neutral sciences like the neurosciences) about systemic racism and its impacts. Leaders, scientists, and educators may lack the knowledge or skills necessary to engage in critical conversations about race and equity. This gap in understanding can result in superficial diversity efforts (some of which are discussed in chapter 5) that fail to address underlying inequities. And finally, policies, practices, and power dynamics within organizations may limit the ability of leaders to implement equitable changes. Color-conscious leadership often requires significant resources, including time, funding, and institutional support. Leaders may face challenges in securing these resources, particularly in organizations where equity is not prioritized. Despite these challenges, the opportunities for transformative change are immense. Color-conscious leadership has the potential to create cultures of the future that prioritize equity and inclusion.[27] Color-conscious leadership is a vital framework for addressing systemic oppression and promoting equity in neurosciences and beyond. By acknowledging the salience of race and implementing practices that prioritize diversity and inclusion, leaders can disrupt inequitable systems and create environments that empower all members of society.

Strategy 3: Intersectional solidarity

[O]ppression and the intolerance of difference come in all shapes and sexes and colors and sexualities; and . . . among those of us who share the goals of liberation and a workable future for our children, there can be no hierarchies of oppression.

Audre Lorde[28]

The last strategy that I would like to emphasize is an approach that bridges intersectional feminist perspectives with coalition building in social movements, namely intersectional solidarity. Intersectional solidarity is a cornerstone of modern social justice movements, emphasizing the need to address multiple, intersecting axes of oppression, such as race, gender, class, disability, and sexuality. This concept has its roots in the works of Black feminists and activists like Kimberlé Crenshaw, who highlighted how overlapping identities create unique forms of disadvantage and require a holistic approach to justice.[29] Intersectionality focuses on the interaction of multiple axes of oppression, such as race, gender, and class, to explain the marginalization experienced by diverse groups, while intersectional solidarity underscores the necessity for solidarity across oppressed identities to address systemic inequalities and ensure equitable representation.[30] As Audre Lorde put forward, "there can be no hierarchies of oppression." Many of us are marginalized and oppressed along many social positions. Furthermore, while some of these positions are visible, like skin color or gender, many are also not (e.g., some disabilities, neurodivergence, having a chronic illness). Effective intersectional solidarity demands confronting power asymmetries along all these dimensions and uniting in solidarity against oppression.

Therefore, I call all scientists, researchers, educators, leaders across institutions and communities to unite and show intersectional solidarity, not only locally but also globally. Intersectional solidarity and coalition building are pivotal in contemporary social movements, addressing the dual challenges of diverse representation and power asymmetries. Intersectional solidarity requires acknowledging and addressing these power asymmetries to form equitable coalitions. Intersectional solidarity offers significant advantages, including broader mobilization, increased legitimacy, and enhanced political leverage. However, achieving this requires deliberate efforts to address systemic inequalities and foster trust.[31] Coalitions must prioritize transformative practices, ensuring that marginalized voices are not only included but central to decision-making processes.[32] Recognizing systemic inequalities and addressing them within coalition structures are vital. This entails equitable resource sharing and inclusive leadership.[33] Creating shared neutral spaces for dialogue and decision making enables groups to address conflicts constructively and develop shared objectives.[34] Regular interaction fosters trust, collective identity, and a shared language of resistance.[35] Additionally, concrete actions demonstrating solidarity, such as public advocacy and mutual support, reinforce coalitional unity.[36]

The Women's March is a – somewhat imperfect – example of intersectional solidarity in action. The Women's March took place in Washington, DC on January 21, 2017, one day after the first inauguration of Donald Trump as president of the United States, to advocate for the intersecting social issues of women's rights, immigration reform, healthcare reform, LGBTQ+ rights, racial equality, workers' rights, environmental justice, and others. Simultaneous "sister marches" were held in cities across the United States and around the world, with an estimated three to five million participants worldwide.[37] In fact, I also joined the march in Atlanta with many of my close friends. I said, however, that this is a somewhat imperfect example because it has also received considerable critique around inclusivity and intersectionality.[38] The Women's March faced initial leadership diversity issues, criticisms of being dominated by whiteness, and controversies over alliances with divisive figures,[39] highlighting challenges in fully enacting its intersectional goals.

Building intersectional solidarity is a complex yet essential task for contemporary social movements. Building coalitions across diverse social, cultural, and political divides poses significant challenges, including managing power imbalances and fostering mutual trust and commitment. It requires acknowledging and addressing power disparities, fostering trust, and creating inclusive spaces for dialogue and decision making. While difficult, these efforts are not just aspirational but necessary for addressing the multifaceted challenges of oppression in the twenty-first century.

Final reflections

This book offers a gateway into the somewhat gargantuan effort to bridge theories and research on race and racism from sociology (and other social sciences) and neurosciences, or in other words to create a neurosociology of race and racism. This work comes at a time when right-wing movements and political leaders are rising in power around the world,[40] while at the same time rhetoric around the declining significance of race and the colorblindness movement is surging.[41] By examining how race, although a socially constructed concept, profoundly impacts the way our brains operate, I hope that this book will contribute to the body of knowledge that counters the narratives on colorblindness.

Neuroscience reveals that racial bias is not hardwired but learned through social exposure and reinforced over time. However, this does not mean that race does not matter. We live in complexly hierarchical and globally unequal societies that reinforce racial boundaries, domination, and exploitation. By deepening our understanding of how larger social forces influence individual minds, we can aspire to refine strategies for mitigating racial prejudice, ultimately contributing to the broader goal of reducing racial inequality. Human brains evolved to prioritize in-group alliances, which, combined with moral frameworks, sustain racial hierarchies and justify inequalities. So, in order to understand how our brains perceive, reinforce, or challenge race and racism, we need to first understand the societal dimensions and the history of race. Thus, the growing need for a new body of knowledge: neurosociology. Decades of sociological research have shown how cultural forces shape personal experiences, but the emerging field of neurosociology allows us to delve deeper into the interplay of social factors and individual processes. By integrating neuroscience and social science, this book offers a hopeful path toward dismantling systemic racism and fostering equity by addressing racial bias at both individual and structural levels. While sociology has increasingly recognized the value of integrating neurological insights into its theories,[42] detailed guidance on how to effectively combine these fields remains limited. So, this book also serves as a model for collaboration between sociologists and neuroscientists in exploring racial attitudes. By examining the social and structural underpinnings of neural and physiological functioning, we can establish connections between macro-level social structures and individual behaviors. This approach helps explain how individuals perpetuate, justify, or challenge these structures. An understanding of how mind, self, and society are interconnected – and of our racialized brain – provides a necessary framework for examining how social forces become embedded within individuals and how these processes sustain systemic racism.

Notes

Introduction

1 In qualitative research, "positionality" is the term used to refer to the way a researcher's identity, background, and social location influence their approach to knowledge production. For scholars of race and inequality, positionality is particularly critical, as it forces us to acknowledge that we are not neutral observers but are embedded in the very systems we study (Choo and Ferree 2010).
2 La Scala et al. 2023.
3 Ahmed 2007.
4 Delatolla 2024.
5 Similar to W. E. B. Du Bois' "double consciousness", which I'll discuss more in chapter 3: Du Bois 1903.
6 Ahmed 2007.
7 Maghbouleh 2017, p. 2.
8 Bonilla-Silva 2010.
9 TenHouten 1997; Bogen et al. 1972.
10 Franks 2010, 2019; Franks and Turner 2013.
11 Franks and Turner 2013.
12 Franks 2010; TenHouten 1997.
13 Ito and Bartholow 2009.
14 Korkın 2020.
15 Sabah TV 2015.
16 Blumer 1986; Mead 2015 [1934].
17 Sauder 2005.

18 Lamont 1992, 2000.

19 Blumer 1986.

20 French sociologist Pierre Bourdieu's concept of "habitus" (Bourdieu 1977) and Sara Ahmed's theory of whiteness as a habit (Ahmed 2007) are both very useful ways of understanding how race and racism are constructed symbolically, yet enacted habitually, through the processing in our brains. Habitus can be thought of as "socially produced cognitive structure" (Lizardo 2004: 380). In this sense, habitus is both inventive and habituated (Swartz 2012). Rooted in past historical conditions, institutional legacies, and norms, habitus reproduces social structure in the form of perception, thought, and action. Habitus is our brains' and, consequently, bodies' unintentional tendency to correct our behaviors to guarantee the correctness and constancy (Ignatow 2007, 2009), translating macro-level structural systems into micro-level actions (Lizardo 2004).

21 Ahmed 2007.

Chapter 1 Is the Brain Colorblind?

1 https://news.meaww.com/white-woman-cosplay-azealia-banks -scathing-attack-on-beyonce-album-cowboy-carter-earns-brick bats-on-internet

2 Schaap, van der Waal, and de Koster 2022.

3 https://www.instagram.com/p/C4s6Zr7rlwA/?utm_source=ig _embed&ig_rid=2acb7d21-347c-47ca-a352-a5cd8dc818cf

4 Legal Defense Fund 2024.

5 Bushnell 2001.

6 Kelly et al. 2005.

7 Bar-Haim et al. 2006; Kelly et al. 2007; Pauker, Williams, and Steele 2016.

8 Anzures et al. 2012.

9 Anzures et al. 2012.

10 Race, Ethnicity, and Genetics Working Group 2005.

11 Rhodes and Baron 2019.

12 Buiatti et al. 2019.

13 Gilmore, Knickmeyer Santelli, and Gao 2018.

14 Liberman, Woodward, and Kinzler 2017.

15 Gibson, Robbins, and Rochat 2015.

16 Gibson, Robbins, and Rochat 2015.

17 Shutts, Pemberton, and Spelke 2013.

18 Kinzler and Spelke 2011.

19 Cristol and Gimbert 2008.

20 Aboud 2003.

21 Hilton and von Hippel 1996.

22 Quadflieg and Macrae 2011.
23 Rogers, Rosario, and Cielto 2020.
24 United States Holocaust Memorial Museum 2024.
25 Feagin and Feagin 2003; Taylor et al. 2019.
26 Jim Crow Museum 2024.
27 Pearl Milling Company 2024.
28 Henrich, Heine, and Norenzayan 2010.
29 Wodtke 2012; Schuman 1997.
30 Wodtke 2012; Schuman 1997.
31 Katz and Braly 1933.
32 Devine and Elliot 1995.
33 Kay et al. 2013.
34 Kay et al. 2013.
35 Kay et al. 2013.
36 Devine 1989.
37 Jones 2025.
38 Anzivino 2025.
39 Jones 2025.
40 Steele and Aronson 1995.
41 Schmader, Johns, and Forbes 2008; Spencer, Logel, and Davies 2016.
42 Osborne 2001.
43 Greenwald, McGhee, and Schwartz 1998.
44 Greenwald and Banaji 1995.
45 Cunningham, Preacher, and Banaji 2001; Dasgupta et al. 2000; Oswald et al. 2013.
46 Correll et al. 2002.
47 Correll et al. 2007.
48 Arkes and Tetlock 2004; Gawronski, Brownstein, and Madva 2022; Ottaway, Hayden, and Oakes 2001.
49 Bandettini 2012.
50 Bennett, Miller, and Wolford 2009.
51 Lyon 2017.
52 Haxby, Hoffman, and Gobbini 2000; Kanwisher et al. 1997.
53 Stolier and Freeman 2017.
54 Papinutto et al. 2016.
55 Herrington et al. 2011.
56 Kanwisher and Yovel 2006; Ratan Murty et al. 2020.
57 Parvizi et al. 2012.
58 Brosch, Bar-David, and Phelps 2013.
59 Lieberman 2007.
60 Anzellotti 2017.
61 Gilbert, Swencionis, and Amodio 2012.
62 Gallate et al. 2011.
63 LeDoux 2007; Meisner, Nair, and Chang 2022.

64 Adolphs, Tranel, and Damasio 1998; Dalgleish 2004; LeDoux 2000.
65 Adolphs, Tranel, and Damasio 1998.
66 Adolphs et al. 1994.
67 Firat et al. 2017; Hart et al. 2000; Lieberman et al. 2005; Ronquillo et al. 2007.
68 Phelps et al. 2000; Stanley, Phelps, and Banaji 2008.
69 Chiao et al. 2008; Lee et al. 2008.
70 Amodio 2014; Kubota 2024; Mitchell, Heatherton, and Macrae 2002; Mitchell, Banaji, and Macrae 2005.
71 Baetens, Ma, and Van Overwalle 2017.
72 Baetens, Ma, and Van Overwalle 2017.
73 Ferrari et al. 2016.
74 Baetens et al. 2014.
75 Liberman, Woodward, and Kinzler 2017.
76 Hehman, Ingbretsen, and Freeman 2014; Li et al. 2016.
77 Li et al. 2016.
78 Crenshaw 1989.
79 Collins 1990.
80 Goff, Thomas, and Jackson 2008.
81 Stolier and Freeman 2016.
82 Duchesne and Trujillo 2021.
83 La Scala et al. 2023.

Chapter 2 The Moral Life of Our Brains
1 Blumer 1958.
2 Allport 1954.
3 Cosmides, Guzmán, and Tooby 2018.
4 Max Planck Institute 2018.
5 Tooby 2020; Tooby and Cosmides 1990.
6 Platten et al. 2010.
7 Hamlin, Wynn, and Bloom 2007.
8 Platten et al. 2010.
9 Platten et al. 2010.
10 Ferera, Baron, and Diesendruck 2018.
11 Ferera, Baron, and Diesendruck 2018.
12 Geraci, Commodari, and Perucchini 2024.
13 Decety, Michalska, and Kinzler 2012.
14 Elenbaas et al. 2022.
15 Byrd 2012.
16 Goff, Thomas, and Jackson 2008.
17 Byrd 2012.
18 Huguley et al. 2019.
19 Huguley et al. 2019.
20 Quintana 2007.

21 Umaña-Taylor et al. 2014.
22 Huguley et al. 2019.
23 Huguley et al. 2019.
24 Graham and Haidt 2012.
25 Schwartz 1992.
26 Firat and McPherson 2010; Hitlin 2008.
27 Blumer 1958; Mead 2015 [1934].
28 West and Zimmerman 1987.
29 Markus and Moya 2010.
30 Sayer 2005, 2010.
31 Kinder and Sears 1981; Sears et al. 2004; Sears and Henry 2003.
32 Lamont 2000.
33 Kinder and Sears 1981; Sears et al. 2004.
34 Gaertner and Dovidio 1977.
35 Kunstman and Plant 2008.
36 Wang, Chen, and Li 2022.
37 Butler, Scammell, and Benson 2016.
38 Elliott and Pais 2006.
39 Beckett 2025.
40 Goff et al. 2014.
41 Stanford University 2020.
42 Harvard Opinion Research Program 2018.
43 Firat and McPherson 2010.
44 Sayer 2005.
45 Ekman 1971; Ekman 1992; Ekman et al. 1987.
46 Turner 2000; Turner and Stets 2006.
47 González-Arias and Aracena 2022.
48 Cacioppo and Gardner 1999.
49 Cahill 1999.
50 Hochschild 1983.
51 Wilkins 2008.
52 Opotow 1990; Leyens, Cortes, and Demoulin 2003.
53 Fiske 2009; Haslam 2006.
54 Cuddy, Rock, and Norton 2007.
55 Lacy and Haspel 2011.
56 Leidner et al., 2010.
57 Piaget 2013.
58 Kohlberg 1963, 1971.
59 Firat and Hitlin 2012; Firat and McPherson 2010.
60 Goleman 1998.
61 Damasio 1994, 1996.
62 Bechara et al. 1994.
63 Bechara et al. 1997.
64 Haidt 2001, 2007.

65 Haidt 2013.
66 Haidt and Hersh 2001.
67 Greene 2007, 2009, 2023.
68 Greene 2001.
69 Bechara et al. 1994; Eslinger and Damasio 1985.
70 Barrash, Tranel, and Anderson 2000.
71 Damasio, Tranel, and Damasio 1990.
72 Anderson et al. 1999, 2006.
73 Kim and Johnson 2015.
74 Cloutier and Gyurovski 2014.
75 Forman et al. 1995.
76 Firat et al. 2017.
77 Bouret and Richmond 2010.
78 Bouret and Richmond 2010; Öngür and Price 2000.
79 Kringelbach 2005; Rolls, Cheng, and Feng 2020.
80 Blood et al. 1999; De Araujo et al. 2003; O'Doherty et al, 2003;
   Rolls, Kringelbach, and De Araujo 2003.
81 Molenberghs and Louis 2018.
82 Molenberghs et al., 2016.
83 Domínguez D et al. 2018.
84 Molenberghs and Louis 2018.
85 Cunningham et al. 2004; Phelps et al. 2000.
86 Schreiber and Iacoboni 2012.
87 Firat et al. 2017.
88 Flynn 1999.
89 Brooks and Tracey 2007; Labrakakis 2023; Wiech et al. 2010.
90 Calder et al. 2007; Verstaen et al. 2016.
91 Papagno et al. 2016; Phillips et al. 1997; Schäfer, Schienle, and
   Vaitl 2005; Wicker et al. 2003; Wright et al. 2004.
92 Harris and Fiske 2006.
93 Lieberman et al. 2005; Phelps et al. 2000; Richeson et al. 2003.
94 Molenberghs 2013.
95 Lamm, Meltzoff, and Decety 2010; Singer et al. 2004; Xu et al.
   2009.
96 Cikara and Fiske 2011.
97 Boyer, Firat, and van Leeuwen 2015.
98 Cosmides, Tooby, and Kurzban 2003.
99 Kurzban, Tooby, and Cosmides 2001.

Chapter 3 Race in the Making

1 Blumer 1958; Bonilla-Silva 1997, 2010.
2 Izard et al. 2008.
3 Brod et al. 2015.
4 Sommers et al. 2006.

5 White et al. 2007.
6 Navarre 2022.
7 Politico 2015.
8 Politico 2015.
9 Fiske and Taylor 2013.
10 Templeton 2013.
11 Gonder et al. 2011.
12 Burbrink et al. 2022.
13 APA 2025.
14 National Museum of African American History and Culture 2025.
15 Shneiderman and Amburgey 2022.
16 Emirbayer and Desmond 2015.
17 US Census Bureau 2024b.
18 US Census Bureau 2024a.
19 Desmond and Emirbayer 2020.
20 Bonilla-Silva 1997.
21 Desmond and Emirbayer 2020, p. 6.
22 Caroline County 2025.
23 *Biography* 2022.
24 Caroline County 2025.
25 Omi and Winant 2020.
26 Brown 2020.
27 Cohn 2010.
28 Parker et al. 2015.
29 Bennett, Barton, and Du Bois 1969.
30 Congress.gov. 2016.
31 Fox and Bloemraad 2015.
32 Fong and Kelly 2024.
33 Compton et al. 2013.
34 US Census Bureau 2024b.
35 Bertrand and Duflo 2017; Bertrand and Mullainathan 2004; Pager, Bonikowski, and Western 2009; Pager and Shepherd 2008; Pager and Western 2012.
36 Bertrand and Mullainathan 2004.
37 Bobo, Kluegel, and Smith 1997.
38 Bobo, Kluegel, and Smith 1997.
39 Bonilla-Silva 2010.
40 Bonilla-Silva 2010.
41 Bonilla-Silva 1997.
42 Wacquant 1997; Loveman 1999; Brubaker 2009.
43 Emirbayer and Desmond 2015.
44 Loveman 1999.
45 Wacquant 1997.

46 Brubaker 2009 further advocates for a unified research paradigm that integrates the study of race, ethnicity, and nationhood into a comparative, global, cross-disciplinary framework.
47 Blumer 1958.
48 Marx 1996 [1867].
49 Du Bois 2018 [1903], p. 9.
50 Maghbouleh 2017.
51 Tehranian 2008, p. 127.
52 Joseph and Golash-Boza 2021.
53 Tajfel 1982; Tajfel and Turner 2004; Turner, Brown, and Tajfel 1979.
54 Hogg 2001.
55 Pierre and Mahalik 2005.
56 Verba and Nie 1987; Shingles 1981. Research also exists, though to a lesser extent, on the United Kingdom: Laniyonu 2019.
57 Shingles 1981; Verba and Nie 1987.
58 Pierre and Mahalik 2005.
59 Hanchard 1991.
60 Feagin 1991.
61 Dirks, Heldman, and Zack 2015.
62 Brown 2009.
63 Dirks, Heldman, and Zack 2015.
64 Dirks, Heldman, and Zack 2015.
65 Lamont 2000.
66 Bonilla-Silva 2019; Brubaker, Loveman, and Stamatov 2004.
67 Izard 2007, 2011.
68 Izard 2007, 2011.
69 Izard et al. 2008; Izard 2009.
70 Izard 2007.
71 Nawa and Ando 2019.
72 Giuliano et al. 2021; Nawa and Ando 2019.
73 Giuliano et al. 2021.
74 Bovy et al. 2020; Brod et al. 2015.
75 Bovy et al. 2020.
76 Ghosh et al. 2014.
77 Nawa and Ando 2019.
78 Izard 2011.
79 Bovy et al. 2020; Nawa and Ando 2019.
80 Kragel et al. 2019.
81 Kragel et al. 2019.
82 Izard 2007, 2011.
83 Bonilla-Silva 2019, p. 2.
84 Firat and McPherson 2010.
85 Giuliano et al. 2021.

86 Brod et al. 2015.
87 Eisenberger 2003.

Chapter 4 The Aftermath of Race
 1 Lorde 1983.
 2 Lorde 2007.
 3 Johns Hopkins 2019.
 4 Beckfield, Olafsdottir, and Bakhtiari 2013; Ruger and Kim 2006.
 5 Here, I am not trying to make a general claim about a direct link between government healthcare funding and universal health coverage. Healthcare systems are inherently complex, influenced by various factors such as population size, economic inequalities, climate, geography, natural disasters, and the quality of education systems. Public health outcomes depend not only on overall government spending on healthcare but also on the equitable distribution of healthcare funds, taking into account these various factors.
 6 Rowland and Telyukov 1991.
 7 Mazur 1969.
 8 Ruger and Kim 2006.
 9 Thoits and Hewitt 2001.
10 Flegal et al. 2012.
11 Egan 2010.
12 Geronimus et al. 1996.
13 Fine, Ibrahim, and Thomas 2005; Krieger 2005.
14 Magesh et al. 2021.
15 Phelan, Link, and Tehranifar 2010; Phelan and Link 2013.
16 Link and Phelan 1995.
17 Clouston, Natale, and Link 2021.
18 Guzman 2024.
19 Sullivan, Hays, and Bennett 2024.
20 Sullivan, Hays, and Bennett 2024.
21 Williams and Sternthal 2010.
22 Kennedy-Moulton et al. 2022.
23 Haskell 2018.
24 Washington and Randall 2022.
25 Williams et al. 2019.
26 James 2020.
27 Butler et al. 2002.
28 Pyke 2010.
29 James 2022; Sosoo, Bernard, and Neblett 2020; Willis et al. 2021.
30 James 2022.

31 Lichter, Thiede, and Brooks 2023.
32 Williams and Collins 2001.
33 Marley 2018.
34 McDaniel et al. 2021; Wylie and McConkey 2019.
35 Benjamins and Middleton 2019; Casagrande et al. 2007; Hausmann et al. 2013; Washington and Randall 2022.
36 Limandjaja et al. 2020.
37 Adelekun, Onyekaba, and Lipoff 2021; Ebede and Papier 2006.
38 Morgan 2021.
39 Brondolo et al. 2003; Goosby, Cheadle, and Mitchell 2018; Pascoe and Richman 2009; Williams 2012.
40 McEwen 1993, 2000, 2004, 2005.
41 McEwen 2000; Pascoe and Richman 2009.
42 Purushothaman and Rein 2023.
43 Eisenberger 2003.
44 Cacioppo et al. 2013.
45 Firat 2022.
46 Peterson et al. 2020.
47 Gover, Harper, and Langton 2020; Su et al. 2020; Tessler, Choi, and Kao 2020.
48 Cohen, Kamarck, and Mermelstein 1983.
49 Kroenke et al. 2009; Kroenke et al. 2016.
50 Spitzer et al. 2006.
51 CDC 2024.
52 Burchard et al. 2003; Fine, Ibrahim, and Thomas 2005.
53 Braun 2002; Rebbeck et al. 2022.
54 Rebbeck et al. 2022.
55 Pearce et al. 2004.
56 Fine, Ibrahim, and Thomas 2005; Rebbeck et al. 2022.
57 Borrell et al. 2021; Fine, Ibrahim, and Thomas 2005.
58 Braun 2002.
59 Fine, Ibrahim, and Thomas 2005; Rebbeck et al. 2022.
60 Burchard et al. 2003; Rebbeck et al. 2022.
61 Aroke et al. 2019; Kuzawa and Sweet 2009; Sullivan 2013.
62 Kurian and Cardarelli 2007; Tajeu et al. 2020.
63 Sluiter et al. 2020; Santos-Lozada 2016; Cao-Lei, Laplante, and King 2016.
64 Oldenburg, O'Shea, and Fry 2020; Provençal and Binder 2015; Kuzawa and Sweet 2009.
65 Kuzawa and Sweet 2009.
66 Aroke et al. 2019.
67 Aroke et al. 2019.
68 Kuzawa and Sweet 2009; Sullivan 2013.
69 Kral et al. 2024.

70 Javanbakht et al. 2015.
71 Javanbakht et al. 2015; Liberzon et al. 2015; Miller et al. 2021.
72 Fine, Ibrahim, and Thomas 2005.
73 Braun 2002; Fine, Ibrahim, and Thomas 2005.
74 Aroke et al. 2019; Kuzawa and Sweet 2009; Sullivan 2013.
75 Barnes, Keyes, and Bates 2013; Keyes 2009; Tobin et al. 2022.
76 Tobin et al. 2022.
77 LaMotte, Elliott, and Mouzon 2023.
78 Fernandez, García-Pérez, and Orozco-Aleman 2023.
79 Bacong and Menjívar 2021; Fernandez, García-Pérez, and Orozco-Aleman 2023; Ruiz et al. 2016.
80 Razum et al. 1998.
81 Teruya and Bazargan-Hejazi 2013.
82 Fernandez, García-Pérez, and Orozco-Aleman 2023; Ruiz, Steffen, and Smith 2013; Ruiz et al. 2016.
83 Bacong and Menjívar 2021; Boen and Hummer 2019.
84 Bacong and Menjívar 2021; Santos-Lozada 2016.
85 Mouzon 2013.
86 Mouzon 2017; Ruiz et al. 2016.
87 Louie et al. 2022; Mouzon 2017.
88 Keyes 2009.
89 Louie et al. 2022; Mouzon 2017.
90 Phelan and Link 2015.
91 Pearlin et al. 2005.
92 Cheadle et al. 2020; Goosby, Cheadle, and Mitchell 2018.
93 Eisenberger 2003.
94 McEwen 2000.
95 Berger and Sarnyai 2015; Kim et al. 2013; Kral et al. 2024.

Chapter 5 Rewiring Our Brains
1 Hamilton 2023.
2 de Kovel, Carrión-Castillo, and Francks 2019.
3 Maguire et al. 2000.
4 Kwok et al. 2011.
5 Forscher et al. 2017.
6 Kalev, Dobbin, and Kelly 2006.
7 Kubota, Banaji, and Phelps 2012; Senholzi and Kubota 2016.
8 Firat 2019.
9 Knutson et al. 2007; Richeson et al. 2003.
10 Richeson et al. 2003.
11 Richeson et al. 2003.
12 Richeson et al. 2003.
13 Amodio 2014.
14 Amodio 2014.

15 Amodio 2014; Devine et al. 2002.
16 Firat and Hitlin 2012.
17 Decety and Jackson 2006; Singer and Lamm 2009.
18 Frith and Frith 2005.
19 Decety and Jackson 2006; Zaki and Ochsner 2012.
20 Cuff et al. 2016; Singer and Lamm 2009.
21 Singer et al. 2004.
22 Contreras-Huerta et al. 2013; Xu et al. 2009.
23 Matthaeus et al. 2024; Petzold et al. 2023; Silveira, Godara, and Singer 2023.
24 Singer 2024.
25 Kok and Singer 2017; Singer and Engert 2019.
26 Kok and Singer 2017; Singer and Engert 2019.
27 Hildebrandt, McCall, and Singer 2017; Silveira, Godara, and Singer 2023.
28 Singer and Engert 2019; Trautwein et al. 2020.
29 Kok and Singer 2017; Singer and Engert 2019.
30 Kok and Singer 2017; Matthaeus et al. 2024; Silveira, Godara, and Singer 2023; Singer and Engert 2019.
31 Petzold et al. 2023; Silveira, Godara, and Singer 2023; Singer and Engert 2019.
32 Devine and Ash 2022; Paluck et al. 2021.
33 Cox and Devine 2019; Devine et al. 2012; Forscher et al. 2017.
34 Cox and Devine 2019; Devine et al. 2012; Forscher et al. 2017.
35 Blair, Ma, and Lenton 2001.
36 Cox and Devine 2019.
37 Devine et al. 2012.
38 Hitlin and Elder 2007; Hitlin and Kirkpatrick Johnson 2015; Hitlin and Long 2009.
39 Emirbayer and Mische 1998.
40 Bandura 1989, 2001, 2006.
41 Bandura 2004, 2005.
42 Firat 2017.
43 Berger 2008.
44 Bandura 2006; Firat 2017; Welzel and Inglehart 2010.
45 Bonilla-Silva 2010.
46 Biran et al. 2006; Panikkath et al. 2014.
47 David 2012.
48 Haggard 2017.
49 Carruthers 2012.
50 Balconi et al. 2021; Balconi, Angioletti, and Crivelli 2023.
51 Cosmides, Tooby, and Kurzban 2003; Kurzban, Tooby, and Cosmides 2001; Tooby and Cosmides 1990.
52 Kurzban, Tooby, and Cosmides 2001.

53 Boyer, Firat, and van Leeuwen 2015.
54 Firat and Boyer 2015.
55 Allport 1954.
56 Pettigrew 1998; Pettigrew et al. 2011; Pettigrew and Tropp 2006.
57 Walker et al. 2008.
58 Cao et al. 2015.
59 Handley, Kubota, and Cloutier 2023.
60 Page-Gould, Mendoza-Denton, and Tropp 2008; Page-Gould, Mendes, and Major 2010; Page-Gould, Mendoza-Denton, and Mendes 2014.
61 Page-Gould, Mendoza-Denton, and Tropp 2008.
62 Lahav, Saltzman, and Schlaug 2007.
63 Hebb 1949.
64 Iacoboni 2009; Keysers and Gazzola 2014.
65 Keysers and Gazzola 2014; Keysers and Perrett 2004.
66 Keysers and Gazzola 2014.
67 Kalev, Dobbin, and Kelly 2006.

Conclusion

1 Mead 2015 [1934].
2 Zuberi 2001; Zuberi and Bonilla-Silva 2008.
3 Parker and Ricard 2022; Webb, Etter, and Kwasa 2022.
4 Webb, Etter, and Kwasa 2022.
5 Wassenaar and van den Brand 2005.
6 Ricard et al. 2023; Webb, Etter, and Kwasa 2022.
7 Ricard et al. 2023.
8 Parker and Ricard 2022; Ricard et al. 2023.
9 Parker and Ricard 2022; Perkins et al. 2023.
10 Perkins et al. 2023; Webb, Etter, and Kwasa 2022.
11 Perkins et al. 2023.
12 Aono, Yaffe, and Kober 2019.
13 La Scala et al. 2023.
14 La Scala et al. 2023.
15 La Scala et al. 2023.
16 Green et al. 2022.
17 La Scala et al. 2023.
18 Alexander 2023.
19 Wilkinson 2022.
20 Flores and Gunzenhauser 2019.
21 Wilkinson 2022.
22 Flores and Gunzenhauser 2019.
23 Mabokela and Madsen 2005.
24 Johnson 2014.

25 Flores and Gunzenhauser 2019.
26 Flores and Gunzenhauser 2019.
27 Wilkinson 2022.
28 Lorde 1983, p. 9.
29 Ciccia and Roggeband 2021; Crenshaw 1989, 1991; Tormos 2017.
30 Ciccia and Roggeband 2021.
31 Gawerc 2021.
32 Ciccia and Roggeband 2021.
33 Ciccia and Roggeband 2021.
34 Gawerc 2021.
35 Gawerc 2021.
36 Einwohner et al. 2021.
37 Chenoweth et al. 2017.
38 Einwohner et al. 2021.
39 Lang et al. 2018.
40 Simon 2024.
41 Bump et al. 2024.
42 Firat 2021; Franks 2010, 2019; Franks and Turner 2013; Kalkhoff, Thye, and Pollock 2016.

References

Aboud, Frances E. 2003. "The Formation of In-Group Favoritism and Out-Group Prejudice in Young Children: Are They Distinct Attitudes?" *Developmental Psychology* 39(1) (January): 48–60. https://doi.org/10.1037/0012-1649.39.1.48

Adelekun, Ademide, Onyekaba, Ginikanwa, and Lipoff, Jules B. 2021. "Skin Color in Dermatology Textbooks: An Updated Evaluation and Analysis." *Journal of the American Academy of Dermatology* 84(1) (January): 194–6. https://doi.org/10.1016/j.jaad.2020.04.084

Adolphs, Ralph, Tranel, Daniel, Damasio, Hanna, and Damasio, Antonio. 1994. "Impaired Recognition of Emotion in Facial Expressions Following Bilateral Damage to the Human Amygdala." *Nature* 372(6507) (December): 669–72. https://doi.org/10.1038/372669a0

Adolphs, Ralph, Tranel, Daniel, and Damasio, Antonio R. 1998. "The Human Amygdala in Social Judgment." *Nature* 393(6684) (June): 470–4. https://doi.org/10.1038/30982

Ahmed, Sara. 2007. "A Phenomenology of Whiteness." *Feminist Theory* 8(2) (August): 149–68. https://doi.org/10.1177/1464700107078139

Alexander, Taifha Natalee. 2023. "Tracking the Attack on Critical Race Theory in Education." US News. www.usnews.com/opinion/articles/2023-04-11/tracking-the-attack-on-critical-race-theory-in-education

Allport, Gordon W. 1954. *The Nature of Prejudice*. Reading, MA: Addison-Wesley.

Amodio, David M. 2014. "The Neuroscience of Prejudice and Stereotyping." *Nature Reviews Neuroscience* 15(10) (October): 670–82. https://doi.org/10.1038/nrn3800

Anderson, Steven W., Barrash, Joseph, Bechara, Antoine, and Tranel, Daniel. 2006. "Impairments of Emotion and Real-World Complex Behavior Following Childhood- or Adult-Onset Damage to Ventromedial Prefrontal Cortex." *Journal of the International Neuropsychological Society* 12(2) (March): 224–35. https://doi.org/10.1017/S1355617706060346

Anderson, Steven W., Bechara, Antoine, Damasio, Hanna, Tranel, Daniel, and Damasio, Antonio R. 1999. "Impairment of Social and Moral Behavior Related to Early Damage in Human Prefrontal Cortex." *Nature Neuroscience* 2(11) (November): 1032–7. https://doi.org/10.1038/14833

Anzellotti, Stefano. 2017. "Anterior Temporal Lobe and the Representation of Knowledge about People." *Proceedings of the National Academy of Sciences of the United States of America* 114(16) (April): 4042–4. https://doi.org/10.1073/pnas.1703438114

Anzivino, Ava. 2025. "*Cowboy Carter* Review." *High Tide* (blog). https://ruhsmedia.com/2024/04/cowboy-carter-review/

Anzures, Gizelle, Wheeler, Andrea, Quinn, Paul C., et al. 2012. "Brief Daily Exposures to Asian Females Reverses Perceptual Narrowing for Asian Faces in Caucasian Infants." *Journal of Experimental Child Psychology* 112(4) (August): 484–95. https://doi.org/10.1016/j.jecp.2012.04.005

Aono, Darby, Yaffe, Gideon, and Kober, Hedy. 2019. "Neuroscientific Evidence in the Courtroom: A Review." *Cognitive Research: Principles and Implications* 4(1) (December): 40. https://doi.org/10.1186/s41235-019-0179-y

APA. 2025. "Race and Ethnicity." American Psychological Association. https://www.apa.org/topics/race-ethnicity

Arkes, Hal R. and Tetlock, Philip E. 2004. "Attributions of Implicit Prejudice, or 'Would Jesse Jackson "Fail" the Implicit Association Test?'" *Psychological Inquiry* 15(4) (October): 257–78. https://doi.org/10.1207/s15327965pli1504_01

Aroke, Edwin N., Joseph, Paule V., Roy, Abhrarup, et al. 2019. "Could Epigenetics Help Explain Racial Disparities in Chronic Pain?" *Journal of Pain Research* (February). https://www.tandfonline.com/doi/abs/10.2147/JPR.S191848

Bacong, Adrian Matias and Menjívar, Cecilia. 2021. "Recasting the Immigrant Health Paradox through Intersections of Legal Status and Race." *Journal of Immigrant and Minority Health* 23(5) (October): 1092–104. https://doi.org/10.1007/s10903-021-01162-2

Baetens, Kris, Ma, Ning, Steen, Johan, and Overwalle, Frank van. 2014. "Involvement of the Mentalizing Network in Social and Non-Social High Construal." *Social Cognitive and Affective Neuroscience* 9(6) (June): 817–24. https://doi.org/10.1093/scan/nst048

Baetens, Kris L. M. R., Ma, Ning, and Overwalle, Frank Van. 2017. "The Dorsal Medial Prefrontal Cortex Is Recruited by High Construal of Non-Social Stimuli." *Frontiers in Behavioral Neuroscience* 11 (March). https://doi.org/10.3389/fnbeh.2017.00044

Bakker, Rembrandt, Tiesinga, Paul, and Kötter, Rolf. 2015. "The Scalable Brain Atlas: Instant Web-Based Access to Public Brain Atlases and Related Content." *Neuroinformatics* 13(3) (July): 353–66. https://doi.org/10.1007/s12021-014-9258-x

Balconi, Michela, Angioletti, Laura, Cassioli, Federico, and Crivelli, Davide. 2021. "Neurocognitive Empowerment in Healthy Aging: A Pilot Study on the Effect of Non-Invasive Brain Stimulation on Executive Functions." *Journal of Cognitive Enhancement* 5(3) (September): 343–50. https://doi.org/10.1007/s41465-020-00203-2

Balconi, Michela, Angioletti, Laura, and Crivelli, Davide. 2023. "Neurofeedback as Neuroempowerment Technique for Affective Regulation and Interoceptive Awareness in Adolescence: Preliminary Considerations Applied to a Psychogenic Pseudosyncope Case." *Frontiers in Rehabilitation Sciences* 4 (June). https://doi.org/10.3389/fresc.2023.1056972

Bandettini, Peter A. 2012. "Twenty Years of Functional MRI: The Science and the Stories." *NeuroImage* (Twenty Years of fMRI) 62(2) (August): 575–88. https://doi.org/10.1016/j.neuroimage.2012.04.026

Bandura, Albert. 1989. "Human Agency in Social Cognitive Theory." *American Psychologist* 44(9): 1175–84. https://doi.org/10.1037/0003-066X.44.9.1175

Bandura, Albert. 2001. "Social Cognitive Theory: An Agentic Perspective." *Annual Review of Psychology* 52(1) (February): 1–26. https://doi.org/10.1146/annurev.psych.52.1.1

Bandura, Albert. 2004. "Health Promotion by Social Cognitive Means." *Health Education & Behavior* 31(2) (April): 143–64. https://doi.org/10.1177/1090198104263660

Bandura, Albert. 2005. "The Primacy of Self-Regulation in Health Promotion." *Applied Psychology* 54(2) (April): 245–54. https://doi.org/10.1111/j.1464-0597.2005.00208.x

Bandura, Albert. 2006. "Toward a Psychology of Human Agency." *Perspectives on Psychological Science* 1(2) (June): 164–80. https://doi.org/10.1111/j.1745-6916.2006.00011.x

Bar-Haim, Yair, Ziv, Talee, Lamy, Dominique, and Hodes, Richard M. 2006. "Nature and Nurture in Own-Race Face Processing." *Psychological Science* 17(2) (February): 159–63. https://doi.org /10.1111/j.1467-9280.2006.01679.x

Barnes, David M., Keyes, Katherine M., and Bates, Lisa M. 2013. "Racial Differences in Depression in the United States: How Do Subgroup Analyses Inform a Paradox?" *Social Psychiatry and Psychiatric Epidemiology* 48(12) (December): 1941–9. https://doi .org/10.1007/s00127-013-0718-7

Barrash, Joseph, Tranel, Daniel, and Anderson, Steven W. 2000. "Acquired Personality Disturbances Associated with Bilateral Damage to the Ventromedial Prefrontal Region." *Developmental Neuropsychology* 18(3) (December): 355–81. https://doi.org/10 .1207/S1532694205Barrash

Beauchamp, Zack. 2024. "Why the Far Right Is Surging All over the World." Vox. https://www.vox.com/politics/361136/far-right-authoritarianism-germany-reactionary-spirit

Bechara, Antoine, Damasio, Antonio R., Damasio, Hanna, and Anderson, Steven W. 1994. "Insensitivity to Future Consequences Following Damage to Human Prefrontal Cortex." *Cognition* 50(1) (April): 7–15. https://doi.org/10.1016/0010-0277(94)90018-3

Bechara, Antoine, Damasio, Hanna, Tranel, Daniel, and Damasio, Antonio R. 1997 "Deciding Advantageously before Knowing the Advantageous Strategy." *Science* 275(5304) (February): 1293–5. https://doi.org/10.1126/science.275.5304.1293

Beckett, Lois. 2025. "The LA Fires Burned Down a Thriving Black Community. Residents Are Afraid of Being 'Erased.'" *The Guardian*, February 16 (US news section). https://www.the guardian.com/us-news/2025/feb/16/california-fires-black-com munity-recovery

Beckfield, Jason, Olafsdottir, Sigrun, and Bakhtiari, Elyas. 2013. "Health Inequalities in Global Context." *American Behavioral Scientist* 57(8) (August): 1014–39. https://doi.org/10.1177/0002 764213487343

Benjamins, Maureen R. and Middleton, Megan. 2019. "Perceived Discrimination in Medical Settings and Perceived Quality of Care: A Population-Based Study in Chicago." *PLOS ONE* 14(4) (April): e0215976. https://doi.org/10.1371/journal.pone.0215976

Bennett, Craig M., Miller, Michael B., and Wolford, George L. 2009. "Neural Correlates of Interspecies Perspective Taking in the Post-Mortem Atlantic Salmon: An Argument for Multiple Comparisons Correction." *NeuroImage* 47(Supp. 1) (Organization for Human Brain Mapping) (July): S39–S41. https://doi.org/10.1016/S1053 -8119(09)71202-9

Bennett, Lerone, Barton, Roland A., and Du Bois, W. E. B. 1969. "WHAT'S IN A NAME? Negro vs. Afro-American vs. Black." *ETC: A Review of General Semantics* 26(4): 399–412.

Berger, Maximus and Sarnyai, Zoltán. 2015. "'More than Skin Deep': Stress Neurobiology and Mental Health Consequences of Racial Discrimination." *Stress* 18(1) (January): 1–10. https://doi.org/10.3109/10253890.2014.989204

Berger, Ronald J. 2008. "Agency, Structure, and the Transition to Disability: A Case Study with Implications for Life History Research." *Sociological Quarterly* 49(2) (May): 309–33. https://doi.org/10.1111/j.1533-8525.2008.00117.x

Bertrand, Marianne and Duflo, Esther. 2017. "Field Experiments on Discrimination," in Abhijit Vinayak Banerjee and Esther Duflo (eds.), *Handbook of Economic Field Experiments*, Vol. 1. Amsterdam: Elsevier, pp. 309–93. https://doi.org/10.1016/bs.hefe.2016.08.004

Bertrand, Marianne and Mullainathan, Sendhil. 2004. "Are Emily and Greg More Employable than Lakisha and Jamal? A Field Experiment on Labor Market Discrimination." *American Economic Review* 94(4) (September): 991–1013. https://doi.org/10.1257/0002828042002561

Biography. 2022. "Richard Loving – Wife, Death and Children." https://www.biography.com/legal-figures/richard-loving

Biran, Iftah, Giovannetti, Tania, Buxbaum, Laurel, and Chatterjee, Anjan. 2006. "The Alien Hand Syndrome: What Makes the Alien Hand Alien?" *Cognitive Neuropsychology* 23(4) (June): 563–82. https://doi.org/10.1080/02643290500180282

Blair, Irene V., Ma, Jennifer E., and Lenton, Alison P. 2001. "Imagining Stereotypes Away: The Moderation of Implicit Stereotypes through Mental Imagery." *Journal of Personality and Social Psychology* 81(5): 828–41. https://doi.org/10.1037/0022-3514.81.5.828

Blood, Anne J., Zatorre, Robert J., Bermudez, Patrick, and Evans, Alan C. 1999. "Emotional Responses to Pleasant and Unpleasant Music Correlate with Activity in Paralimbic Brain Regions." *Nature Neuroscience* 2(4) (April): 382–7. https://doi.org/10.1038/7299

Blumer, Herbert. 1958. "Race Prejudice as a Sense of Group Position." *Pacific Sociological Review* 1(1) (March): 3–7. https://doi.org/10.2307/1388607

Blumer, Herbert. 1986. *Symbolic Interactionism: Perspective and Method.* Berkeley, CA: University of California Press.

Bobo, Lawrence, Kluegel, James R., and Smith, Ryan A. 1997. "Laissez-Faire Racism: The Crystallization of a Kinder,

Gentler, Antiblack Ideology," in Steven A. Tuch and Martin Jack (eds.), *Racial Attitudes in the 1990s*. London: Bloomsbury Publishing, pp. 15–42. https://www.torrossa.com/en/resources/an/5531707

Boen, Courtney E. and Hummer, Robert A. 2019. "Longer-but Harder-Lives? The Hispanic Health Paradox and the Social Determinants of Racial, Ethnic, and Immigrant-Native Health Disparities from Midlife through Late Life." *Journal of Health and Social Behavior* 60(4) (December): 434–52. https://doi.org/10.1177/0022146519884538

Bogen, J. E., DeZure, R., TenHouten, W. D. and Marsh, J. F., Jr. 1972. "The Other Side of the Brain, IV: The A/P Ratio." *Bulletin of the Los Angeles Neurological Societies* 37: 49961

Bonilla-Silva, Eduardo. 1997. "Rethinking Racism: Toward a Structural Interpretation." *American Sociological Review* 62(3) (June): 465. https://doi.org/10.2307/2657316

Bonilla-Silva, Eduardo. 2010. *Racism without Racists: Color-Blind Racism and the Persistence of Racial Inequality in the United States*, 3rd edn. Lanham: Rowman & Littlefield Publishers.

Bonilla-Silva, Eduardo. 2019. "Feeling Race: Theorizing the Racial Economy of Emotions." *American Sociological Review* 84(1) (February): 1–25. https://doi.org/10.1177/0003122418816958

Borrell, Luisa N., Elhawary, Jennifer R., Fuentes-Afflick, Elena, et al. 2021. "Race and Genetic Ancestry in Medicine – A Time for Reckoning with Racism." *New England Journal of Medicine* 384(5) (February): 474–80. https://doi.org/10.1056/NEJMms2029562

Bourdieu, Pierre. 1977. *Outline of a Theory of Practice*. Trans. by Richard Nice. Cambridge: Cambridge University Press. https://doi.org/10.1017/CBO9780511812507

Bouret, Sebastien and Richmond, Barry J. 2010. "Ventromedial and Orbital Prefrontal Neurons Differentially Encode Internally and Externally Driven Motivational Values in Monkeys." *Journal of Neuroscience* 30(25) (June): 8591–601. https://doi.org/10.1523/JNEUROSCI.0049-10.2010

Bovy, Leonore, Berkers, Ruud, M. W. J., Pottkämper, Julia C. M., et al. 2020. "Transcranial Magnetic Stimulation of the Medial Prefrontal Cortex Decreases Emotional Memory Schemas." *Cerebral Cortex* 30(6) (May): 3608–16. https://doi.org/10.1093/cercor/bhz329

Boyer, Pascal, Firat, Rengin, and van Leeuwen, Florian. 2015. "Safety, Threat, and Stress in Intergroup Relations: A Coalitional Index Model." *Perspectives on Psychological Science* 10(4) (July): 434–50. https://doi.org/10.1177/1745691615583133

Braun, Lundy. 2002. "Race, Ethnicity, and Health: Can Genetics Explain Disparities?" *Perspectives in Biology and Medicine* 45(2): 159–74. https://doi.org/10.1353/pbm.2002.0023

Brod, Garvin, Lindenberger, Ulman, Werkle-Bergner, Markus, and Shing, Yee Lee. 2015. "Differences in the Neural Signature of Remembering Schema-Congruent and Schema-Incongruent Events." *NeuroImage* 117 (August): 358–66. https://doi.org/10.1016/j.neuroimage.2015.05.086

Brondolo, Elizabeth, Rieppi, Ricardo, Kelly, Kim P., and Gerin, William. 2003. "Perceived Racism and Blood Pressure: A Review of the Literature and Conceptual and Methodological Critique." *Annals of Behavioral Medicine* 25(1) (January): 55–65. https://doi.org/10.1207/S15324796ABM2501_08

Brooks, Jonathan C. W. and Tracey, Irene. 2007. "The Insula: A Multidimensional Integration Site for Pain." *PAIN* 128(1) (March): 1. https://doi.org/10.1016/j.pain.2006.12.025

Brosch, Tobias, Bar-David, Eyal, and Phelps, Elizabeth A. 2013. "Implicit Race Bias Decreases the Similarity of Neural Representations of Black and White Faces." *Psychological Science* 24(2) (February): 160–6. https://doi.org/10.1177/0956797612451465

Brown, Anna. 2020. "The Changing Categories the US Census Has Used to Measure Race." *Pew Research Center* (blog), February 25. https://www.pewresearch.org/short-reads/2020/02/25/the-changing-categories-the-u-s-has-used-to-measure-race/

Brown, Michelle. 2009. *The Culture of Punishment: Prison, Society, and Spectacle* (Alternative Criminology Series). New York: New York University Press.

Brubaker, Rogers. 2009. "Ethnicity, Race, and Nationalism." *Annual Review of Sociology* 35: 21–42. https://doi.org/10.1146/annurev-soc-070308-115916

Brubaker, Rogers, Loveman, Mara, and Stamatov, Peter. 2004. "Ethnicity as Cognition." *Theory and Society* 33(1) (February): 31–64. https://doi.org/10.1023/B:RYSO.0000021405.18890.63

Buiatti, Marco, Di Giorgio, Elisa, Piazza, Manuela, et al. 2019. "Cortical Route for Facelike Pattern Processing in Human Newborns." *Proceedings of the National Academy of Sciences* 116(10) (March): 4625–30. https://doi.org/10.1073/pnas.1812419116

Bump, Philip, Alemany, Jacqueline, Sotomayor, Marianna, et al. 2024. "Why the 'Colorblindness' Movement Is Peaking Now." *Washington Post*, March 14. https://www.washingtonpost.com/politics/2024/03/14/race-colorblindness-trap/

Burbrink, Frank T., Crother, Brian I., Murray, Christopher M., et al.

2022. "Empirical and Philosophical Problems with the Subspecies Rank." *Ecology and Evolution* 12(7): e9069. https://doi.org/10.1002/ece3.9069

Burchard, Esteban González, Ziv, Elad, Coyle, Natasha, et al. 2003. "The Importance of Race and Ethnic Background in Biomedical Research and Clinical Practice." *New England Journal of Medicine* 348(12) (March): 1170–5. https://doi.org/10.1056/NEJMsb025007

Bushnell, Ian W. R. 2001. "Mother's Face Recognition in Newborn Infants: Learning and Memory." *Infant and Child Development* 10(1–2): 67–74. https://doi.org/10.1002/icd.248

Butler, Cleve, Tull, Eugene S., Chambers, Earle C., and Taylor, Jerome. 2002. "Internalized Racism, Body Fat Distribution, and Abnormal Fasting Glucose among African-Caribbean Women in Dominica, West Indies." *Journal of the National Medical Association* 94(3) (March): 143.

Butler, Lindsey J., Scammell, Madeleine K., and Benson, Eugene B. 2016. "The Flint, Michigan, Water Crisis: A Case Study in Regulatory Failure and Environmental Injustice." *Environmental Justice* 9(4) (August): 93–7. https://doi.org/10.1089/env.2016.0014

Byrd, Christy M. 2012. "The Measurement of Racial/Ethnic Identity in Children: A Critical Review." *Journal of Black Psychology* 38(1) (February): 3–31. https://doi.org/10.1177/0095798410397544

Cacioppo, John T. and Gardner, Wendi L. 1999. "Emotion." *Annual Review of Psychology* 50(1) (February): 191–214. https://doi.org/10.1146/annurev.psych.50.1.191

Cacioppo, Stephanie, Frum, Chris, Asp, Erik, Weiss, Robin M., Lewis, James W., and Cacioppo, John T. 2013. "A Quantitative Meta-Analysis of Functional Imaging Studies of Social Rejection." *Scientific Reports* 3(1) (December): 2027. https://doi.org/10.1038/srep02027

Cahill, Spencer E. 1999. "Emotional Capital and Professional Socialization: The Case of Mortuary Science Students (and Me)." *Social Psychology Quarterly* 62(2): 101–16. https://doi.org/10.2307/2695852

Calder, Andrew J., Beaver, John D., Davis, Matthew H., van Ditzhuijzen, Jasper, Keane, John, and Lawrence, Andrew D. 2007. "Disgust Sensitivity Predicts the Insula and Pallidal Response to Pictures of Disgusting Foods." *European Journal of Neuroscience* 25(11) (June). https://doi.org/10.1111/j.1460-9568.2007.05604.x

Cao, Yuan, Contreras-Huerta, Luis Sebastian, McFadyen, Jessica, and Cunnington, Ross. 2015. "Racial Bias in Neural Response to Others' Pain Is Reduced with Other-Race Contact." *Cortex* (special issue: Neuro-cognitive Mechanisms of Social Interaction) 70 (September): 68–78. https://doi.org/10.1016/j.cortex.2015.02.010

Cao-Lei, Lei, Laplante, David P., and King, Suzanne. 2016. "Prenatal Maternal Stress and Epigenetics: Review of the Human Research." *Current Molecular Biology Reports* 2(1) (March): 16–25. https://doi.org/10.1007/s40610-016-0030-x

Caroline County. 2025. "The Lovings." https://co.caroline.va.us /308/The-Lovings

Carruthers, Glenn. 2012. "A Metacognitive Model of the Sense of Agency over Thoughts." *Cognitive Neuropsychiatry* (July). https://www.tandfonline.com/doi/full/10.1080/13546805.2011 .627275

Casagrande, Sarah Stark, Gary, Tiffany L., LaVeist, Thomas A., Gaskin, Darrell J., and Cooper, Lisa A. 2007. "Perceived Discrimination and Adherence to Medical Care in a Racially Integrated Community." *Journal of General Internal Medicine* 22(3) (March): 389–95. https://doi.org/10.1007/s11606-006-00 57-4

U.S. Centers for Disease Control and Prevention (CDC). 2024. "2020 NHIS Questionnaires, Datasets, and Documentation." National Health Interview Survey, November 21. https:// www.cdc.gov/nchs/nhis/documentation/2020-nhis.html

Cheadle, Jacob E., Goosby, Bridget J., Jochman, Joseph C., Tomaso, Cara C., Kozikowski Yancey, Chelsea B., and Nelson, Timothy D. 2020. "Race and Ethnic Variation in College Students' Allostatic Regulation of Racism-Related Stress." *Proceedings of the National Academy of Sciences* 117(49) (December): 31053–62. https://doi.org/10.1073/pnas.1922025117

Chenoweth, Erica, Pressman, Jeremy, Kornfield, Meryl, et al. 2017. "This Is What We Learned by Counting the Women's Marches." *The Washington Post*, February 7. https://www.washingtonpost.com /news/monkey-cage/wp/2017/02/07/this-is-what-we-learned-by -counting-the-womens-marches/

Chiao, Joan Y., Iidaka, Tetsuya, Gordon, Heather L., et al. 2008. "Cultural Specificity in Amygdala Response to Fear Faces." *Journal of Cognitive Neuroscience* 20(12) (December): 2167–74. https://doi.org/10.1162/jocn.2008.20151

Choo, Hae Yeon and Ferree, Myra Marx. 2010. "Practicing Intersectionality in Sociological Research: A Critical Analysis of Inclusions, Interactions, and Institutions in the Study of Inequalities." *Sociological Theory* 28(2) (June): 129–49. https:// doi.org/10.1111/j.1467-9558.2010.01370.x

Ciccia, Rossella and Roggeband, Conny. 2021. "Unpacking Intersectional Solidarity: Dimensions of Power in Coalitions." *European Journal of Politics and Gender* 4(2): 181–98. https://doi.org/10.1332/251510821X16145402377609

Cikara, Mina and Fiske, Susan T. 2011. "Bounded Empathy: Neural Responses to Outgroup Targets' (Mis)Fortunes." *Journal of Cognitive Neuroscience* 23(12) (December): 3791–803. https://doi.org/10.1162/jocn_a_00069

Clark, Margaret L. and Pearson, Willie. 1982. "Racial Stereotypes Revisited." *International Journal of Intercultural Relations* 6(4) (January): 381–93. https://doi.org/10.1016/0147-1767(82)90020-7

Clouston, Sean A. P., Natale, Ginny, and Link, Bruce G. 2021. "Socioeconomic Inequalities in the Spread of Coronavirus-19 in the United States: A Examination of the Emergence of Social Inequalities." *Social Science & Medicine* 268 (January): 113554. https://doi.org/10.1016/j.socscimed.2020.113554

Cloutier, Jasmin and Gyurovski, Ivo. 2014. "Ventral Medial Prefrontal Cortex and Person Evaluation: Forming Impressions of Others Varying in Financial and Moral Status." *NeuroImage* 100 (October): 535–43. https://doi.org/10.1016/j.neuroimage.2014.06.024

Cohen, Sheldon, Kamarck, Tom, and Mermelstein, Robin. 1983. "A Global Measure of Perceived Stress." *Journal of Health and Social Behavior* 24(4) (December): 385. https://doi.org/10.2307/2136404

Cohn, D'Vera. 2010. "Race and the Census: The 'Negro' Controversy." *Pew Research Center* (blog), January 21. https://www.pewresearch.org/social-trends/2010/01/21/race-and-the-census-the-negro-controversy/

Collins, Patricia Hill. 1990. *Black Feminist Thought: Knowledge, Consciousness, and the Politics of Empowerment*. Boston: Unwin Hyman.

Compton, Elizabeth, Bentley, Michael, Ennis, Sharon and Rastogi, Sonya. 2013. *2010 Census Race and Hispanic Origin Alternative Questionnaire Experiment*. CPEX-211 (2nd reissue). Washington, DC: US Census Bureau. https://www.census.gov/programs-surveys/decennial-census/decade/2010/program-management/cpex/2010-cpex-211.html

Congress.gov. 2016. [D-NY-6]. "Text – H.R.4238 – 114th Congress (2015–2016): To Amend the Department of Energy Organization Act and the Local Public Works Capital Development and Investment Act of 1976 to Modernize Terms Relating to Minorities." Legislation, May 20. https://www.congress.gov/bill/114th-congress/house-bill/4238/text

Contreras-Huerta, Luis Sebastian, Baker, Katharine S., Reynolds, Katherine J., Batalha, Luisa, and Cunnington, Ross. 2013. "Racial Bias in Neural Empathic Responses to Pain." *PLOS ONE* 8(12) (December): e84001. https://doi.org/10.1371/journal.pone.008 4001

Correll, Joshua, Park, Bernadette, Judd, Charles M., and Wittenbrink, Bernd. 2002. "The Police Officer's Dilemma: Using Ethnicity to Disambiguate Potentially Threatening Individuals." *Journal of Personality and Social Psychology* 83(6): 1314–29. https://doi.org/10.1037/0022-3514.83.6.1314

Correll, Joshua, Park, Bernadette, Judd, Charles M., Wittenbrink, Bernd, Sadler, Melody S., and Keesee, Tracie. 2007. "Across the Thin Blue Line: Police Officers and Racial Bias in the Decision to Shoot." *Journal of Personality and Social Psychology* 92(6): 1006–23. https://doi.org/10.1037/0022-3514.92.6.1006

Cosmides, Leda, Guzmán, Ricardo Andrés, and Tooby, John. 2018. "The Evolution of Moral Cognition," in Aaron Zimmerman, Karen Jones, and Mark Timmons (eds.), *The Routledge Handbook of Moral Epistemology*. Abingdon, UK: Routledge, pp. 174–228.

Cosmides, Leda, Tooby, John, and Kurzban, Robert. 2003. "Perceptions of Race." *Trends in Cognitive Sciences* 7(4) (April): 173–9. https://doi.org/10.1016/S1364-6613(03)00057-3

Cox, William T. L. and Devine, Patricia G. 2019. "12 – The Prejudice Habit-Breaking Intervention: An Empowerment-Based Confrontation Approach," in Robyn K. Mallett and Margo J. Monteith (eds.), *Confronting Prejudice and Discrimination*. Cambridge, MA: Academic Press, pp. 249–74. https://doi.org/10.1016/B978-0-12-814715-3.00015-1

Crenshaw, Kimberle. 1989. "Demarginalizing the Intersection of Race and Sex: A Black Feminist Critique of Antidiscrimination Doctrine, Feminist Theory and Antiracist Politics." *University of Chicago Legal Forum* 1(art. 8).

Crenshaw, Kimberle. 1991. "Mapping the Margins: Intersectionality, Identity Politics, and Violence against Women of Color." *Stanford Law Review* 43(6): 1241–99. https://doi.org/10.2307/1229039

Cristol, Dean and Gimbert, Belinda. 2008. "Racial Perceptions of Young Children: A Review of Literature Post-1999." *Early Childhood Education Journal* 36(2) (October): 201–7. https://doi .org/10.1007/s10643-008-0251-6

Cuddy, Amy J. C., Rock, Mindi S., and Norton, Michael I. 2007. "Aid in the Aftermath of Hurricane Katrina: Inferences of Secondary Emotions and Intergroup Helping." *Group Processes & Intergroup Relations* 10(1) (January): 107–18. https://doi.org /10.1177/1368430207071344

Cuff, Benjamin M. P., Brown, Sarah J., Taylor, Laura, and Howat, Douglas J. 2016. "Empathy: A Review of the Concept." *Emotion Review* 8(2) (April): 144–53. https://doi.org/10.1177/1754073914558466

Cunningham, William A., Johnson, Marcia K., Raye, Carol L., Gatenby, J. Chris, Gore, John C., and Banaji, Mahzarin R. 2004. "Separable Neural Components in the Processing of Black and White Faces." *Psychological Science* 15(12) (December): 806–13. https://doi.org/10.1111/j.0956-7976.2004.00760.x

Cunningham, William A., Preacher, Kristopher J., and Banaji, Mahzarin R. 2001. "Implicit Attitude Measures: Consistency, Stability, and Convergent Validity." *Psychological Science* 12(2) (March): 163–70. https://doi.org/10.1111/1467-9280.00328

Dalgleish, Tim. 2004. "The Emotional Brain." *Nature Reviews Neuroscience* 5(7) (July): 583–9. https://doi.org/10.1038/nrn1432

Damasio, Antonio R. 1994. *Descartes' Error: Emotion, Reason, and the Human Brain*. New York: Putnam.

Damasio, Antonio R. 1996. "The Somatic Marker Hypothesis and the Possible Functions of the Prefrontal Cortex." *Philosophical Transactions of the Royal Society of London. Series B: Biological Sciences* 35(1346) (October): 1413–20. https://doi.org/10.1098/rstb.1996.0125

Damasio, Antonio R., Tranel, Daniel, and Damasio, Hanna. 1990. "Individuals with Sociopathic Behavior Caused by Frontal Damage Fail to Respond Autonomically to Social Stimuli." *Behavioural Brain Research* 41(2) (December): 81–94. https://doi.org/10.1016/0166-4328(90)90144-4

Dasgupta, Nilanjana, McGhee, Debbie E., Greenwald, Anthony G., and Banaji, Mahzarin R. 2000. "Automatic Preference for White Americans: Eliminating the Familiarity Explanation." *Journal of Experimental Social Psychology* 36(3) (May): 316–28. https://doi.org/10.1006/jesp.1999.1418

David, Nicole. 2012. "New Frontiers in the Neuroscience of the Sense of Agency." *Frontiers in Human Neuroscience* 6 (June). https://doi.org/10.3389/fnhum.2012.00161

De Araujo, Ivan E. T., Rolls, Edmund T., Kringelbach, Morten L., McGlone, Francis, and Phillips, Nicola. 2003. "Taste-Olfactory Convergence, and the Representation of the Pleasantness of Flavour, in the Human Brain." *European Journal of Neuroscience* 18(7): 2059–68. https://doi.org/10.1046/j.1460-9568.2003.02915.x

Decety, Jean and Jackson, Philip L. 2006. "A Social-Neuroscience Perspective on Empathy." *Current Directions in Psychological*

Science 15(2) (April): 54–8. https://doi.org/10.1111/j.0963-7214
.2006.00406.x

Decety, Jean, Michalska, Kalina J., and Kinzler, Katherine D.
2012. "The Contribution of Emotion and Cognition to Moral
Sensitivity: A Neurodevelopmental Study." *Cerebral Cortex*
22(1) (January): 209–20. https://doi.org/10.1093/cercor/bhr111

de Kovel, Carolien G. F., Carrión-Castillo, Amaia, and Francks,
Clyde. 2019. "A Large-Scale Population Study of Early Life
Factors Influencing Left-Handedness." *Scientific Reports* 9(1)
(January): 584. https://doi.org/10.1038/s41598-018-37423-8

Delatolla, Andrew. 2024. "A Global Phenomenology of Whiteness:
Turkey, Europe and Institutional Global Racism." *Sociology Lens*
37(3): 312–28. https://doi.org/10.1111/johs.12470

Desmond, Matthew and Emirbayer, Mustafa. 2020. *Race in
America*, 2nd edn. New York: W. W. Norton & Company.

Devine, Patricia G. 1989. "Stereotypes and Prejudice: Their
Automatic and Controlled Components." *Journal of Personality
and Social Psychology* 56(1): 5–18. https://doi.org/10.1037/0022
-3514.56.1.5

Devine, Patricia G. and Ash, Tory L. 2022. "Diversity Training Goals,
Limitations, and Promise: A Review of the Multidisciplinary
Literature." *Annual Review of Psychology* 73 (January): 403–29.
https://doi.org/10.1146/annurev-psych-060221-122215

Devine, Patricia G. and Elliot, Andrew J. 1995. "Are Racial
Stereotypes Really Fading? The Princeton Trilogy Revisited."
Personality and Social Psychology Bulletin 21(11): 1139–50.
https://doi.org/10.1177/01461672952111002

Devine, Patricia G., Forscher, Patrick S., Austin, Anthony J., and
Cox, William T. L. 2012. "Long-Term Reduction in Implicit
Race Bias: A Prejudice Habit-Breaking Intervention." *Journal of
Experimental Social Psychology* 48(6) (November): 1267–78.
https://doi.org/10.1016/j.jesp.2012.06.003

Devine, Patricia G., Plant, E. A., Amodio, David M., Harmon-Jones,
Eddie, and Vance, Stephanie L. 2002. "The Regulation of Explicit
and Implicit Race Bias: The Role of Motivations to Respond
without Prejudice." *Journal of Personality and Social Psychology*
82(5): 835–48. https://doi.org/10.1037/0022-3514.82.5.835

Dirks, Danielle, Heldman, Caroline, and Zack, Emma. 2015. "'She's
White and She's Hot, So She Can't Be Guilty': Female Criminality,
Penal Spectatorship, and White Protectionism." *Contemporary
Justice Review* 18(2) (April): 160–77. https://doi.org/10.1080/10
282580.2015.1025626

Domínguez D, Juan F., Nunspeet, Félice van, Gupta, Ayushi, et
al. 2018. "Lateral Orbitofrontal Cortex Activity Is Modulated

by Group Membership in Situations of Justified and Unjustified Violence." *Social Neuroscience* 13(6) (November): 739–55. https://doi.org/10.1080/17470919.2017.1392342

Du Bois, W. E. B. 2018 [1903]. The Souls of Black Folk. Myers Education Press, LLC. https://search.ebscohost.com/login.aspx?direct=true&scope=site&db=nlebk&db=nlabk&AN=1804164

Duchesne, Annie and Trujillo, Anelis Kaiser. 2021. "Reflections on Neurofeminism and Intersectionality Using Insights from Psychology." *Frontiers in Human Neuroscience* 15 (September). https://doi.org/10.3389/fnhum.2021.684412

Ebede, Tobechi and Papier, Art. 2006. "Disparities in Dermatology Educational Resources." *Journal of the American Academy of Dermatology* 55(4) (October): 687–90. https://doi.org/10.1016/j.jaad.2005.10.068

Egan, Brent M. 2010. "US Trends in Prevalence, Awareness, Treatment, and Control of Hypertension, 1988–2008." *JAMA* 303(20) (May): 2043. https://doi.org/10.1001/jama.2010.650

Einwohner, Rachel L., Kelly-Thompson, Kaitlin, Sinclair-Chapman, Valeria, et al. 2021. "Active Solidarity: Intersectional Solidarity in Action." *Social Politics: International Studies in Gender, State & Society* 28(3) (September): 704–29. https://doi.org/10.1093/sp/jxz052

Eisenberger, Naomi I. 2003. "Does Rejection Hurt? An fMRI Study of Social Exclusion." *Science* 302(5643) (October): 290–2. https://doi.org/10.1126/science.1089134

Ekman, Paul. 1971. "Universals and Cultural Differences in Facial Expressions of Emotion." *Nebraska Symposium on Motivation* 19: 207–83.

Ekman, Paul. 1992. "Are There Basic Emotions?" *Psychological Review* 99(3): 550–3. https://doi.org/10.1037/0033-295X.99.3.550

Ekman, Paul, Friesen, Wallace V, O'Sullivan, Maureen, et al. 1987. "Universals and Cultural Differences in the Judgments of Facial Expressions of Emotion." *Journal of Personality and Social Psychology* 53(4): 712–17. https://doi.org/10.1037/0022-3514.53.4.712

Elenbaas, Laura, Luken Raz, Katherine, Ackerman, Amanda, and Kneeskern, Ellen. 2022. "'This Kid Looks Like He Has Everything': 3- to 11-Year-Old Children's Concerns for Fairness and Social Preferences when Peers Differ in Social Class and Race." *Child Development* 93(5): 1527–39. https://doi.org/10.1111/cdev.13778

Elliott, James R. and Pais, Jeremy. 2006. "Race, Class, and Hurricane Katrina: Social Differences in Human Responses to

Disaster." *Social Science Research* 35(2) (June): 295–321. https:// doi.org/10.1016/j.ssresearch.2006.02.003

Emirbayer, Mustafa and Desmond, Matthew. 2015. *The Racial Order*. Chicago, IL: University of Chicago Press. https://doi.org /10.7208/chicago/9780226253664.001.0001

Emirbayer, Mustafa and Mische, Ann. 1998. "What Is Agency?" *American Journal of Sociology* 103(4) (January): 962–1023. https://doi.org/10.1086/231294

Eslinger, Paul J. and Damasio, Antonio R. 1985. "Severe Disturbance of Higher Cognition after Bilateral Frontal Lobe Ablation: Patient EVR." *Neurology* 35(12) (December): 1731. https://doi.org/10 .1212/WNL.35.12.1731

Feagin, Joe R. 1991. "The Continuing Significance of Race: Antiblack Discrimination in Public Places." *American Sociological Review* 56(1): 101–16. https://doi.org/10.2307/2095676

Feagin, Joe R. and Feagin, Clairece Booher. 2003. *Racial and Ethnic Relations*, 7th edn. Upper Saddle River, NJ: Prentice Hall.

Ferera, Matar, Baron, Andrew Scott, and Diesendruck, Gil. 2018. "Collaborative and Competitive Motivations Uniquely Impact Infants' Racial Categorization." *Evolution and Human Behavior* 39(5) (September): 511–19. https://doi.org/10.1016/j.evolhum behav.2018.05.002

Fernandez, José, García-Pérez, Mónica, and Orozco-Aleman, Sandra. 2023. "Unraveling the Hispanic Health Paradox." *Journal of Economic Perspectives* 37(1) (February): 145–68. https://doi.org/10.1257/jep.37.1.145

Ferrari, Chiara, Lega, Carlotta, Vernice, Mirta, et al. 2016. "The Dorsomedial Prefrontal Cortex Plays a Causal Role in Integrating Social Impressions from Faces and Verbal Descriptions." *Cerebral Cortex* 26(1) (January): 156–65. https://doi.org/10.1093/cercor /bhu186

Fine, Michael J., Ibrahim, Said A., and Thomas, Stephen B. 2005. "The Role of Race and Genetics in Health Disparities Research." *American Journal of Public Health* 95(12) (December): 2125–8. https://doi.org/10.2105/AJPH.2005.076588

Firat, Rengin B. 2017. "Discrimination and Well-Being: The Moderating Effects of Agentic Value Orientations." *Social Indicators Research* 134(1) (October): 167–94. https://doi.org/10 .1007/s11205-016-1425-z

Firat, Rengin B. 2019. "Opening the 'Black Box': Functions of the Frontal Lobes and Their Implications for Sociology." *Frontiers in Sociology* 4 (February): 3. https://doi.org/10.3389/fsoc.2019 .00003

Firat, Rengin B. 2021. "A Neurosociological Theory of Culturally and Structurally Situated Cognition and Ethno-Racial Stress." *Frontiers in Sociology* 6. https://doi.org/10.3389/fsoc.2021.69 5042

Firat, Rengin B. 2022. "Individualistic Values Moderate Neural Responses to Social Exclusion among African American Respondents: An FMRI Study," in W. Kalkhoff, S. R. Thye, and E. J. Lawler (eds.), "Advances in Group Processes," *Advances in Group Processes* 39: 155–86. https://doi.org/10.1108/S0882-614 520220000039008

Firat, Rengin B. and Boyer, Pascal. 2015. "Coalitional Affiliation as a Missing Link between Ethnic Polarization and Well-Being: An Empirical Test from the European Social Survey." *Social Science Research* 53 (September): 148–61. https://doi.org/10.1016/j. ssresearch.2015.05.006

Firat, Rengin and Hitlin, Steven. 2012. "Morally Bonded and Bounded: A Sociological Introduction to Neurology," in W. Kalkhoff, S. R. Thye, and E. J. Lawler (eds.), *Advances in Group Processes* 29 (Biosociology and Neurosociology): 165–99.

Firat, Rengin and McPherson, Chad Michael. 2010. "Toward an Integrated Science of Morality," in Steven Hitlin and Stephen Vaisey (eds.), *Handbook of the Sociology of Morality*. New York: Springer, pp. 361–84. https://doi.org/10.1007/978-1-4419-6896-8_19

Firat, Rengin B., Hitlin, Steven, Magnotta, Vincent, and Tranel, Daniel. 2017. "Putting Race in Context: Social Class Modulates Processing of Race in the Ventromedial Prefrontal Cortex and Amygdala." *Social Cognitive and Affective Neuroscience* 12(8) (August): 1314–24. https://doi.org/10.1093/scan/nsx052

Fiske, Susan T. 2009. "From Dehumanization and Objectification to Rehumanization." *Annals of the New York Academy of Sciences* 1167(1): 31–4. https://doi.org/10.1111/j.1749-6632.2009.04544 .x

Fiske, Susan T. and Taylor, Shelley E. 2013. *Social Cognition: From Brains to Culture*, 2nd edn. Los Angeles: SAGE.

Flegal, Katherine M., Carroll, Margaret D., Kit, Brian K., and Ogden, Cynthia L. 2012. "Prevalence of Obesity and Trends in the Distribution of Body Mass Index among US Adults, 1999–2010." *JAMA* 307(5) (February): 491. https://doi.org/10. 1001/jama.2012.39

Flores, Osly J. and Gunzenhauser, Michael G. 2019. "The Problems with Colorblind Leadership Revealed: A Call for Race-Conscious Leaders." *International Journal of Qualitative Studies in*

Education 32(8) (September): 963–81. https://doi.org/10.1080 /09518398.2019.1635278

Flynn, Frederick G. 1999. "Anatomy of the Insula Functional and Clinical Correlates." *Aphasiology* 13(1) (January): 55–78. https:// doi.org/10.1080/026870399402325

Fong, Clara and Kelly, Percival. 2024. "Making the Census Work for Latinos" (Brennan Center for Justice), December 20. https:// www.brennancenter.org/our-work/analysis-opinion/making-census-work-latinos

Forman, Steven D., Cohen, Jonathan D., Fitzgerald, Michael, Eddy, William F., Mintun, Mark A., and Noll, Douglas C. 1995. "Improved Assessment of Significant Activation in Functional Magnetic Resonance Imaging (fMRI): Use of a Cluster-Size Threshold." *Magnetic Resonance in Medicine* 33(5) (May): 636–47. https://doi.org/10.1002/mrm.1910330508

Forscher, Patrick S., Mitamura, Chelsea, Dix, Emily L., Cox, William T. L., and Devine, Patricia G. 2017. "Breaking the Prejudice Habit: Mechanisms, Timecourse, and Longevity." *Journal of Experimental Social Psychology* 72 (September): 133–46. https:// doi.org/10.1016/j.jesp.2017.04.009

Fox, Cybelle and Bloemraad, Irene. 2015. "Beyond 'White by Law': Explaining the Gulf in Citizenship Acquisition between Mexican and European Immigrants, 1930." *Social Forces* 94(1) (September): 181–207. https://doi.org/10.1093/sf/sov009

Franks, David D. 2010. *Neurosociology: The Nexus between Neuroscience and Social Psychology*. New York: Springer.

Franks, David D. 2019. *Neurosociology: Fundamentals and Current Findings*. (SpringerBriefs in Sociology). Dordrecht: Springer Netherlands.. https://doi.org/10.1007/978-94-024-1600-8

Franks, David D. and Turner, Jonathan H. (eds.). 2013. *Handbook of Neurosociology*. (Handbooks of Sociology and Social Research). Dordrecht: Springer Netherlands, https://doi.org/10.1007/978-94 -007-4473-8

Frith, Chris and Frith, Uta. 2005. "Theory of Mind." *Current Biology* 15(17) (September): R644–5. https://doi.org/10.1016 /j.cub.2005.08.041

Gaertner, Samuel L. and Dovidio, John F. 1977. "The Subtlety of White Racism, Arousal, and Helping Behavior." *Journal of Personality and Social Psychology* 35(10): 691–707. https://doi .org/10.1037/0022-3514.35.10.691

Gallate, Jason, Wong, Cara, Ellwood, Sophie, Chi, Richard, and Snyder, Allan. 2011. "Noninvasive Brain Stimulation Reduces Prejudice Scores on an Implicit Association Test." *Neuropsychology* 25(2): 185–92. https://doi.org/10.1037/a0021102

Gawerc, Michelle I. 2021. "Coalition-Building and the Forging of Solidarity across Difference and Inequality." *Sociology Compass* 15(3): e12858. https://doi.org/10.1111/soc4.12858

Gawronski, Bertram, Brownstein, Michael, and Madva, Alex. 2022. "How Should We Think about Implicit Measures and Their Empirical 'Anomalies'?" *WIREs Cognitive Science* 13(3): e1590. https://doi.org/10.1002/wcs.1590

Geraci, Alessandra, Commodari, Elena, and Perucchini, Paola. 2024. "Early Intergroup Coalition: Toddlers Attribute Fair Distributions to Black Rather than White Distributors." *Social Development* 33(4): e12740. https://doi.org/10.1111/sode.12740

Geronimus, Arline T., Bound, John, Waidmann, Timothy A., Hillemeier, Marianne M., and Burns, Patricia B. 1996. "Excess Mortality among Blacks and Whites in the United States." *New England Journal of Medicine* 335(21) (November): 1552–8. https://doi.org/10.1056/NEJM199611213352102

Ghosh, Vanessa E., Moscovitch, Morris, Colella, Brenda Melo, and Gilboa, Asaf. 2014. "Schema Representation in Patients with Ventromedial PFC Lesions." *Journal of Neuroscience* 34(36) (September): 12057–70. https://doi.org/10.1523/JNEUROSCI.07 40-14.2014

Gibson, Bentley, Robbins, Erin, and Rochat, Philippe. 2015. "White Bias in 3–7-Year-Old Children across Cultures." *Journal of Cognition & Culture* 15(3/4) (June): 344–73. https://doi.org /10.1163/15685373-12342155

Gilbert, Gustave M. 1951. "Stereotype Persistence and Change among College Students." *Journal of Abnormal and Social Psychology* 46(2) (April): 245–54. https://doi.org/10.1037/h005 3696

Gilbert, Sam J., Swencionis, Jillian K., and Amodio, David M. 2012. "Evaluative vs. Trait Representation in Intergroup Social Judgments: Distinct Roles of Anterior Temporal Lobe and Prefrontal Cortex." *Neuropsychologia* 50(14) (December): 3600–11. https://doi.org/10.1016/j.neuropsychologia.2012.09.002

Gilmore, John H., Knickmeyer Santelli, Rebecca, and Gao, Wei. 2018. "Imaging Structural and Functional Brain Development in Early Childhood." *Nature Reviews. Neuroscience* 19(3) (February): 123. https://doi.org/10.1038/nrn.2018.1

Giuliano, Ariana E., Bonasia, Kyra, Ghosh, Vanessa E., Moscovitch, Morris, and Gilboa, Asaf. 2021. "Differential Influence of Ventromedial Prefrontal Cortex Lesions on Neural Representations of Schema and Semantic Category Knowledge." *Journal of Cognitive Neuroscience* (June): 1–28. https://doi.org /10.1162/jocn_a_01746

Goff, Phillip Atiba, Jackson, Matthew Christian, Di Leone, Brooke Allison Lewis, Culotta, Carmen Marie, and DiTomasso, Natalie Ann. 2014. "The Essence of Innocence: Consequences of Dehumanizing Black Children." *Journal of Personality and Social Psychology* 106(4)): 526–45. https://doi.org/10.1037/a0035663

Goff, Phillip Atiba, Thomas, Margaret A., and Jackson, Matthew Christian. 2008. "'Ain't I a Woman?' Towards an Intersectional Approach to Person Perception and Group-Based Harms." *Sex Roles* 59(5) (September): 392–403. https://doi.org/10.1007/s111 99-008-9505-4

Goleman, Daniel. 1998. *Working with Emotional Intelligence*. New York: Bantam Books.

Gonder, Mary Katherine, Locatelli, Sabrina, Ghobrial, Lora, et al. 2011. "Evidence from Cameroon Reveals Differences in the Genetic Structure and Histories of Chimpanzee Populations." *Proceedings of the National Academy of Sciences* 108(12) (March): 4766–71. https://doi.org/10.1073/pnas.1015422108

González-Arias, Mauricio and Aracena, Daniela. 2022. "Are the Concepts of Emotion Special? A Comparison between Basic-Emotion, Secondary-Emotion, Abstract, and Concrete Words." *Frontiers in Psychology* 13. https://doi.org/10.3389/fpsyg.2022.915165

Goosby, Bridget J., Cheadle, Jacob E., and Mitchell, Colter. 2018. "Stress-Related Biosocial Mechanisms of Discrimination and African American Health Inequities." *Annual Review of Sociology* 44(1) (July): 319–40. https://doi.org/10.1146/annurev-soc-060116-053403

Gover, Angela R., Harper, Shannon B., and Langton, Lynn. 2020. "Anti-Asian Hate Crime during the COVID-19 Pandemic: Exploring the Reproduction of Inequality." *American Journal of Criminal Justice* 45(4) (August): 647–67. https://doi.org/10.1007/s12103-020-09545-1

Graham, Jesse and Haidt, Jonathan. 2012. "Sacred Values and Evil Adversaries: A Moral Foundations Approach," in M. Mikulincer and P. R. Shaver (eds.), *The Social Psychology of Morality: Exploring the Causes of Good and Evil* (Herzliya Series on Personality and Social Psychology). Washington, DC: American Psychological Association, pp. 11–31. https://doi.org/10.1037/13091-001

Green, Kayla H., van de Groep, Ilse H., Te Brinke, Lysanne W., van der Cruijsen, Renske, van Rossenberg, Fabienne, and El Marroun, Hanan. 2022. "A Perspective on Enhancing Representative Samples in Developmental Human Neuroscience:

Connecting Science to Society." *Frontiers in Integrative Neuroscience* 16 (September). https://doi.org/10.3389/fnint.2022.981 657

Greene, Joshua. 2001. "An fMRI Investigation of Emotional Engagement in Moral Judgment." *Science* 293(5537) (September): 2105–8. https://doi.org/10.1126/science.1062872

Greene, Joshua D. 2007. "Why Are VMPFC Patients More Utilitarian? A Dual-Process Theory of Moral Judgment Explains." *Trends in Cognitive Sciences* 11(8) (August): 322–3. https://doi .org/10.1016/j.tics.2007.06.004

Greene, Joshua D. 2009. "Dual-Process Morality and the Personal/ Impersonal Distinction: A Reply to McGuire, Langdon, Coltheart, and Mackenzie." *Journal of Experimental Social Psychology* 45(3) (May): 581–4. https://doi.org/10.1016/j.jesp.2009.01.003

Greene, Joshua D. 2023. "The Dual-Process Theory of Moral Judgment Does Not Deny that People Can Make Compromise Judgments." *Proceedings of the National Academy of Sciences* 120(6) (February): e2220396120. https://doi.org/10.1073/pnas .2220396120

Greenwald, Anthony G. and Banaji, Mahzarin R. 1995. "Implicit Social Cognition: Attitudes, Self-Esteem, and Stereotypes." *Psychological Review* 102(1): 4–27. https://doi.org/10.1037/00 33-295X.102.1.4

Greenwald, Anthony G., McGhee, Debbie E., and Schwartz, Jordan L. K. 1998. "Measuring Individual Differences in Implicit Cognition: The Implicit Association Test." *Journal of Personality and Social Psychology* 74(6): 1464–80. https://doi.org/10.1037 /0022-3514.74.6.1464

Guzman, Gloria. 2024. "Median Household Income Increased in 2023 for First Time since 2019." US Census. https://www.cen sus.gov/library/stories/2024/09/household-income-race-hispanic .html

Haggard, Patrick. 2017. "Sense of Agency in the Human Brain." *Nature Reviews Neuroscience* 18(4) (April): 196–207. https://doi .org/10.1038/nrn.2017.14

Haidt, Jonathan. 2001. "The Emotional Dog and Its Rational Tail: A Social Intuitionist Approach to Moral Judgment." *Psychological Review* 108(4): 814–34. https://doi.org/10.1037/0033-295X.108 .4.814

Haidt, Jonathan. 2007. "The New Synthesis in Moral Psychology." *Science* 316(5827) (May): 998–1002. https://doi.org/10.1126/ science.1137651

Haidt, Jonathan. 2013. "Moral Psychology and the Law: How Intuitions Drive Reasoning, Judgment, and the Search for

Evidence." Meador Lecture Series 2011–2012. *Alabama Law Review* 64(4): 867–80.

Haidt, Jonathan and Hersh, Matthew A. 2001. "Sexual Morality: The Cultures and Emotions of Conservatives and Liberals." *Journal of Applied Social Psychology* 31(1): 191–221. https://doi.org/10.1111/j.1559-1816.2001.tb02489.x

Hamilton, Jon. 2023. "Meet the 'Glass-Half-Full Girl' Whose Brain Rewired after Losing a Hemisphere." NPR, March 2 (sec. Treatments). https://www.npr.org/sections/health-shots/2023/03/22/1165131907/neuroplasticity-plasticity-glass-half-full-girl

Hamlin, J. Kiley, Wynn, Karen, and Bloom, Paul. 2007. "Social Evaluation by Preverbal Infants." *Nature* 450(7169) (November): 557–9. https://doi.org/10.1038/nature06288

Hanchard, Michael. 1991. "Racial Consciousness and Afro-diasporic Experiences: Antonio Gramsci Reconsidered." *Socialism and Democracy* 7(3) (December): 83–106. https://doi.org/10.1080/08854309108428108

Handley, Grace, Kubota, Jennifer T., and Cloutier, Jasmin. 2023. "Reading the Mind in the Eyes of Black and White People: Interracial Contact and Perceived Race Affects Brain Activity when Inferring Mental States." *NeuroImage* 269 (April): 119910. https://doi.org/10.1016/j.neuroimage.2023.119910

Harris, Lasana T. and Fiske, Susan T. 2006. "Dehumanizing the Lowest of the Low: Neuroimaging Responses to Extreme Out-Groups." *Psychological Science* 17(10) (October): 847–53. https://doi.org/10.1111/j.1467-9280.2006.01793.x

Hart, Allen J., Whalen, Paul J., Shin, Lisa M., McInerney, Sean C., Fischer, Håkan, and Rauch, Scott L. 2000. "Differential Response in the Human Amygdala to Racial Outgroup vs Ingroup Face Stimuli." *NeuroReport* 11(11) (August): 2351–4. https://doi.org/10.1097/00001756-200008030-00004

Harvard Opinion Research Program. 2018. "Discrimination in America." https://content.sph.harvard.edu/wwwhsph/sites/94/2018/01/NPR-RWJF-HSPH-Discrimination-Final-Summary.pdf/

Haskell, Rob. 2018. "Serena Williams on Her Comeback." Vogue Cover Interview. https://www.vogue.com/article/serena-williams-vogue-cover-interview-february-2018

Haslam, Nick. 2006. "Dehumanization: An Integrative Review." *Personality and Social Psychology Review* 10(3) (August): 252–64. https://doi.org/10.1207/s15327957pspr1003_4

Hausmann, Leslie R. M., Kwoh, C. Kent, Hannon, Michael J., and Ibrahim, Said A. 2013. "Perceived Racial Discrimination in Health Care and Race Differences in Physician Trust." *Race and*

Social Problems 5(2) (June): 113–20. https://doi.org/10.1007/s12 552-013-9092-z

Haxby, James V., Hoffman, Elizabeth A., and Gobbini, M. I. 2000. "The Distributed Human Neural System for Face Perception." *Trends in Cognitive Sciences* 4(6) (June): 223–33. https://doi.org /10.1016/S1364-6613(00)01482-0

Hebb, D. O. 1949. "The First Stage of Perception: Growth of the Assembly." *The Organization of Behavior* 4(60): 78–60.

Hehman, Eric, Ingbretsen, Zachary A., and Freeman, Jonathan B. 2014. "The Neural Basis of Stereotypic Impact on Multiple Social Categorization." *NeuroImage* 101 (November): 704–11. https:// doi.org/10.1016/j.neuroimage.2014.07.056

Henrich, Joseph, Heine, Steven J., and Norenzayan, Ara. 2010. "The Weirdest People in the World?" *Behavioral and Brain Sciences* 33(2–3) (June): 61–83. https://doi.org/10.1017/S01405 25X0999152X

Herrington, John D., Taylor, James M., Grupe, Daniel W., Curby, Kim M., and Schultz, Robert T. 2011. "Bidirectional Communication between Amygdala and Fusiform Gyrus during Facial Recognition." *NeuroImage* 56(4) (June): 2348–55. https:// doi.org/10.1016/j.neuroimage.2011.03.072

Hildebrandt, Lea K., McCall, Cade, and Singer, Tania. 2017. "Differential Effects of Attention-, Compassion-, and Socio-Cognitively Based Mental Practices on Self-Reports of Mindfulness and Compassion." *Mindfulness* 8(6) (December): 1488–1512. https://doi.org/10.1007/s12671-017-0716-z

Hilton, James L. and von Hippel, William. 1996. "Stereotypes." *Annual Review of Psychology* 47 (February): 237–71. https://doi .org/10.1146/annurev.psych.47.1.237

Hitlin, Steven. 2008. *Moral Selves, Evil Selves: The Social Psychology of Conscience*, 1st edn. New York: Palgrave Macmillan.

Hitlin, Steven and Elder, Glen H. 2007. "Time, Self, and the Curiously Abstract Concept of Agency." *Sociological Theory* 25(2) (June): 170–91. https://doi.org/10.1111/j.1467-9558.2007 .00303.x

Hitlin, Steven and Kirkpatrick Johnson, Monica. 2015. "Reconceptualizing Agency within the Life Course: The Power of Looking Ahead." *American Journal of Sociology* 120(5): 1429–72. https://doi.org/10.1086/681216

Hitlin, Steven and Long, Charisse. 2009. "Agency as a Sociological Variable: A Preliminary Model of Individuals, Situations, and the Life Course." *Sociology Compass* 3(1): 137–60. https://doi.org /10.1111/j.1751-9020.2008.00189.x

Hochschild, Arlie Russell. 1983. *The Managed Heart:*

Commercialization of Human Feeling. Berkeley, CA: University of California Press.

Hogg, Michael A. 2001. "Social Categorization, Depersonalization, and Group Behavior," in Michael Hogg and Scott Tindale (eds.), *Blackwell Handbook of Social Psychology: Group Processes.* Hoboken, NJ: John Wiley & Sons, pp. 56–85. https://doi.org/10.1002/9780470998458.ch3

Huguley, James P., Wang, Ming-Te, Vasquez, Ariana C., and Guo, Jiesi. 2019. "Parental Ethnic–Racial Socialization Practices and the Construction of Children of Color's Ethnic–Racial Identity: A Research Synthesis and Meta-Analysis." *Psychological Bulletin* 145(5): 437–58. https://doi.org/10.1037/bul0000187

Iacoboni, Marco. 2009. "Imitation, Empathy, and Mirror Neurons." *Annual Review of Psychology* 60 (January): 653–70. https://doi.org/10.1146/annurev.psych.60.110707.163604

Ignatow, Gabriel. 2007. "Theories of Embodied Knowledge: New Directions for Cultural and Cognitive Sociology?" *Journal for the Theory of Social Behaviour* 37(2) (June): 115–35. https://doi.org/10.1111/j.1468-5914.2007.00328.x

Ignatow, Gabriel. 2009. "Why the Sociology of Morality Needs Bourdieu's Habitus." *Sociological Inquiry* 79(1): 98–114. https://doi.org/10.1111/j.1475-682X.2008.00273.x

Ito, Tiffany A. and Bartholow, Bruce D. 2009. "The Neural Correlates of Race." *Trends in Cognitive Sciences* 13(12) (December): 524–31. https://doi.org/10.1016/j.tics.2009.10.002

Izard, Carroll E. 2007. "Basic Emotions, Natural Kinds, Emotion Schemas, and a New Paradigm." *Perspectives on Psychological Science* 2(3) (September): 260–80. https://doi.org/10.1111/j.1745-6916.2007.00044.x

Izard, Carroll E. 2009. "Emotion Theory and Research: Highlights, Unanswered Questions, and Emerging Issues." *Annual Review of Psychology* 60(1) (January): 1–25. https://doi.org/10.1146/annurev.psych.60.110707.163539

Izard, Carroll E. 2011. "Forms and Functions of Emotions: Matters of Emotion–Cognition Interactions." *Emotion Review* 3(4) (October): 371–8. https://doi.org/10.1177/1754073911410737

Izard, Carroll, Stark, Kevin, Trentacosta, Christopher, and Schultz, David. 2008. "Beyond Emotion Regulation: Emotion Utilization and Adaptive Functioning." *Child Development Perspectives* 2(3): 156–63. https://doi.org/10.1111/j.1750-8606.2008.00058.x

James, Drexler. 2020. "Health and Health-Related Correlates of Internalized Racism among Racial/Ethnic Minorities: A Review of the Literature." *Journal of Racial and Ethnic Health Disparities*

7(4) (August): 785–806. https://doi.org/10.1007/s40615-020-00726-6

James, Drexler. 2022. "An Initial Framework for the Study of Internalized Racism and Health: Internalized Racism as a Racism-Induced Identity Threat Response." *Social and Personality Psychology Compass* 16(11): e12712. https://doi.org/10.1111/spc3.12712

Javanbakht, Arash, King, Anthony P., Evans, Gary W., et al. 2015. "Childhood Poverty Predicts Adult Amygdala and Frontal Activity and Connectivity in Response to Emotional Faces." *Frontiers in Behavioral Neuroscience* 9 (June). https://doi.org/10.3389/fnbeh.2015.00154

Jim Crow Museum. 2024. "The Mammy Caricature." https://jimcrowmuseum.ferris.edu/mammies/homepage.htm

Johns Hopkins Bloomberg School of Public Health. 2019. "US Health Care Spending Highest among Developed Countries." Bloomberg School of Public Health, January 7. https://publichealth.jhu.edu/2019/us-health-care-spending-highest-among-developed-countries

Johnson, Lauri. 2014. "Culturally Responsive Leadership for Community Empowerment." *Multicultural Education Review* 6(2) (January): 145–70. https://doi.org/10.1080/2005615X.2014.11102915

Jones, Amyri. 2025. "Opinion: Beyoncé's Grammy Award-Winning Album Is Just a Gimmick." *Reveille* (blog), February 6. https://lsureveille.com/248440/opinion/beyonce-didnt-deserve-album-of-the-year/

Joseph, Tiffany and Golash-Boza, Tanya. 2021. "Double Consciousness in the 21st Century: Du Boisian Theory and the Problem of Racialized Legal Status." *Social Sciences* 10(9) (September): 345. https://doi.org/10.3390/socsci10090345

Kalev, Alexandra, Dobbin, Frank, and Kelly, Erin. 2006. "Best Practices or Best Guesses? Assessing the Efficacy of Corporate Affirmative Action and Diversity Policies." *American Sociological Review* 71(4) (August): 589–617. https://doi.org/10.1177/000312240607100404

Kalkhoff, Will, Thye, Shane R., and Pollock, Joshua. 2016. "Developments in Neurosociology." *Sociology Compass* 10(3): 242–58. https://doi.org/10.1111/soc4.12355

Kanwisher, Nancy, Woods, Roger P., Iacoboni, Marco, and Mazziotta, John C. 1997. "A Locus in Human Extrastriate Cortex for Visual Shape Analysis." *Journal of Cognitive Neuroscience* 9(1) (January): 133–42. https://doi.org/10.1162/jocn.1997.9.1.133

Kanwisher, Nancy and Yovel, Galit. 2006. "The Fusiform Face Area: A Cortical Region Specialized for the Perception of Faces." *Philosophical Transactions of the Royal Society B: Biological Sciences* 361(1476) (November): 2109–28. https://doi.org/10.1098/rstb.2006.1934

Katz, Daniel and Braly, Kenneth. 1933. "Racial Stereotypes of One Hundred College Students." *Journal of Abnormal and Social Psychology* 28(3): 280–90. https://doi.org/10.1037/h0074049

Kay, Aaron C., Day, Martin V., Zanna, Mark P., and Nussbaum, A. David. 2013. "The Insidious (and Ironic) Effects of Positive Stereotypes." *Journal of Experimental Social Psychology* 49(2) (March): 287–91. https://doi.org/10.1016/j.jesp.2012.11.003

Kelly, David J., Liu, Shaoying, Ge, Liezhong, et al. 2007. "Cross-Race Preferences for Same-Race Faces Extend beyond the African versus Caucasian Contrast in 3-Month-Old Infants." *Infancy: The Official Journal of the International Society on Infant Studies* 11(1): 87–95. https://pmc.ncbi.nlm.nih.gov/articles/PMC2575407

Kelly, David J., Quinn, Paul C., Slater, Alan M., et al. 2005. "Three-Month-Olds, but Not Newborns, Prefer Own-Race Faces." *Developmental Science* 8(6): F31–6. https://doi.org/10.1111/j.1467-7687.2005.0434a.x

Kennedy-Moulton, Kate, Miller, Sarah, Persson, Petra, Rossin-Slater, Maya, Wherry, Laura, and Aldana, Gloria. 2022. "Maternal and Infant Health Inequality: New Evidence from Linked Administrative Data." National Bureau of Economic Research Working Paper Series (November). https://doi.org/10.3386/w30693

Keyes, Corey L. M. 2009. "The Black–White Paradox in Health: Flourishing in the Face of Social Inequality and Discrimination." *Journal of Personality* 77(6) (December): 1677–1706. https://doi.org/10.1111/j.1467-6494.2009.00597.x

Keysers, Christian and Gazzola, Valeria. 2014. "Hebbian Learning and Predictive Mirror Neurons for Actions, Sensations and Emotions." *Philosophical Transactions of the Royal Society B: Biological Sciences* 369(1644) (June): 20130175. https://doi.org/10.1098/rstb.2013.0175

Keysers, Christian and Perrett, David I. 2004. "Demystifying Social Cognition: A Hebbian Perspective." *Trends in Cognitive Sciences* 8(11) (November): 501–7. https://doi.org/10.1016/j.tics.2004.09.005

Kim, Kyungmi and Johnson, Marcia K. 2015. "Activity in Ventromedial Prefrontal Cortex during Self-Related Processing: Positive Subjective Value or Personal Significance?" *Social*

Cognitive and Affective Neuroscience 10(4) (April): 494–500. https://doi.org/10.1093/scan/nsu078

Kim, Pilyoung, Evans, Gary W., Angstadt, Michael, et al. 2013. "Effects of Childhood Poverty and Chronic Stress on Emotion Regulatory Brain Function in Adulthood." *Proceedings of the National Academy of Sciences* 110(46) (November): 18442–7. https://doi.org/10.1073/pnas.1308240110

Kinder, Donald R. and Sears, David O. 1981. "Prejudice and Politics: Symbolic Racism versus Racial Threats to the Good Life." *Journal of Personality and Social Psychology* 40(3): 414–31. https://doi.org/10.1037/0022-3514.40.3.414

Kinzler, Katherine D. and Spelke, Elizabeth S. 2011. "Do Infants Show Social Preferences for People Differing in Race?" *Cognition* 119(1) (April): 1–9. https://doi.org/10.1016/j.cognition.2010.10.019

Knutson, Kristine M., Mah, Linda, Manly, Charlotte F., and Grafman, Jordan. 2007. "Neural Correlates of Automatic Beliefs about Gender and Race." *Human Brain Mapping* 28(10) (October): 915–30. https://doi.org/10.1002/hbm.20320

Kohlberg, Lawrence. 1963. "The Development of Children's Orientations toward a Moral Order I: Sequence in the Development of Moral Thought." *Vita Humana* 6(1/2): 11–33. http://www.jstor.org/stable/26762149

Kohlberg, Lawrence. 1971. "Stages of Moral Development as a Basis for Moral Education," in Clive M. Beck, Brian S. Crittenden, and Edmund Sullivan (eds.), *Moral Education*. Toronto: University of Toronto Press, pp. 23–92. https://doi.org/10.3138/9781442656758-004

Kok, Bethany E. and Singer, Tania. 2017. "Phenomenological Fingerprints of Four Meditations: Differential State Changes in Affect, Mind-Wandering, Meta-Cognition, and Interoception before and after Daily Practice across 9 Months of Training." *Mindfulness* 8(1) (February): 218–31. https://doi.org/10.1007/s12671-016-0594-9

Korkın, Erhan. 2020. "Merkez-Çevre Ayrımından Beyaz-Zenci Türk Ayrımına Türk Siyasal Hayatında Sosyal Bölünme." *Akademik İzdüşüm Dergisi* 5(2): 250–65.

Kragel, Philip A., Reddan, Marianne C., LaBar, Kevin S., and Wager, Tor D. 2019. "Emotion Schemas Are Embedded in the Human Visual System." *Science Advances* 5(7) (July): eaaw4358. https://doi.org/10.1126/sciadv.aaw4358

Kral, Tammi R. A., Williams, Claire Y., Wylie, Abigail C., et al. 2024. "Intergenerational Effects of Racism on Amygdala and Hippocampus Resting State Functional Connectivity." *Scientific*

Reports 14(1) (July): 17034. https://doi.org/10.1038/s41598-024 -66830-3

Krieger, Nancy. 2005. "Stormy Weather: Race, Gene Expression, and the Science of Health Disparities." *American Journal of Public Health* 95(12) (December): 2155–60. https://doi.org/ 10.2105/AJPH.2005.067108

Kringelbach, Morten L. 2005. "The Human Orbitofrontal Cortex: Linking Reward to Hedonic Experience." *Nature Reviews Neuroscience* 6(9) (September): 691–702. https://doi.org/10.10 38/nrn1747

Kroenke, Kurt, Strine, Tara W., Spitzer, Robert L., Williams, Janet B.W., Berry, Joyce T., and Mokdad, Ali H. 2009. "The PHQ-8 as a Measure of Current Depression in the General Population." *Journal of Affective Disorders* 114(1–3) (April): 163–73. https://doi.org/10.1016/j.jad.2008.06.026

Kroenke, Kurt, Wu, Jingwei, Yu, Zhangsheng, et al. 2016. "Patient Health Questionnaire Anxiety and Depression Scale: Initial Validation in Three Clinical Trials." *Psychosomatic Medicine* 78(6): 716–27. https://doi.org/10.1097/PSY.0000000000000322

Kubota, Jennifer T. 2024. "Uncovering Implicit Racial Bias in the Brain: The Past, Present & Future." *Daedalus* 153(1) (March): 84–105. https://doi.org/10.1162/daed_a_02050

Kubota, Jennifer T., Banaji, Mahzarin R., and Phelps, Elizabeth A. 2012. "The Neuroscience of Race." *Nature Neuroscience* 15(7) (July): 940–8. https://doi.org/10.1038/nn.3136

Kunstman, Jonathan W. and Plant, E. Ashby. 2008. "Racing to Help: Racial Bias in High Emergency Helping Situations." *Journal of Personality and Social Psychology* 95(6): 1499–1510. https:// doi.org/10.1037/a0012822

Kurian, Anita K. and Cardarelli, Kathryn M. 2007. "Racial and Ethnic Differences in Cardiovascular Disease Risk Factors: A Systematic Review." *Ethnicity & Disease* 17(1): 143–52.

Kurzban, Robert, Tooby, John, and Cosmides, Leda. 2001. "Can Race Be Erased? Coalitional Computation and Social Categorization." *Proceedings of the National Academy of Sciences* 98, no. 26 (December): 15387–92. https://doi.org/10.10 73/pnas.251541498

Kuzawa, Christopher W. and Sweet, Elizabeth. 2009. "Epigenetics and the Embodiment of Race: Developmental Origins of US Racial Disparities in Cardiovascular Health." *American Journal of Human Biology* 21(1): 2–15. https://doi.org/10.1002/ajhb.20822

Kwok, Veronica, Niu, Zhendong, Kay, Paul, et al. 2011. "Learning New Color Names Produces Rapid Increase in Gray Matter in the Intact Adult Human Cortex." *Proceedings of the National*

Academy of Sciences 108(16) (April): 6686–8. https://doi.org/10
.1073/pnas.1103217108

La Scala, Shayna, Mullins, Jordan L., Firat, Rengin B., Emotional Learning Research Community Advisory Board, and Michalska, Kalina J. 2023. "Equity, Diversity, and Inclusion in Developmental Neuroscience: Practical Lessons from Community-Based Participatory Research." *Frontiers in Integrative Neuroscience* 16 (March). https://doi.org/10.3389/fnint.2022.1007249

Labrakakis, Charalampos. 2023. "The Role of the Insular Cortex in Pain." *International Journal of Molecular Sciences* 24(6) (March): 5736. https://doi.org/10.3390/ijms24065736

Lacy, Michael G. and Haspel, Kathleen C. 2011. "Apocalypse: The Media's Framing of Black Looters, Shooters, and Brutes in Hurricane Katrina's Aftermath," in Michael G. Lacy and Kent A. Ono (eds.), *Critical Rhetorics of Race*. New York: New York University Press. https://doi.org/10.18574/nyu/9780814762226.003.0001

Lahav, Amir, Saltzman, Elliot, and Schlaug, Gottfried. 2007. "Action Representation of Sound: Audiomotor Recognition Network while Listening to Newly Acquired Actions." *Journal of Neuroscience* 27(2) (January): 308–14. https://doi.org/10.1523/JNEUROSCI.4822-06.2007

Lamm, Claus, Meltzoff, Andrew N., and Decety, Jean. 2010. "How Do We Empathize with Someone Who Is Not Like Us? A Functional Magnetic Resonance Imaging Study." *Journal of Cognitive Neuroscience* 22(2) (February): 362–76. https://doi.org/10.1162/jocn.2009.21186

Lamont, Michèle. 1992. *Money, Morals, and Manners: The Culture of the French and American Upper-Middle Class* (Morality and Society series). Chicago, IL: University of Chicago Press.

Lamont, Michèle. 2000. *The Dignity of Working Men: Morality and the Boundaries of Race, Class, and Immigration*. New York and Cambridge, MA: Russell Sage Foundation and Harvard University Press.

LaMotte, Megan E., Elliott, Marta, and Mouzon, Dawne M. 2023. "Revisiting the Black–White Mental Health Paradox during the Coronavirus Pandemic." *Journal of Racial and Ethnic Health Disparities* 10(6) (December): 2802–15. https://doi.org/10.1007/s40615-022-01457-6

Lang, Marissa J., Alexander, Keith L., Duggan, Paul, et al. 2018. "Anger over Farrakhan Ties Prompts Calls for Women's March Leaders to Resign." *Washington Post*, November 22. https://www.washingtonpost.com/local/anger-over-farrakhan-ties-

prompts-calls-for-womens-march-leaders-to-resign/2018/11/21/
6d925942-edb4-11e8-8679-934a2b33be52_story.html

Laniyonu, Ayobami. 2019. "A Comparative Analysis of Black Racial Group Consciousness in the United States and Britain." *Journal of Race, Ethnicity, and Politics* 4(1) (March): 117–47. https://doi.org/10.1017/rep.2018.28

LeDoux, Joseph E. 2000. "Emotion Circuits in the Brain." *Annual Review of Neuroscience* 23(1) (March): 155–84. https://doi.org /10.1146/annurev.neuro.23.1.155

LeDoux, Joseph. 2007. "The Amygdala." *Current Biology* 17(20) (October 23): R868–74. https://doi.org/10.1016/j.cub.2007.08 .005

Lee, Kyoung-Uk, Khang, Hyun Soo, Kim, Ki-Tae, et al. 2008. "Distinct Processing of Facial Emotion of Own-Race versus Other-Race." *NeuroReport* 19(10) (July): 1021–5. https://doi.org /10.1097/WNR.0b013e3283052df2

Legal Defense Fund. 2024. "The Significance of 'The Doll Test.'" https://www.naacpldf.org/brown-vs-board/significance-doll-test/

Leidner, Bernhard, Castano, Emanuele, Zaiser, Erica, and Giner-Sorolla, Roger. 2010. "Ingroup Glorification, Moral Disengagement, and Justice in the Context of Collective Violence." *Personality and Social Psychology Bulletin* 36(8) (August): 1115–29. https://doi.org/10.1177/0146167210376391

Leyens, Jacques-Philippe, Cortes, Brezo, Demoulin, Stéphanie, et al. 2003. "Emotional Prejudice, Essentialism, and Nationalism: The 2002 Tajfel Lecture." *European Journal of Social Psychology* 33(6) (November): 703–17. https://doi.org/10.1002/ejsp.170

Li, Tianyi, Cardenas-Iniguez, Carlos, Correll, Joshua, and Cloutier, Jasmin. 2016. "The Impact of Motivation on Race-Based Impression Formation." *NeuroImage* 124(A) (January): 1–7. https://doi.org/10.1016/j.neuroimage.2015.08.035

Liberman, Zoe, Woodward, Amanda L., and Kinzler, Katherine D. 2017. "The Origins of Social Categorization." *Trends in Cognitive Sciences* 21(7) (July): 556–68. https://doi.org/10.1016 /j.tics.2017.04.004

Liberzon, Israel, Ma, Sean T., Okada, Go, Ho, S. Shaun, Swain, James E., and Evans, Gary W. 2015. "Childhood Poverty and Recruitment of Adult Emotion Regulatory Neurocircuitry." *Social Cognitive and Affective Neuroscience* 10(11) (November): 1596–606. https://doi.org/10.1093/scan/nsv045

Lichter, Daniel T., Thiede, Brian C., and Brooks, Matthew M. 2023. "Racial Diversity and Segregation: Comparing Principal Cities, Inner-Ring Suburbs, Outlying Suburbs, and the Suburban

Fringe." *Russell Sage Foundation Journal of the Social Sciences* 9(1): 26–51. https://doi.org/10.7758/RSF.2023.9.1.02

Lieberman, Matthew D. 2007. "Social Cognitive Neuroscience: A Review of Core Processes." *Annual Review of Psychology* 58(1) (January): 259–89. https://doi.org/10.1146/annurev.psych.58. 110405.085654

Lieberman, Matthew D., Hariri, Ahmad, Jarcho, Johanna M., Eisenberger, Naomi I., and Bookheimer, Susan Y. 2005. "An fMRI Investigation of Race-Related Amygdala Activity in African-American and Caucasian–American Individuals." *Nature Neuroscience* 8(6) (June): 720–2. https://doi.org/10.1038/nn1465

Limandjaja, Grace C., Niessen, Frank B., Scheper, Rik J., and Gibbs, Susan. 2020. "The Keloid Disorder: Heterogeneity, Histopathology, Mechanisms and Models." *Frontiers in Cell and Developmental Biology* 8 (May): 1–26. https://doi.org/10.3389/fcell.2020.00360

Link, Bruce G. and Phelan, Jo. 1995. "Social Conditions as Fundamental Causes of Disease." *Journal of Health and Social Behavior* 35: 80. https://doi.org/10.2307/2626958

Lizardo, Omar. 2004. "The Cognitive Origins of Bourdieu's Habitus." *Journal for the Theory of Social Behaviour* 34(4): 375–401. https://doi.org/10.1111/j.1468-5914.2004.00255.x

Lorde, Audre. 1983. "There Is No Hierarchy of Oppressions." *Interracial Books for Children Bulletin* 14(3/4): 9–10. https://digital.library.wisc.edu/1711.dl/ZV6IH7UCTMVC28H

Lorde, Audre. 2007. *Sister Outsider: Essays and Speeches.* Berkeley, CA: Crossing Press.

Louie, Patricia, Upenieks, Laura, Erving, Christy L., and Tobin, Courtney S. Thomas. 2022. "Do Racial Differences in Coping Resources Explain the Black–White Paradox in Mental Health? A Test of Multiple Mechanisms." *Journal of Health and Social Behavior* 63(1) (March): 55–70. https://doi.org/10.1177/00221465211041031

Loveman, Mara. 1999. "Is 'Race' Essential?" *American Sociological Review* 64(6): 891–8. https://doi.org/10.2307/2657409

Lyon, Louisa. 2017. "Dead Salmon and Voodoo Correlations: Should We Be Sceptical about Functional MRI?" *Brain* 140(8) (August): e53. https://doi.org/10.1093/brain/awx180

Mabokela, Reitumetse Obakeng and Madsen, Jean A. 2005. "'Color-blind' and 'Color-conscious' Leadership: A Case Study of Desegregated Suburban Schools in the USA." *International Journal of Leadership in Education* 8(3) (January): 187–206. https://doi.org/10.1080/13603120500107313

Madon, Stephanie, Guyll, Max, Aboufadel, Kathy, et al. 2001.

"Ethnic and National Stereotypes: The Princeton Trilogy Revisited and Revised." *Personality and Social Psychology Bulletin* 27(8) (August): 996–1010. https://doi.org/10.1177/014616720127 8007

Magesh, Shruti, John, Daniel, Li, Wei Tse, et al. 2021. "Disparities in COVID-19 Outcomes by Race, Ethnicity, and Socioeconomic Status: A Systematic Review and Meta-Analysis." *JAMA Network Open* 4(11) (November): e2134147. https://doi.org/10.1001/jamanetworkopen.2021.34147

Maghbouleh, Neda. 2017. *The Limits of Whiteness: Iranian Americans and the Everyday Politics of Race.* Redwood City, CA: Stanford University Press.

Maguire, Eleanor A., Gadian, David G., Johnsrude, Ingrid S., et al. 2000. "Navigation-Related Structural Change in the Hippocampi of Taxi Drivers." *Proceedings of the National Academy of Sciences of the United States of America* 97(8) (April): 4398–403. https://doi.org/10.1073/pnas.070039597

Majka, Piotr, Kublik, Ewa, Furga, Grzegorz, and Krzysztof Wójcik, Daniel. 2012. "Common Atlas Format and 3D Brain Atlas Reconstructor: Infrastructure for Constructing 3D Brain Atlases." *Neuroinformatics* 10(2) (April): 181–97. https://doi.org/10.1007/s12021-011-9138-6

Markus, Hazel Rose and Moya, Paula M. (eds.). 2010. *Doing Race: 21 Essays for the 21st Century.* New York: W. W. Norton & Co.

Marley, Tennille Larzelere. 2018. "Segregation, Reservations, and American Indian Health." *Wicazo Sa Review* 33(2): 49–61. https://doi.org/10.5749/wicazosareview.33.2.0049

Marx, Karl. 1996 [1867]. *Das Kapital: A Critique of Political Economy.* Gateway edn. Skeptical Reader Series. Washington, DC: Regnery Publishing.

Matthaeus, Hannah, Heim, Christine, Voelkle, Manuel C., and Singer, Tania. 2024. "Reducing Neuroendocrine Psychosocial Stress Response through Socio-Emotional Dyadic but Not Mindfulness Online Training." *Frontiers in Endocrinology* 15 (June): 1–12. https://doi.org/10.3389/fendo.2024.1277929

Max Planck Institute. 2018. "Our Fractured African Roots." https://www.shh.mpg.de/1007846/human-evolution

Maykovich, Minako Kurokawa. 1972. "Reciprocity in Racial Stereotypes: White, Black, and Yellow." *American Journal of Sociology* 77(5): 876–97.

Mazur, Peter D. 1969. "Expectancy of Life at Birth in 36 Nationalities of the Soviet Union: 1958–60." *Population Studies* 23(2) (July): 225–46. https://doi.org/10.1080/00324728.1969.10405279

McDaniel, Marla, Richardson, Audrey, Gonzalez, Dulce, Caraveo, Clara Alvarez, Wagner, Laura, and Skopec, Laura. 2021. *Black and African American Adults' Perspectives on Discrimination and Unfair Judgment in Health Care.* Washington, DC: Urban Institute. https://www.urban.org/sites/default/files/publication/104568/black-and-african-american-adults-perspectives-on-discrimination-and-unfair-judgment-in-health-care_0.pdf

McEwen, Bruce S. 1993. "Stress and the Individual: Mechanisms Leading to Disease." *Archives of Internal Medicine* 153(18) (September): 2093. https://doi.org/10.1001/archinte.1993.00410180039004

McEwen, Bruce S. 2000. "Allostasis and Allostatic Load Implications for Neuropsychopharmacology." *Neuropsychopharmacology* 22(2) (February): 108–24. https://doi.org/10.1016/S0893-133X(99)00129-3

McEwen, Bruce S. 2004. "Protection and Damage from Acute and Chronic Stress: Allostasis and Allostatic Overload and Relevance to the Pathophysiology of Psychiatric Disorders." *Annals of the New York Academy of Sciences* 1032(1) (December): 1–7. https://doi.org/10.1196/annals.1314.001

McEwen, Bruce S. 2005. "Stressed or Stressed Out: What Is the Difference?" *Journal of Psychiatry and Neuroscience* 30(5) (September): 315–18.

Mead, George Herbert. 2015 [1934]. *Mind, Self, and Society: The Definitive Edition*, ed. by Charles W. Morris and annotated by Daniel R. Huebner and Hans Joas. Chicago, IL: University of Chicago Press.

Meisner, Olivia C., Nair, Amrita, and Chang, Steve W. C. 2022. "Amygdala Connectivity and Implications for Social Cognition and Disorders." *Handbook of Clinical Neurology* 187: 381–403. https://doi.org/10.1016/B978-0-12-823493-8.00017-1

Miller, Gregory E., White, Stuart F., Chen, Edith, and Nusslock, Robin. 2021. "Association of Inflammatory Activity with Larger Neural Responses to Threat and Reward among Children Living in Poverty." *American Journal of Psychiatry* 178(4) (April): 313–20. https://doi.org/10.1176/appi.ajp.2020.20050635

Mitchell, Jason P., Banaji, Mahzarin R., and Macrae, C. Neil. 2005. "The Link between Social Cognition and Self-Referential Thought in the Medial Prefrontal Cortex." *Journal of Cognitive Neuroscience* 17(8) (August): 1306–15. https://doi.org/10.1162/0898929055002418

Mitchell, Jason P., Heatherton, Todd F., and Macrae, C. Neil. 2002. "Distinct Neural Systems Subserve Person and Object Knowledge." *Proceedings of the National Academy of Sciences*

99(23) (November): 15238–43. https://doi.org/10.1073/pnas. 232395699

Molenberghs, Pascal. 2013. "The Neuroscience of In-Group Bias." *Neuroscience & Biobehavioral Reviews* 37(8) (September): 1530–6. https://doi.org/10.1016/j.neubiorev.2013.06.002

Molenberghs, Pascal, Gapp, Joshua, Wang, Bei, Louis, Winnifred, R., and Decety, Jean. 2016. "Increased Moral Sensitivity for Outgroup Perpetrators Harming Ingroup Members." *Cerebral Cortex* 26(1) (January): 225–33. https://doi.org/10.1093/cercor /bhu195

Molenberghs, Pascal and Louis, Winnifred R. 2018. "Insights from fMRI Studies into Ingroup Bias." *Frontiers in Psychology* 9 (October): 1–12. https://doi.org/10.3389/fpsyg.2018.01868

Morgan, Tierra. 2021. "Keloid Coverage in Health Care Insurance – Is It Racism?" Lexington Plastic Surgeons, September 23. https://lexingtonplasticsurgeons.com/keloid-coverage-in-health-care-insurance-is-it-racism/

Mouzon, Dawne M. 2013. "Can Family Relationships Explain the Race Paradox in Mental Health? Family and the Race Paradox in Mental Health." *Journal of Marriage and Family* 75(2) (April): 470–85. https://doi.org/10.1111/jomf.12006

Mouzon, Dawne M. 2017. "Religious Involvement and the Black–White Paradox in Mental Health." *Race and Social Problems* 9(1) (March): 63–78. https://doi.org/10.1007/s12552-017-9198-9

National Museum of African American History and Culture. 2025. "Historical Foundations of Race." https://dogoodroseville.com/ wp-content/uploads/2020/08/Historical-Foundations-Of-Race-Document.pdf

Navarre, Brianna. 2022. "Inside Poland's Drastic Immigration Reversal." US News. www.usnews.com/news/best-countries/ articles/2022-03-08/the-russia-ukraine-conflict-highlights-polands-complicated-history-with-refugees

Nawa, Norberto Eiji and Ando, Hiroshi. 2019. "Effective Connectivity within the Ventromedial Prefrontal Cortex-Hippocampus-Amygdala Network during the Elaboration of Emotional Autobiographical Memories." *NeuroImage* 189 (April): 316–28. https://doi.org/10.1016/j.neuroimage.2019.01 .042

O'Doherty, John, Winston, James, Critchley, Hugo, Perrett, David, Burt, David M., and Dolan, Raymond J. 2003. "Beauty in a Smile: The Role of Medial Orbitofrontal Cortex in Facial Attractiveness." *Neuropsychologia, The Cognitive Neuroscience of Social Behavior* 41(2) (January): 147–55. https://doi.org/10. 1016/S0028-3932(02)00145-8

Oldenburg, Kirsi S., O'Shea, T. Michael, and Fry, Rebecca C. 2020. "Genetic and Epigenetic Factors and Early Life Inflammation as Predictors of Neurodevelopmental Outcomes." *Seminars in Fetal and Neonatal Medicine* 25(3) (June): 101115. https://doi.org/10.1016/j.siny.2020.101115

Omi, Michael and Winant, Howard. 2020. "Racial Formation," in Steven Seidman and Jeffrey C. Alexander (eds.), *The New Social Theory Reader*, 2nd edn, pp. 405–15. https://www.taylorfrancis.com/chapters/edit/10.4324/9781003060963-68/racial-formation-michael-omi-howard-winant

Öngür, D. and Price, J. L. 2000. "The Organization of Networks within the Orbital and Medial Prefrontal Cortex of Rats, Monkeys and Humans." *Cerebral Cortex* 10(3) (March): 206–19. https://doi.org/10.1093/cercor/10.3.206

Opotow, Susan. 1990. "Moral Exclusion and Injustice: An Introduction." *Journal of Social Issues* 46(1): 1–20. https://doi.org/10.1111/j.1540-4560.1990.tb00268.x

Osborne, Jason W. 2001. "Testing Stereotype Threat: Does Anxiety Explain Race and Sex Differences in Achievement?" *Contemporary Educational Psychology* 26(3) (July): 291–310. https://doi.org/10.1006/ceps.2000.1052

Oswald, Frederick L., Mitchell, Gregory, Blanton, Hart, Jaccard, James, and Tetlock, Philip E. 2013. "Predicting Ethnic and Racial Discrimination: A Meta-Analysis of IAT Criterion Studies." *Journal of Personality and Social Psychology* 105(2): 171–92. https://doi.org/10.1037/a0032734

Ottaway, Scott A., Hayden, Davis C., and Oakes, Mark A. 2001. "Implicit Attitudes and Racism: Effects of Word Familiarity and Frequency on the Implicit Association Test." *Social Cognition* 19(2) (April): 97–144. https://doi.org/10.1521/soco.19.2.97.20706

Page-Gould, Elizabeth, Mendes, Wendy Berry, and Major, Brenda. 2010. "Intergroup Contact Facilitates Physiological Recovery Following Stressful Intergroup Interactions." *Journal of Experimental Social Psychology* 46(5) (September): 854–8. https://doi.org/10.1016/j.jesp.2010.04.006

Page-Gould, Elizabeth, Mendoza-Denton, Rodolfo, and Mendes, Wendy Berry. 2014. "Stress and Coping in Interracial Contexts: The Influence of Race-Based Rejection Sensitivity and Cross-Group Friendship in Daily Experiences of Health." *Journal of Social Issues* 70(2): 256–78. https://doi.org/10.1111/josi.12059

Page-Gould, Elizabeth, Mendoza-Denton, Rodolfo, and Tropp, Linda R. 2008. "With a Little Help from My Cross-Group Friend: Reducing Anxiety in Intergroup Contexts through Cross-

Group Friendship." *Journal of Personality and Social Psychology* 95(5): 1080–94. https://doi.org/10.1037/0022-3514.95.5.1080

Pager, Devah, Bonikowski, Bart, and Western, Bruce. 2009. "Discrimination in a Low-Wage Labor Market: A Field Experiment." *American Sociological Review* 74(5) (October): 777–99. https://doi.org/10.1177/000312240907400505

Pager, Devah and Shepherd, Hana. 2008. "The Sociology of Discrimination: Racial Discrimination in Employment, Housing, Credit, and Consumer Markets." *Annual Review of Sociology* 34(1) (August): 181–209. https://doi.org/10.1146/annurev.soc.33.040406.131740

Pager, Devah and Western, Bruce. 2012. "Identifying Discrimination at Work: The Use of Field Experiments." *Journal of Social Issues* 68(2) (June): 221–37. https://doi.org/10.1111/j.1540-4560.2012.01746.x

Paluck, Elizabeth Levy, Porat, Roni, Clark, Chelsey S., and Green, Donald P. 2021. "Prejudice Reduction: Progress and Challenges." *Annual Review of Psychology* 72 (January): 533–60. https://doi.org/10.1146/annurev-psych-071620-030619

Panikkath, Ragesh, Panikkath, Deepa, Mojumder, Deb, and Nugent, Kenneth. 2014. "The Alien Hand Syndrome." *Proceedings (Baylor University. Medical Center)* 27(3) (July): 219–20.

Papagno, Costanza, Pisoni, Alberto, Mattavelli, Giulia, et al. 2016. "Specific Disgust Processing in the Left Insula: New Evidence from Direct Electrical Stimulation." *Neuropsychologia* 84 (April): 29–35. https://doi.org/10.1016/j.neuropsychologia.2016.01.036

Papinutto, Nico, Galantucci, Sebastiano, Mandelli, Maria Luisa, et al. 2016. "Structural Connectivity of the Human Anterior Temporal Lobe: A Diffusion Magnetic Resonance Imaging Study." *Human Brain Mapping* 37(6) (March): 2210–22. https://doi.org/10.1002/hbm.23167

Parker, Kim, Horowitz, Juliana Menasce, Morin, Rich, and Lopez, Mark Hugo. 2015. "Chapter 1: Race and Multiracial Americans in the US Census." *Pew Research Center* (blog), June 11. https://www.pewresearch.org/social-trends/2015/06/11/chapter-1-race-and-multiracial-americans-in-the-u-s-census/

Parker, Termara C. and Ricard, Jocelyn A. 2022. "Structural Racism in Neuroimaging: Perspectives and Solutions." *Lancet Psychiatry* 9(5) (May): e22. https://doi.org/10.1016/S2215-0366(22)00079-7

Parvizi, Josef, Jacques, Corentin, Foster, Brett L., et al. 2012. "Electrical Stimulation of Human Fusiform Face-Selective Regions Distorts Face Perception." *Journal of Neuroscience*

32(43) (October): 14915–20. https://doi.org/10.1523/JNEUROS
CI.2609-12.2012

Pascoe, Elizabeth A. and Richman, Laura Smart. 2009. "Perceived
Discrimination and Health: A Meta-Analytic Review."
Psychological Bulletin 135(4): 531–54. https://doi.org/10.1037
/a0016059

Pauker, Kristin, Williams, Amanda, and Steele, Jennifer R.
2016: "Children's Racial Categorization in Context." *Child
Development Perspectives* 10(1) (March): 33–8. https://doi.org
/10.1111/cdep.12155

Pearce, Neil, Foliaki, Sunia, Sporle, Andrew, and Cunningham,
Chris. 2004. "Genetics, Race, Ethnicity, and Health." *British
Medical Journal* 328(7447) (April): 1070–2. https://doi.org/10.11
36/bmj.328.7447.1070

Pearl Milling Company. 2024. "Why Is Aunt Jemima Removing
the Image from the Packaging and Changing Its Name?" https://
contact.pepsico.com/pearlmillingcompany/article/why-is-aunt
-jemima-removing-the-image-from-the-packaging-and-cha

Pearlin, Leonard I., Schieman, Scott, Fazio, Elena M., and Meersman,
Stephen C. 2005. "Stress, Health, and the Life Course: Some
Conceptual Perspectives." *Journal of Health and Social Behavior*
46(2) (June): 205–19. https://doi.org/10.1177/00221465050460
0206

Perkins, Emily R., Bradford, Daniel E., Verona, Edelyn, Hamilton,
Roy H., and Joyner, Keanan J. 2023. "The Intersection of
Racism and Neuroscience Technology: A Cautionary Tale for the
Criminal Legal System." *Policy Insights from the Behavioral and
Brain Sciences* 10(2) (October): 279–86. https://doi.org/10.1177
/23727322231196299

Peterson, Laurel M., Stock, Michelle L., Monroe, Janet,
Molloy-Paolillo, Brianne K., and Lambert, Sharon F. 2020. "Racial
Exclusion Causes Acute Cortisol Release among Emerging-Adult
African Americans: The Role of Reduced Perceived Control."
Journal of Social Psychology 160(5) (September): 658–74. https://
doi.org/10.1080/00224545.2020.1729685

Pettigrew, Thomas F. 1998. "Intergroup Contact Theory." *Annual
Review of Psychology* 49 (February): 65–85. https://doi.org/10
.1146/annurev.psych.49.1.65

Pettigrew, Thomas F. and Tropp, Linda R. 2006. "A Meta-Analytic
Test of Intergroup Contact Theory." *Journal of Personality and
Social Psychology* 90(5): 751–83. https://doi.org/10.1037/0022
-3514.90.5.751

Pettigrew, Thomas F., Tropp, Linda R., Wagner, Ulrich, and Christ,
Oliver. 2011. "Recent Advances in Intergroup Contact Theory."

International Journal of Intercultural Relations 35(3) (May): 271–80. https://doi.org/10.1016/j.ijintrel.2011.03.001

Petzold, Paul, Silveira, Sarita, Godara, Malvika, Matthaeus, Hannah, and Singer, Tania. 2023. "A Randomized Trial on Differential Changes in Thought and Affect after Mindfulness versus Dyadic Practice Indicates Phenomenological Fingerprints of App-Based Interventions." *Scientific Reports* 13(1) (August): 13843. https://doi.org/10.1038/s41598-023-40636-1

Phelan, Jo C. and Link, Bruce G. 2013. "Fundamental Cause Theory," in William C. Cockerham (ed.), *Medical Sociology on the Move*. Dordrecht: Springer Netherlands, pp. 105–25. https://doi.org/10.1007/978-94-007-6193-3_6

Phelan, Jo C. and Link, Bruce G. 2015. "Is Racism a Fundamental Cause of Inequalities in Health?" *Annual Review of Sociology* 41(1) (August): 311–30. https://doi.org/10.1146/annurev-soc-073014-112305

Phelan, Jo C., Link, Bruce G., and Tehranifar, Parisa. 2010. "Social Conditions as Fundamental Causes of Health Inequalities: Theory, Evidence, and Policy Implications." *Journal of Health and Social Behavior* 51(1), suppl. (March): S28–40. https://doi.org/10.1177/0022146510383498

Phelps, Elizabeth A., O'Connor, Kevin J., Cunningham, William A., et al. 2000. "Performance on Indirect Measures of Race Evaluation Predicts Amygdala Activation." *Journal of Cognitive Neuroscience* 12(5) (September): 729–38. https://doi.org/10.1162/089892900562552

Phillips, Michael L., Young, Andrew W., Senior, Chris, et al. 1997. "A Specific Neural Substrate for Perceiving Facial Expressions of Disgust." *Nature* 389(6650) (October): 495–8. https://doi.org/10.1038/39051

Piaget, Jean. 2013. *The Moral Judgment of the Child*. London: Routledge. https://doi.org/10.4324/9781315009681

Pierre, Martin R. and Mahalik, James R. 2005. "Examining African Self-Consciousness and Black Racial Identity as Predictors of Black Men's Psychological Well-Being." *Cultural Diversity and Ethnic Minority Psychology* 11(1) (February): 28–40. https://doi.org/10.1037/1099-9809.11.1.28

Platten, Lara, Hernik, Mikołaj, Fonagy, Peter, and Pasco Fearon, R. 2010. "Knowing Who Likes Who: The Early Developmental Basis of Coalition Understanding." *European Journal of Social Psychology* 40(4): 569–80. https://doi.org/10.1002/ejsp.752

Politico. 2015. "The Top 10 Wackiest Anti-Refugee Remarks," October 19. https://www.politico.eu/article/toxic-news-refugees-migrants-eu/

Provençal, Nadine and Binder, Elisabeth B. 2015. "The Effects of Early Life Stress on the Epigenome: From the Womb to Adulthood and Even Before." *Experimental Neurology* (Epigenetics in Neurodevelopment and Neurological Diseases) 268 (June): 10–20. https://doi.org/10.1016/j.expneurol.2014.09.001

Purushothaman, Deepa and Rein, Valerie. 2023. "Workplace Toxicity Is Not Just a Mental Health Issue." *MIT Sloan Management Review*, January 18. https://sloanreview.mit.edu/article/workplace-toxicity-is-not-just-a-mental-health-issue/

Pyke, Karen D. 2010. "What Is Internalized Racial Oppression and Why Don't We Study It? Acknowledging Racism's Hidden Injuries." *Sociological Perspectives* 53(4) (December): 551–72. https://doi.org/10.1525/sop.2010.53.4.551

Quadflieg, Susanne and Macrae, C. Neil. 2011. "Stereotypes and Stereotyping: What's the Brain Got to Do with It?" *European Review of Social Psychology* 22(1) (March): 215–73. https://doi.org/10.1080/10463283.2011.627998

Quintana, Stephen M. 2007. "Racial and Ethnic Identity: Developmental Perspectives and Research." *Journal of Counseling Psychology* 54(3) (July): 259–70. https://doi.org/10.1037/0022-0167.54.3.259

Race, Ethnicity, and Genetics Working Group. 2005. "The Use of Racial, Ethnic, and Ancestral Categories in Human Genetics Research." *American Journal of Human Genetics* 77(4) (October): 519–32. https://doi.org/10.1086/491747

Ratan Murty, N. Apurva, Teng, Santani, Beeler, David, Mynick, Anna, Oliva, Aude, and Kanwisher, Nancy. 2020. "Visual Experience Is Not Necessary for the Development of Face-Selectivity in the Lateral Fusiform Gyrus." *Proceedings of the National Academy of Sciences* 117(37) (September): 23011–20. https://doi.org/10.1073/pnas.2004607117

Razum, Oliver, Zeeb, Hajo, Akgün, H. Seval, and Yilmaz, Selma. 1998. "Low Overall Mortality of Turkish Residents in Germany Persists and Extends into a Second Generation: Merely a Healthy Migrant Effect?" *Tropical Medicine and International Health* 3(4) (April): 297–303. https://doi.org/10.1046/j.1365-3156.1998.00233.x

Rebbeck, Timothy R., Mahal, Brandon, Maxwell, Kara N., Garraway, Isla P., and Yamoah, Kosj. 2022. "The Distinct Impacts of Race and Genetic Ancestry on Health." *Nature Medicine* 28(5) (May): 890–3. https://doi.org/10.1038/s41591-022-01796-1

Rhodes, Marjorie and Baron, Andrew. 2019. "The Development of Social Categorization." *Annual Review of Developmental*

Psychology 1(1) (December): 359–86. https://doi.org/10.1146/annurev-devpsych-121318-084824

Ricard, Jonathan A., Parker, Taylor C., Dhamala, Eram, Kwasa, James, Allsop, Abigail, and Holmes, Andrew J. 2023. "Confronting Racially Exclusionary Practices in the Acquisition and Analyses of Neuroimaging Data." *Nature Neuroscience* 26(1) (January): 4–11. https://doi.org/10.1038/s41593-022-01218-y

Richeson, Jennifer A., Baird, Abigail A., Gordon, Heather L., et al. 2003. "An fMRI Investigation of the Impact of Interracial Contact on Executive Function." *Nature Neuroscience* 6 (December): 1323–8. https://doi.org/10.1038/nn1156

Rogers, Leoandra, Onnie, Rosario, R. Josiah, and Cielto, Janene. 2020. "The Role of Stereotypes: Racial Identity and Learning," in S. Nasir, C. D. Lee, R. Pea, and M. McKinney de Royston (eds.), *Handbook of the Cultural Foundations of Learning*. New York: Routledge, pp. 62–78. http://www.scopus.com/inward/record.url?scp=85101038258&partnerID=8YFLogxK

Rolls, Edmund T., Cheng, Wei and Feng, Jianfeng. 2020. "The Orbitofrontal Cortex: Reward, Emotion and Depression." *Brain Communications* 2(2) (July): fcaa196. https://doi.org/10.1093/braincomms/fcaa196

Rolls, Edmund T., Kringelbach, Morten L., and De Araujo, Ivan E. T. 2003. "Different Representations of Pleasant and Unpleasant Odours in the Human Brain." *European Journal of Neuroscience* 18(3): 695–703. https://doi.org/10.1046/j.1460-9568.2003.02779.x

Ronquillo, Jaclyn, Denson, Thomas F., Lickel, Brian, Lu, Zhong-Lin, Nandy, Anirvan, and Maddox, Keith B. 2007. "The Effects of Skin Tone on Race-Related Amygdala Activity: An fMRI Investigation." *Social Cognitive and Affective Neuroscience* 2(1) (March): 39–44. https://doi.org/10.1093/scan/nsl043

Rowland, Diane and Telyukov, Alexandre V. 1991. "Soviet Health Care from Two Perspectives." *Health Affairs* 10(3) (January): 71–86. https://doi.org/10.1377/hlthaff.10.3.71

Ruger, Jennifer Prah and Kim, Hae-Jung. 2006. "Global Health Inequalities: An International Comparison." *Journal of Epidemiology & Community Health* 60(11) (November): 928–36. https://doi.org/10.1136/jech.2005.041954

Ruiz, John M., Hamann, Heidi A., Mehl, Matthias R., and O'Connor, Mary-Frances. 2016. "The Hispanic Health Paradox: From Epidemiological Phenomenon to Contribution Opportunities for Psychological Science." *Group Processes & Intergroup Relations* 19(4) (July): 462–76. https://doi.org/10.1177/1368430216638540

Ruiz, John M., Steffen, Patrick, and Smith, Timothy B. 2013. "Hispanic Mortality Paradox: A Systematic Review and Meta-Analysis of the Longitudinal Literature." *American Journal of Public Health* 103(3) (March): e52–60. https://doi.org/10.2105/AJPH.2012.301103

Sabah TV. 2015. "Cumhurbaşkanı Erdoğan: 'Zenci bir Türk olmaktan şeref duyuyorum.'" https://www.sabah.com.tr/video/turkiye/cumhurbaskani-erdogan-zenci-bir-turk-olmaktan-seref-duyuyorum

Santos-Lozada, Alexis R. 2016. "Self-Rated Mental Health and Race/Ethnicity in the United States: Support for the Epidemiological Paradox." *PeerJ* 4: e2508. https://doi.org/10.7717/peerj.2508

Sauder, Michael. 2005. "Symbols and Contexts: An Interactionist Approach to the Study of Social Status." *Sociological Quarterly* 46(2) (May): 279–98. https://doi.org/10.1111/j.1533-8525.2005.00013.x

Sayer, Andrew. 2005. *The Moral Significance of Class.* New York: Cambridge University Press.

Sayer, Andrew. 2010. "Class and Morality," in Steven Hitlin and Stephen Vaisey (eds.), *Handbook of the Sociology of Morality.* Handbooks of Sociology and Social Research. New York: Springer, pp. 163–78. https://doi.org/10.1007/978-1-4419-6896-8_9

Schaap, Julian, van der Waal, Jeroen, and de Koster, Willem. 2022. "Black Rap, White Rock: Non-Declarative Culture and the Racialization of Cultural Categories." *Sociological Inquiry* 92(4): 1281–305. https://doi.org/10.1111/soin.12461

Schäfer, Axel, Schienle, Anne, and Vaitl, Dieter. 2005. "Stimulus Type and Design Influence Hemodynamic Responses towards Visual Disgust and Fear Elicitors." *International Journal of Psychophysiology* (Neurobiology of Fear and Disgust) 57(1) (July): 53–9. https://doi.org/10.1016/j.ijpsycho.2005.01.011

Schmader, Toni, Johns, Michael, and Forbes, Chad. 2008. "An Integrated Process Model of Stereotype Threat Effects on Performance." *Psychological Review* 115(2) (April): 336–56. https://doi.org/10.1037/0033-295X.115.2.336

Schreiber, Darren and Iacoboni, Marco. 2012. "Huxtables on the Brain: An fMRI Study of Race and Norm Violation." *Political Psychology* 33(3) (June): 313–30. https://doi.org/10.1111/j.1467-9221.2012.00879.x

Schuman, Howard. 1997. *Racial Attitudes in America: Trends and Interpretations.* Cambridge, MA: Harvard University Press.

Schwartz, Shalom H. 1992. "Universals in the Content and Structure of Values: Theoretical Advances and Empirical Tests in

20 Countries." *Advances in Experimental Social Psychology* 25: 1–65. https://doi.org/10.1016/S0065-2601(08)60281-6

Sears, David O. and Henry, P. J. "The Origins of Symbolic Racism." 2003. *Journal of Personality and Social Psychology* 85(2): 259–75. https://doi.org/10.1037/0022-3514.85.2.259

Sears, David O., van Laar, Colette, Carrillo, Mary, and Kosterman, Rick. 2004. "Is It Really Racism? The Origins of White Americans' Opposition to Race-Targeted Policies," in John T. Jost and Jim Sidanius (eds.), *Political Psychology*. New York: Psychology Press, pp. 358–78.

Senholzi, Keith B. and Kubota, Jennifer T. 2016. "The Neural Mechanisms of Prejudice Intervention," in John R. Absher and Jasmin Cloutier (eds.), *Neuroimaging Personality, Social Cognition, and Character*. San Diego: Academic Press, pp. 337–54. https://doi.org/10.1016/B978-0-12-800935-2.00018-X

Shingles, Richard D. 1981. "Black Consciousness and Political Participation: The Missing Link." *American Political Science Review* 75(1) (March): 76–91. https://doi.org/10.2307/1962160

Shneiderman, Sara and Amburgey, Emily. 2022. "Ethnicity." *Cambridge Encyclopedia of Anthropology*, August 22. https://www.anthroencyclopedia.com/entry/ethnicity

Shutts, Kristin, Pemberton, Caroline K., and Spelke, Elizabeth S. 2013. "Children's Use of Social Categories in Thinking about People and Social Relationships." *Journal of Cognition and Development: Official Journal of the Cognitive Development Society* 14(1) (January): 35–62. https://doi.org/10.1080/15248372.2011.638686

Silveira, Sarita, Godara, Malvika, and Singer, Tania. 2023. "Boosting Empathy and Compassion through Mindfulness-based and Socioemotional Dyadic Practice: Randomized Controlled Trial with App-Delivered Trainings." *Journal of Medical Internet Research* 25(1) (July): e45027. https://doi.org/10.2196/45027

Simon, Scott. 2024. "Right Wing Movements Are Growing in Europe. How Do They Differ from Those in the U.S.?" NPR, July 6, sec. Europe. https://www.npr.org/2024/07/06/nx-s1-5026953/right-wing-movements-are-growing-in-europe-how-do-they-differ-from-those-in-the-u-s

Singer, Tania. 2024. "The ReSource Project." https://taniasinger.de/the-resource-project/

Singer, Tania and Engert, Veronika. 2019. "It Matters What You Practice: Differential Training Effects on Subjective Experience, Behavior, Brain and Body in the *ReSource Project*." *Current Opinion in Psychology* (Mindfulness) 28 (August): 151–8. https://doi.org/10.1016/j.copsyc.2018.12.005

Singer, Tania and Lamm, Claus. 2009. "The Social Neuroscience of Empathy." *Annals of the New York Academy of Sciences* 1156(1) (March): 81–96. https://doi.org/10.1111/j.1749-6632.2009.044 18.x

Singer, Tania, Seymour, Ben, O'Doherty, John, Kaube, Holger, Dolan, Raymond J., and Frith, Chris D. 2004 "Empathy for Pain Involves the Affective but Not Sensory Components of Pain." *Science* 303(5661) (February): 1157–62. https://doi.org/10.1126 /science.1093535

Sluiter, Femke, Rodriguez, Angela C. Incollingo, Nephew, Benjamin C., Cali, Ryan, Murgatroyd, Chris, and Santos, Hudson P. 2020. "Pregnancy Associated Epigenetic Markers of Inflammation Predict Depression and Anxiety Symptoms in Response to Discrimination." *Neurobiology of Stress* 13 (November): 100273. https://doi.org/10.1016/j.ynstr.2020.100273

Sommers, Samuel R., Apfelbaum, Evan P., Dukes, Kristin N., Toosi, Negin, and Wang, Elsie J. 2006. "Race and Media Coverage of Hurricane Katrina: Analysis, Implications, and Future Research Questions." *Analyses of Social Issues and Public Policy* 6(1): 39–55. https://doi.org/10.1111/j.1530-2415.2006.00103.x

Sosoo, Effua E., Bernard, Donte L., and Neblett, Enrique W. 2020. "The Influence of Internalized Racism on the Relationship between Discrimination and Anxiety." *Cultural Diversity & Ethnic Minority Psychology* 26(4) (October): 570–80. https://doi .org/10.1037/cdp0000320

Spencer, Steven J., Logel, Christine, and Davies, Paul G. 2016. "Stereotype Threat." *Annual Review of Psychology* 67 (January): 415–37. https://doi.org/10.1146/annurev-psych-073115-103235

Spitzer, Robert L., Kroenke, Kurt, Williams, Janet B. W., and Löwe, Bernd. 2006. "A Brief Measure for Assessing Generalized Anxiety Disorder: The GAD-7." *Archives of Internal Medicine* 166(10) (May): 1092. https:// doi.org/10.1001/archinte.166.10.1092

Stanford University. 2020. "'Amadou Diallo': Say Their Names." Spotlight at Stanford, August 5. https://exhibits.stanford.edu/say theirnames/feature/amadou-diallo

Stanley, Damian, Phelps, Elizabeth, and Banaji, Mahzarin. 2008. "The Neural Basis of Implicit Attitudes." *Current Directions in Psychological Science* 17(2) (April): 164–70. https://doi.org/10 .1111/j.1467-8721.2008.00568.x

Steele, Claude M. and Aronson, Joshua. 1995. "Stereotype Threat and the Intellectual Test Performance of African Americans." *Journal of Personality and Social Psychology* 69(5): 797–811. https://doi.org/10.1037/0022-3514.69.5.797

Stolier, Ryan M. and Freeman, Jonathan B. 2016. "Neural Pattern Similarity Reveals the Inherent Intersection of Social Categories." *Nature Neuroscience* 19(6) (June): 795–7. https://doi.org/10.10 38/nn.4296

Stolier, Ryan M. and Freeman, Jonathan B. 2017. "A Neural Mechanism of Social Categorization." *Journal of Neuroscience* 37(23) (June): 5711–21. https://doi.org/10.1523/JNEUROSCI. 3334-16.2017

Su, Zhaohui, McDonnell, Dean, Ahmad, Junaid, et al. 2020. "Time to Stop the Use of 'Wuhan Virus', 'China Virus' or 'Chinese Virus' across the Scientific Community." *BMJ Global Health* 5(9) (September): e003746. https://doi.org/10.1136/bmjgh-2020-003746

Sullivan, Briana, Hays, Donald, and Bennett, Neil. 2024. "Wealth by Race of Householder." US Census. https://www.census.gov/ library/stories/2024/04/wealth-by-race.html

Sullivan, Shannon. 2013. "Inheriting Racist Disparities in Health: Epigenetics and the Transgenerational Effects of White Racism." *Critical Philosophy of Race* 1(2): 190–218. https://dx.doi.org/ 10.5325/critphilrace.1.2.0190

Swartz, David. 2012. *Culture & Power: The Sociology of Pierre Bourdieu*. Chicago, IL: University of Chicago Press.

Tajeu, Gabriel S., Safford, Monika M., Howard, George, et al. 2020. "Black–White Differences in Cardiovascular Disease Mortality: A Prospective US Study, 2003–2017." *American Journal of Public Health* 110(5) (May): 696–703. https://doi.org/10.2105/AJPH. 2019.305543

Tajfel, Henri (ed.). 1982. *Social Identity and Intergroup Relations* (European Studies in Social Psychology). Cambridge, UK and New York: Cambridge University Press and Paris: Editions de la Maison des sciences de l'homme.

Tajfel, Henri and Turner, John C. 2004. "The Social Identity Theory of Intergroup Behavior," in John T. Jost and Jim Sidanius (eds.), *Political Psychology*. New York: Psychology Press, pp. 276–93. https://doi.org/10.4324/9780203505984-16

Taylor, Evi, Guy-Walls, Patricia, Wilkerson, Patricia, and Addae, Rejoice. 2019. "The Historical Perspectives of Stereotypes on African-American Males." *Journal of Human Rights and Social Work* 4(3) (September): 213–25. https://doi.org/10.1007/s41134 -019-00096-y

Tehranian, John. 2008. *Whitewashed: America's Invisible Middle Eastern Minority*. New York: New York University Press. https:// doi.org/10.18574/nyu/9780814784235.001.0001

Templeton, Alan R. 2013. "Biological Races in Humans." *Studies in History and Philosophy of Science Part C: Studies in History and Philosophy of Biological and Biomedical Sciences* 44(3) (September): 262–71. https://doi.org/10.1016/j.shpsc.2013.04.010

TenHouten, Warren. 1997. "Neurosociology." *Journal of Social and Evolutionary Systems* 20(1) (January): 7–37. https://doi.org/10.1016/S1061-7361(97)90027-8

Teruya, Stacey A. and Bazargan-Hejazi, Shahrzad. 2013. "The Immigrant and Hispanic Paradoxes: A Systematic Review of Their Predictions and Effects." *Hispanic Journal of Behavioral Sciences* 35(4) (November): 486–509. https://doi.org/10.1177/0739986313499004

Tessler, Hannah, Choi, Meera, and Kao, Grace. 2020. "The Anxiety of Being Asian American: Hate Crimes and Negative Biases during the COVID-19 Pandemic." *American Journal of Criminal Justice* 45(4) (August): 636–46. https://doi.org/10.1007/s12103-020-09541-5

Thoits, Peggy A. and Hewitt, Lyndi N. 2001. "Volunteer Work and Well-Being." *Journal of Health and Social Behavior* 42(2) (June): 115. https://doi.org/10.2307/3090173

Tobin, Courtney S. Thomas, Erving, Christy L., Hargrove, Taylor W., and Satcher, Lacee A. 2022. "Is the Black–White Mental Health Paradox Consistent across Age, Gender, and Psychiatric Disorders?" *Aging & Mental Health* 26(1): 196–204. https://www.tandfonline.com/doi/full/10.1080/13607863.2020.1855627

Thomas, W. I. and Thomas, D. S. 1928. *The Child in America: Behavior Problems and Programs*. New York: Alfred A. Knopf. http://catalog.hathitrust.org/api/volumes/oclc/514305.html

Tooby, John. 2020. "Evolutionary Psychology as the Crystalizing Core of a Unified Modern Social Science." *Evolutionary Behavioral Sciences* 14(4): 390–403. https://doi.org/10.1037/ebs0000250

Tooby, John and Cosmides, Leda. 1990. "The Past Explains the Present." *Ethology and Sociobiology* 11(4–5) (July): 375–424. https://doi.org/10.1016/0162-3095(90)90017-Z

Tormos, Francisco. 2017. "Intersectional Solidarity." *Politics, Groups, and Identities* 5(4) (October): 707–20. https://doi.org/10.1080/21565503.2017.1385494

Trautwein, Fynn-Mathis, Kanske, Philipp, Böckler, Anne, and Singer, Tania. 2020. "Differential Benefits of Mental Training Types for Attention, Compassion, and Theory of Mind." *Cognition* 194 (January): 104039. https://doi.org/10.1016/j.cognition.2019.104039

Turner, Jonathan. 2000. *On the Origins of Human Emotions:*

A Sociological Inquiry into the Evolution of Human Affect. Redwood City, CA: Stanford University Press.

Turner, Jonathan H. and Stets, Jan E. (2006). "Sociological Theories of Human Emotions." *Annual Review of Sociology* 32(1): 25–52. https://doi.org/10.1146/annurev.soc.32.061604.123130

Turner, Turner, John C., Brown, Rupert J., and Tajfel, Henri. 1979. "Social Comparison and Group Interest in Ingroup Favouritism." *European Journal of Social Psychology* 9(2): 187–204. https://doi.org/10.1002/ejsp.2420090207

Umaña-Taylor, Adriana J., Quintana, Stephen M., Lee, Richard M., et al. 2014. "Ethnic and Racial Identity during Adolescence and into Young Adulthood: An Integrated Conceptualization." *Child Development* 85(1) (January): 21–39. https://doi.org/10.1111/cdev.12196

United States Holocaust Memorial Museum. 2024. "500 Years of Antisemitic Propaganda: The Katz-Ehrenthal Collection." https://www.ushmm.org/collections/the-museums-collections/collections-highlights/500-years-of-antisemitic-propaganda

US Census Bureau. 2024a. "Households with a White, Non-Hispanic Householder Were Ten Times Wealthier than Those with a Black Householder in 2021." Census.gov. https://www.census.gov/library/stories/2024/04/wealth-by-race.html

US Census Bureau. 2024b. "What Updates to OMB's Race/Ethnicity Standards Mean for the Census Bureau." Census.gov. https://www.census.gov/newsroom/blogs/random-samplings/2024/04/updates-race-ethnicity-standards.html

Verba, Sidney and Nie, Norman H. 1987. *Participation in America: Political Democracy and Social Equality.* Chicago: University of Chicago Press.

Verstaen, Alice, Eckart, Janet A., Muhtadie, Luma, et al. 2016. "Insular Atrophy and Diminished Disgust Reactivity." *Emotion* 16(6) (September): 903–12. https://doi.org/10.1037/emo0000195

Wacquant, Loïc. 1997. "For an Analytic of Racial Domination," in Diane E. Davis (ed.), *Political Power and Social Theory* 11: 221–34.

Walker, Pamela M., Silvert, Laetitia, Hewstone, Miles, and Nobre, Anna C. 2008. "Social Contact and Other-Race Face Processing in the Human Brain." *Social Cognitive and Affective Neuroscience* 3(1) (March): 16–25. https://doi.org/10.1093/scan/nsm035

Wang, Rui, Chen, Xi, and Li, Xun. 2022. "Something in the Pipe: The Flint Water Crisis and Health at Birth." *Journal of Population Economics* 35(4) (October): 1723–49. https://doi.org/10.1007/s00148-021-00876-9

Washington, Ariel and Randall, Jill. 2022. "'We're Not Taken Seriously': Describing the Experiences of Perceived Discrimination in Medical Settings for Black Women." *Journal of Racial and Ethnic Health Disparities* 10(2) (March): 883. https://doi.org/10.1007/s40615-022-01276-9

Wassenaar, Erik B. and van den Brand, Jaap G. H. 2005. "Reliability of Near-Infrared Spectroscopy in People with Dark Skin Pigmentation." *Journal of Clinical Monitoring and Computing* 19(3) (June): 195–9. https://doi.org/10.1007/s10877-005-1655-0

Webb, E. Kate, Etter, J. Arthur, and Kwasa, Jasmine A. 2022. "Addressing Racial and Phenotypic Bias in Human Neuroscience Methods." *Nature Neuroscience* 25(4) (April): 410–14. https://doi.org/10.1038/s41593-022-01046-0

Weber, Max. 1978 (1922). *Economy and Society: An Outline of Interpretive Sociology*, ed. by Guenther Roth and Claus Wittich. Berkeley: University of California Press.

Welzel, Christian and Inglehart, Ronald. 2010. "Agency, Values, and Well-Being: A Human Development Model." *Social Indicators Research* 97(1) (May): 43–63. https://doi.org/10.1007/s11205-009-9557-z

West, Candace and Zimmerman, Don. 1987. "Doing Gender." *Gender & Society* 1(2): 125–51. https://doi.org/10.1177/0891243287001002002

White, Ismail K., Philpot, Tasha S., Wylie, Kristin, and McGowen, Ernest. 2007. "Feeling the Pain of My People: Hurricane Katrina, Racial Inequality, and the Psyche of Black America." *Journal of Black Studies* 37(4) (March): 523–38. https://doi.org/10.1177/0021934706296191

Wicker, Bruno, Keysers, Christian, Plailly, Jane, Royet, Jean-Pierre, Gallese, Vittorio, and Rizzolatti, Giacomo. 2003. "Both of Us Disgusted in My Insula." *Neuron* 40(3) (October): 655–64. https://doi.org/10.1016/S0896-6273(03)00679-2

Wiech, Katja, Lin, Chia-shu, Brodersen, Kay H., Bingel, Ulrike, Ploner, Markus, and Tracey, Irene. 2010. "Anterior Insula Integrates Information about Salience into Perceptual Decisions about Pain." *Journal of Neuroscience* 30(48) (December): 16324–31. https://doi.org/10.1523/JNEUROSCI.2087-10.2010

Wilkins, Amy C. 2008. "'Happier than Non-Christians': Collective Emotions and Symbolic Boundaries among Evangelical Christians." *Social Psychology Quarterly* 71(3) (September): 281–301. https://doi.org/10.1177/019027250807100308

Wilkinson, Bethaney. 2022. "Becoming a Race Conscious Leader." *Leader to Leader* 106: 13–18. https://doi.org/10.1002/ltl.20669

Williams, David R. 2012. "Miles to Go before We Sleep: Racial Inequities in Health." *Journal of Health and Social Behavior* 53(3) (September): 279–95. https://doi.org/10.1177/0022146512455804

Williams, David R. and Collins, Chiquita. 2001. "Racial Residential Segregation: A Fundamental Cause of Racial Disparities in Health." *Public Health Reports* 116(5) (September): 404–16. https://doi.org/10.1016/S0033-3549(04)50068-7

Williams, David R., Lawrence, Jourdyn A., Davis, Brigette A., and Vu, Cecilia. 2019. "Understanding How Discrimination Can Affect Health." *Health Services Research* 54(S2): 1374–88. https://doi.org/10.1111/1475-6773.13222

Williams, David R. and Sternthal, Michelle. 2010. "Understanding Racial-Ethnic Disparities in Health: Sociological Contributions." *Journal of Health and Social Behavior* 51(1) (March suppl): S15–27. https://doi.org/10.1177/0022146510383838

Willis, Henry A., Sosoo, Effua E., Bernard, Donte L., Neal, Aaron, and Neblett, Enrique W. 2021. "The Associations between Internalized Racism, Racial Identity, and Psychological Distress." *Emerging Adulthood (Print)* 9(4) (August): 384–400. https://doi.org/10.1177/21676968211005598

Wodtke, Geoffrey T. 2012. "The Impact of Education on Inter-Group Attitudes: A Multiracial Analysis." *Social Psychology Quarterly* 75(1) (March): 80–106. https://doi.org/10.1177/0190272511430234

Wright, Paul, He, Guoshi, Shapira, Naomi A., Goodman, Wayne K., and Liu, Yijun. 2004. "Disgust and the Insula: fMRI Responses to Pictures of Mutilation and Contamination." *NeuroReport* 15(15) (October): 2347. https://doi.org/10.1097/00001756-200410250-00009

Wylie, Lloy and McConkey, Stephanie. 2019. "Insiders' Insight: Discrimination against Indigenous Peoples through the Eyes of Health Care Professionals." *Journal of Racial and Ethnic Health Disparities* 6(1): 37–45. https://doi.org/10.1007/s40615-018-0495-9

Xu, Xiaojing, Zuo, Xiangyu, Wang, Xiaoying, and Han, Shihui. 2009. "Do You Feel My Pain? Racial Group Membership Modulates Empathic Neural Responses." *Journal of Neuroscience* 29(26) (July): 8525–9. https://doi.org/10.1523/JNEUROSCI.2418-09.2009

Zaki, Jamil and Ochsner, Kevin N. 2012. "The Neuroscience of Empathy: Progress, Pitfalls and Promise." *Nature Neuroscience* 15(5) (May): 675–80. https://doi.org/10.1038/nn.3085

Zuberi, Tukufu. 2001. *Thicker Than Blood: How Racial Statistics Lie.* Minneapolis, MN: University of Minnesota Press.

Zuberi, Tukufu and Bonilla-Silva, Eduardo. 2008. *White Logic, White Methods: Racism and Methodology.* Lanham, MD: Rowman & Littlefield.

Index